She

Understanding Feminine Psychology

RObert A. JohNSON

SHe

UNdERSTANdiNG FEMiNiNE Psychology

*An interpretation based on the myth
of Amor and Psyche and using Jungian
psychological concepts*

PERENNIAL LIBRARY
Harper & Row, Publishers
New York, Hagerstown, San Francisco, London

To John Sanford,
certainly the godfather
of this work

A hardcover edition of this book is published by Religious Publishing Company. It is here reprinted by arrangement.

Designed by Stephanie Krasnow

First PERENNIAL LIBRARY edition published 1977

INTERNATIONAL STANDARD BOOK NUMBER: 0–06–080416–5

    84   10

Acknowledgments

My great appreciation to Glenda Taylor and Helen Macey for the heroic tasks of transcriptions, additions, editing, and typing the lecture tapes into readable form. My gratitude to the many people of the parish of St. Paul in San Diego for their contributions to the evolution of this book.

Introduction

The story of Amor and Psyche is one of the best elucidations available of the psychology of the feminine personality. It is an ancient, pre-Christian myth, first recorded in classical Greek times, having enjoyed a long oral tradition before that; it is still pertinent for us today.

That it should be so is not strange, for, as the chemistry of the human body is the same today as it was in Greek times, so also is the unconscious psychological dynamic of human personality. Basic human needs, both physical and psychological, remain fixed, although the form in which they are satisfied may vary from time to time.

This is why when we want to study the basic patterns of human behavior and personality it is instructive to go to the earliest sources where their portrayal is apt to be so direct and so simple we cannot fail to comprehend them. Then, perhaps, if we can understand the basic structure, we can begin to see the variations peculiar to our own time.

Myths are rich sources of psychological insight. Great literature, as all great art, records and portrays the human condition with indelible accuracy. Myths are a special kind of literature. They are usually not written or created by a single individual, but are the product of the collective imagination and experience of an entire age and culture. Myths seem to develop gradually: Certain motifs emerge, are elaborated, and finally are rounded out as people tell and retell certain stories that catch and hold their interest. Thus themes that are universal are kept alive, while those elements peculiar to single individuals usually drop away. Myths, therefore, portray a collective image. They tell about things that are true for all men.

This belies our current rationalistic society's definition of myth as something untrue or imaginary. "Why, that's a myth; it's not true at all," we hear. But actually, for the reasons suggested above, a myth is profoundly and universally true.

A myth may be a fantasy; it may be a product of the imagination, but it is nonetheless true and real. It depicts levels of reality that include the outer rational world as well as the less understood inner world within the psyche of each individual.

This confusion concerning the narrow definition of reality may be illustrated by the thinking of a small child after a nightmare. A parent may say, to be comforting, "It was only a dream; the monster was not real." But the child is unconvinced, and rightly so. To him it was real, as alive and real as any outer experience. The monster he dreamed about was in his head and not in his bedroom, but it had, nonetheless, an awesome reality, with power over the child's emotional and physical reactions. It had an inner reality for him that cannot and should not be denied.

A myth is a product of the collective imagination and not of scientific or rational development, but it is profoundly real. Because of its manner of development, through years of retelling and refining by countless people, it carries a powerful collective meaning.

Myths have been carefully studied by many psychologists. C. G. Jung, for example, in his studies of the underlying structure of the human personality, paid particular attention to myths. He found in them an expression of basic psychological patterns. We may hope to do the same with our study of "Amor and Psyche."

But first we must learn to think mythologically, a delightful and thrilling process. Powerful things happen when we touch the mythological thinking that myths, fairy tales, and our own dreams bring to us. The terms and settings of the old myths are strange; they seem archaic and distant to us, but if we listen to them carefully and take them seriously, we begin to hear and to understand. Sometimes it is necessary to translate a symbolic meaning, but this is not difficult once we see how it can be done.

Many psychologists who have read "Amor and Psyche" have interpreted it as a statement of the feminine personality. Perhaps it would be wise at the very beginning of this study to say that we are speaking of femininity wherever it is found, in men as well as in women.

Jung, in one of his most profound insights, showed that, just as genetically every man has recessive female chromosomes and hormones, so too every man has a group of feminine psychological characteristics that make up a minority element within him. A woman likewise has a psychological masculine minority component within her. The man's feminine side Jung called the *anima;* the woman's masculine side he called the *animus.*

Much has been written about the anima and the animus, and we will have more to say about both of them later. At this point, suffice it to say that whenever we speak of the feminine aspects of the Amor and Psyche myth, we are speaking not only about women, but also about the man's anima, his feminine side. The connection may be more obvious to a woman, since femininity is her major psychological quality, yet there will also be something of a parallel to a man's anima.

1

Let us begin then with our story of Amor and Psyche. It seems that there was a kingdom. There is always a kingdom; that is the beginning of everything. There is a king and a queen, and they have three daughters. The two eldest daughters are ordinary princesses (if a princess can be ordinary); they are not very remarkable.

The third daughter, who is named Psyche, is an extraordinary person. She is beautiful, charming, so like a goddess in her bearing, her speech, and her whole personality that a cult of worship has sprung up around her. People have begun to say, "Here is the new Aphrodite. Here is a new goddess."

Now Aphrodite was an age-old goddess of femininity who had reigned since the beginning; no one knew just how long. But people began saying that Psyche was taking her place. In the poetic and beautiful terms of the myth, the ashes of the sacramental fires in the temple of Aphrodite grew cold.

The different origins of these two, Aphrodite and Psyche, are significant. When the genitals of the god Uranus were severed and fell into the sea, the sea was fertilized and Aphrodite was born. Her birth was immortalized in a magnificent painting by Botticelli called *Birth of Venus*. (Venus is the Roman name for Aphrodite.) The painting depicts Venus being borne in upon a wave, standing on a shell; it is an exquisitely beautiful thing. On the other hand, it was rumored that Psyche was born when a dewdrop from the sky fell upon the land. Here we begin our mythological unraveling.

The difference between these two births, if properly understood, reveals the different natures of these two goddesses. Aphrodite is a goddess born out of the sea; she is primeval, oceanic femininity. She is of a preconscious evolutionary time; she is at home at the bottom of the sea and holds court there. As Erich Neumann has said, she is the goddess of swamp fertility. In psychological terms she reigns in the unconscious, symbolized by the waters of the sea. She is therefore scarcely approachable on normal, conscious, human terms. One can hardly cope with oceanic femininity; one might as well argue with a tidal wave. It is difficult to touch or come to terms with the Aphrodite nature, as it is primitive femininity. One can admire or worship or be crushed by it, or one can go the way of this myth, Psyche's way of evolving to a new level of femininity. Those are the choices.

Every woman has an Aphrodite in her who is easily recognized, her chief characteristics being vanity, conniving lust, fertility, and tyranny when she is crossed.

There are marvelous stories about Aphrodite and her court. She has a servant who walks before her carrying a mirror so that she may constantly admire herself. Someone continually makes perfume for her. She is jealous and will stand no competition whatsoever. She is always arranging marriages and is never satisfied until everyone is busily serving her aims of fertility. Women who are matchmakers and who are not satisfied if any bachelor is left loose are Aphrodites.

Actually, one sees Aphrodite everywhere. At every supermarket, Aphrodite parks her grocery cart squarely in the middle of the aisle and says, "If you won't court me, you will at least bump into me." That is Aphrodite.

It is very embarrassing for a modern, reasonably intelligent woman to discover her own Aphrodite nature and all of the primitive, instinctive tricks she plays. There are women who get into a rage if their husbands deviate so much as an inch from the straight and narrow line they have dictated. This is Aphrodite.

Naturally, when a new kind of femininity appears on the stage of evolution, Aphrodite, goddess of the old femininity, is going to be irate. For she is beyond morality; she is before the time of morality. She will use any means at her disposal to down an opponent. She is, in fact, a thorough bitch. Every woman knows this through her own sudden regressions to her Aphrodite nature, for a woman is a terrifying figure when she falls into it. Every male around her trembles, for men are terrified of Aphrodite. It is a calmer household where someone can gently say, "Now look, sweet, remember Aphrodite?"

Yet Aphrodite is a valuable person. She is that basic, instinctive motherhood necessary for reproduction of the species. As time goes on, we will see that she does not crush Psyche; on the contrary, she does all that is right to make Psyche grow, though she is so unpleasant about it one does not feel like giving her a great deal of credit.

One of the beautiful things about the structure of the unconscious in human personality is that when it is time for growth, the old ways, the old habits pave the way and welcome the new. They *seem* to persecute the new growth at every point, but who knows—perhaps that is the correct way to bring a new consciousness to birth.

There is a story about the first elephant born in captivity. Its keeper was horrified when the other elephants in the compound gathered in a circle and tossed the baby to each other. The keeper thought they were killing it, but they were only making it breathe.

Often, when new growth occurs, the most dreadful things seem to happen, but then one sees that they were exactly what was required. Aphrodite, who is criticized at every turn, does everything to make Psyche's evolution possible. One can be optimistic after the fact, but it is devilishly painful while it is happening. There is a sort of chaotic evolutionary warfare within one during this time. The old way, the Aphrodite nature in this case, is regressive, pulling one back into unconsciousness, yet at the same time forcing one forward into new life sometimes at great risk. It may be that evolution could be accomplished in another way; it may be that at times Aphrodite is the only element that can bring about growth. There are women, for example, who would not grow unless they had a tyrant of a mother-in-law. (Aphrodite turns up regularly in mothers-in-law. The wicked stepmother is also a parallel.)

Most of the turmoil for a modern woman is the collision between her Aphrodite nature and her Psyche nature. It may help her to have a framework for understanding the process because, if she can see what is happening, she is already well on her way to a new consciousness. Recognizing Aphrodite can be of great value to her. When a man can recognize Aphrodite in a woman and know what to do or what not to do, he is better off as well.

2

Now that we have learned something of the nature of Aphrodite, the older, more primitive level of femininity, let us look at the new arrival on the scene, Psyche. Psyche was born when a dewdrop fell on the land. The land is the symbol for consciousness, so we see a change from the ocean to the land. Instead of oceanic proportions of unconsciousness, we have the manageable waters of a dewdrop.

Psyche's nature is so magnificent, so unworldly, so virginal and pure that she is worshiped, *but she is not courted.* This is a horribly lonely experience and poor Psyche can find no husband.

In this sense, there is a Psyche in every woman, and it is intensely lonely. Every woman is, in part, a king's daughter—too lovely, too perfect, too deep for the ordinary world. When a woman finds herself lonely and not understood, when she finds that people are good to her but stay just a little distance away, she has found the Psyche nature in her own person. It is terribly painful. Women are often excruciatingly aware of this situation without knowing its origin, which is the Psyche nature, and there is nothing that can be done about it. That part of one will remain untouched, unrelated, unmarried most of one's life.

All manner of nonsense goes on when a woman tries to bring her Psyche nature into the everyday give and take of a relationship. If the Psyche nature is a large part of a woman, she has a painful task on her hands. She bursts into tears and says, "But nobody understands." And it is true; nobody understands. Every woman has this quality within her; it makes no difference what her station in life may be. If one knows of this quality and can touch it in a woman, the great beauty of a Psyche can be made conscious in her and a noble evolution may begin.

If a woman is very beautiful, the problem is compounded. Marilyn Monroe is a good example. She was worshiped far and wide, yet she never succeeded in relating closely to anyone. Finally, she found it intolerable. Such a person seems to be the carrier of a goddesslike quality, an almost unapproachable perfection. If one understands, perhaps one can set in motion the evolution that was required of Psyche, but it is not easy.

I once saw a film in which two horribly disfigured people in an institution fell in love with each other. Through the magic of fantasy they made each infinitely beautiful to the other, and a love affair went on between these two handsome, beautiful people. At the end of the movie, the camera blurred back to show the two originally disfigured faces, but the audience knew where they had been: They had seen the god and goddess within.

Psyche is the distress of her parents because, while her two older sisters are married happily to neighboring kings, no one asks for Psyche's hand. They only worship her. The king goes to an oracle, who happens to be dominated by Aphrodite, and she, irate and jealous of Psyche, has the oracle deliver a terrible judgment that Psyche is to be married to Death, the ugliest, the most horrible, the most awful creature possible. Psyche is to be taken to the top of a mountain, chained to a rock, and left to be ravished by this dreadful creature, Death.

The pronouncements of the oracles were received without recourse in Greek society; they were considered absolutely final. So Psyche's parents don't question this decision. They make a wedding procession, which is a funeral cortege, take Psyche as instructed, and chain her to the rock at the top of the mountain. There are floods of tears; wedding finery and funeral darkness are mixed together. Then the parents extinguish the torches and leave Psyche alone in the dark.

What can we make of this? Psyche is to be married. Her husband will come, but this is an unhappy occasion because her husband is Death itself. The maiden dies on her wedding day; her wedding is a funeral. But this is instructive. Many of our wedding customs are actually funeral customs. In primitive weddings, marriage was celebrated as such; it was at once a funeral, a transformation, and a joyous outburst. Many of our customs stem from primitive times when weddings were abductions and the best man and his friends were abductors. The bridesmaids were protectors of the virginity of the bride. If a man could not win a woman in this way, he was not worthy of her. Funeral rites and abduction ceremonies are still present in our weddings. One is not inclined to remind people of this on wedding days, but many a bride cries on her wedding day. Instinctively she knows that the maiden in her is dying.

One of the problems with marriage is that we no longer

recognize or observe this duality in custom or ritual, and all manner of trouble comes from this fact. But the dual impact of marriage is simply inescapable. It is as much ours as it was the ancient Greeks', yet it is ignored. We do not have a place for the girl's dying experience in the wedding. We try to make it all happy and white and pink and joyous, but somewhere we should reckon with the dying part. If we do not, that component will have to be "lived out" at a later, perhaps less appropriate time. This is generally experienced by the woman as a fierce resentment against her marriage.

I have seen a picture of a Turkish wedding party in which boys of eight or nine each had one foot bound to his thigh and was hopping on one leg. This was to remind everyone that pain was present at the wedding as well as joy.

Some African weddings are not valid unless the bride arrives with scars and wounds evident on her. We would call that barbaric, and it is, but elemental reality had best be observed somewhere along the way. Perhaps the girl who comes to her mother a few hours before the wedding and bursts into tears is wise. For if the sacrificial element of a wedding is given its due, the joy of the marriage is possible. Aphrodite does not like maidens to die at the hands of men. It is not her nature to be subject to a man. So the Aphrodite in a woman is either crying or fuming or both at her wedding.

Here again we observe the paradox of evolution mentioned earlier. It is Aphrodite who condemns Psyche to death but who is also the matchmaker who brings about weddings in the first place. Yet Aphrodite also weeps and rages at the wedding for the possible loss of the bride's freedom and individuality, for the loss of her virginity.

The forward push of evolution toward marriage is accompanied by a regressive tug of longing for the autonomy and freedom of things as they were before.

A wedding is a powerful time. All manner of elemental forces are loose. I once saw a cartoon that summed up the archetypal power of a wedding with great genius. It showed the thoughts of each of the parents. The father of the bride is angry at that fellow who is audacious enough to snatch his darling daughter away from him; the father of the groom is triumphant at the supremacy of the males of the community, for a day at least; the mother of the bride is horrified at the beast of a groom who is intruding; the mother of the groom is horrified at the creature who has seduced her pure son away from her. All of the archetypes (those ancient, embedded patterns of thought and behavior laid down in the unconscious of the human psyche through countless years of evolution) were depicted in this cartoon.

3

In order to destroy Psyche, as she wishes to do, Aphrodite has to have help, and she engages the assistance of her son Eros, the god of love. Eros, Amor, and Cupid are various names that have been given to the god of love. Since Cupid has been degraded to the level of valentine cards and Amor has been shorn of his dignity, let us use the name Eros for this noble god.

Eros carries his quiver of arrows and is the bane of everyone on Olympus; not even Zeus himself escapes the power of Eros. Yet Eros is under his mother's thumb. Aphrodite instructs him to enflame Psyche with love for the loathsome beast who will come to claim her, thus ending Psyche's challenge to Aphrodite. One of Aphrodite's characteristics is that she is constantly regressive. She wants things to go back where they were; she wants evolution to go backward. She is the voice of tradition, and ironically it is a beautiful voice when intelligently used.

There are many levels from which to view Eros. He may be seen as the outer man, the husband or the male in every relationship; or he may be seen as the woman's animus, her own inner masculinity. We will speak to both of these aspects of Eros in our myth as we continue.

Eros goes to do his mother's bidding, but just as he glimpses Psyche, he accidentally pricks his finger on one of his own arrows and falls in love with her. He decides on the spot to take Psyche as his own bride and asks his friend, the West Wind, to lift her very gently down from the top of the mountain into the Valley of Paradise. The West Wind does this, and Psyche, who was expecting the worst, finds herself in a heaven on earth instead. She does not ask Eros any questions. Imagine landing in an alabaster hall with servants, music, fine food, entertainment, and beauty all day long! Of course she doesn't ask any questions. It has been enough to be delivered from facing Death; she does not want or need any more consciousness now. Sometimes one feels that there has been enough of evolution for the present and asks nothing more.

The experience of Psyche on the death mountain is a strange thing. There are women of fifty who have never been to the death mountain, though they may be grandmothers. The dewy quality is not off the world for them even in middle age. There are also young girls of sixteen who know all about that experience, have been through it and survived it, and have a terrifying wisdom in their eyes.

These things do not happen automatically at any age. I knew a girl of sixteen who had a baby out of season. She went off to have it privately and quietly, and the baby was adopted. She never saw it. She came back and nothing had happened to that girl; she had not learned a thing. Several years later she was married, and if anybody could be called virgin, she could. Psychologically she had not been touched, even though she had had a baby.

So the Psyche in each woman terminates her naiveté at

vastly different times in life; it is not just when she marries. Many girls are through it by sixteen, which is bitter; one should not be chained on the mountain at sixteen.

Marriage is a totally different thing to a man than to a woman. The man is adding to his stature; his world is getting stronger and he has come up a peg. He generally does not understand that he is killing the Psyche in his newfound wife and that he has to. If she behaves strangely, or collapses, or if something goes dreadfully wrong, he usually doesn't understand that marriage is a totally different experience for her than for him.

Anyway, our Psyche of the myth finds that her paradise is magnificent. She has everything one could wish. Her god-husband Eros is with her every night. He puts only one restriction on her: He extracts from her the promise that she will not look at him and will not inquire into any of his ways. She may have anything she wishes, she may live in her paradise, but she must not ask to know him. Psyche agrees to this. She wants to be his wife and to do whatever he wishes.

Nearly every man wants this of his wife: if she will just not ask for consciousness, if she will just do things his way. He wants the old patriarchal marriage, where the man decides all the important issues, the woman says yes to him, and there is no trouble. Every man harbors within him the hope that this is how it will be, and for a little while there is the possibility that the marriage will go forward in this way.

For some reason, the Psyche in every woman has to go through a stage, at least briefly, in which she is totally subject to a man. It is an archetypal level that cannot be avoided. A woman need not stay there long, but she must have the experience briefly. This may be an echo of some primitive patriarchal practice in which she is subject to the man. There are remnants of the patriarchal world in our customs, such as the woman's bearing the man's name. Psyche goes through such a patriarchal experience. Eros insists that she not ask any questions, she agrees, and they are content in paradise.

Every immature Eros is a paradise maker. It is adolescent to carry a girl off and promise her that she will live happily ever after. That is Eros in a secretive stage; he wants his paradise, but no responsibility, no conscious relationship. There is a bit of this in every man. The feminine demand for evolution—and most evolution comes from the feminine element in the myths, either from the woman or the animal—is a terrifying thing to a man. He would like it just to be a paradise. But all paradises are suspect; they just do not work well. It is Eros's childishness or boyishness (Eros is pure *puer eternis*) that makes this demand.

Listen to lovers build a paradise. It is such fun and so beautiful. Someone listening to such people could say, "Look, it isn't going to go like that at all." But they wouldn't listen; they are in paradise.

There is something in the unconscious of a man that wishes to make an agreement with his wife that she shall ask no questions of him. A man's attitude toward marriage is that it should be there for him to come home to but should not be an encumbrance; he wants to be free to forget about it when he wants to focus elsewhere. This is a great shock to a woman when she discovers it. Marriage is a total commitment for a woman; for a man this is not so. I remember a woman who told me she cried for days when she discovered that their marriage was merely a detail in her husband's life, though it was her whole life. She had discovered her husband in his Eros, his paradise-making nature.

4

All paradises fail; each one has a serpent of some kind in it. That is the nature of paradise; it demands that its opposite shall appear quickly. Our own Christian paradise of Eden had a serpent in it. Psyche's paradise had its awakening element in it also.

It seems that Psyche's two sisters, who had been mourning her loss—though not vigorously, it had been noticed—hear that Psyche is living in a garden paradise and that she has a god as a husband. Their jealousy knows no bounds. They come to the crag where Psyche had been chained and call down to her in the garden. They send the best of wishes and inquiries about her health.

Psyche naively reports all this to Eros. He warns her over and over that she is in great danger. He tells her that if she pays attention to her inquiring sisters there will be a disaster, and he tells her what the disaster will be. If Psyche continues unquestioning, her child (which is now on the way) will be a god, but if she breaks her vow of not questioning, the child will be born a mortal and a girl. And he, Eros, will go away.

Psyche listens and again agrees not to ask questions.

But the sisters keep coming and calling. Finally, Psyche draws from Eros permission to let them come and visit her. Soon after, the sisters are wafted down from the high crag by the West Wind and deposited safely in the lovely garden. They admire everything, they are fed and shown about, and of course, they are green with envy at their sister's good fortune. They ask many questions. Poor Psyche, not up to this interrogation, says that her husband is a very young man with the first down of beard on his face and that he spends his time hunting. She heaps extravagant presents upon her sisters and sends them home.

Eros again and yet again warns Psyche, but she allows her sisters to come back. This time, forgetting what she has told them before, she says her husband is a middle-aged man with graying hair who is prominent in the affairs of the world. When the sisters leave, they discuss all this and between them devise a venomous plan. When they come the third time, they tell Psyche that her husband is actually a serpent, a loathsome creature, and that when the baby is born, he plans to devour both her and the child!

The sisters propose a plan to avert this. They advise Psyche to get a lamp, put it in a covered vessel, and have it ready in the bedchamber. They also tell her to take the sharpest knife available and have it beside her on the couch. In the middle of the night, when her husband is fast asleep, she must sever the head of this loathsome creature with her knife.

Psyche is taken in by all this and makes these preparations: a light that can be uncovered in the middle of the night and a knife that she whets to fine sharpness.

Eros comes to the couch after dark and falls asleep beside Psyche. In the night she takes the cover off the lamp, grasps the knife, stands over her husband, and looks at him. To her utter amazement, bewilderment, and guilt, she sees that he is a god, the god of love, and the most beautiful creature on all of Mt. Olympus. She is so shaken and terrified by this that she thinks of killing herself. She fumbles with the knife and drops it. She pricks herself accidentally on one of Eros's arrows and, of course, falls in love with him.

She jostles the lamp and a drop of oil from it falls on Eros's right shoulder, and he wakes in pain from the hot oil. He sees what has happened and, being a winged creature, takes flight. Poor Psyche clings to him and is carried a little way with him out of paradise. But she soon falls to the earth in exhaustion and desolation. Eros alights nearby. He says that she has disobeyed; she has broken her covenant. He tells her that, as he had warned her, her child will be born a mortal and that he, Eros, will go away and punish her by his absence. Then he flies away.

This is a drama reproduced and replayed in marriage after marriage countless times. What does this archaic, poetic, mythic language tell us about woman and her relationship to man?

The sisters are those nagging voices within and often without. Once I was tuning a harpsichord of a friend and couldn't help overhearing the conversation of a coffee klatch going on in the kitchen. Several women were egging each other on to criticize their husbands and their marriages. Here were the two sisters. It affected me so much that I quietly packed up and left. I could not stay in the presence of that venomous talk. Here were the sisters at work.

There is, of course, the positive side, too. The sisters cause Psyche to become conscious, to know Eros as he is, but this consciousness is won at such high cost! It means overturning the old order. And this is often so. For consciousness we are apt to pay a Promethean cost.

I am personally terrified of the sister quality in a woman, but it is useful and essential in its place. It does not necessarily follow that one becomes conscious because the nagging sisters appear. One can get stuck there and go no further. One can get stuck at any point. There are women, for example, who are chained on the mountain of death all the rest of their lives. Their relationship with men is then colored by their picture of man as a frightening emissary of death.

Some women do experience love as the devouring dragon, and in that case the sisters are telling the truth. Neumann says that Psyche was devoured by death. Eros comes, and beautiful as he is, he *is* death to her. All husbands are death to their wives in that they destroy them as maidens and force them into an evolution toward mature womanhood. It is paradoxical, but one is both grateful and resentful to the person who sets one on the path of evolution. The oracle was right. A man is death to a woman in an archetypal sense. When a man sees an anguished look on his wife's face, this is a time for him to be gentle and cautious; it may be that she is just waking up to the fact that she is dying a little as a maiden. He can make it easier for her at this moment if he understands.

Usually a man doesn't understand this death-resurrection in a woman as he has no parallel to it in his own life. Marriage is not a sacrificial matter to a man, but that is its chief characteristic for a woman. She looks at her husband in horror one day because she realizes she is caught, trapped, at his mercy. If she has children with a man, she is so much more tied to him.

The truth is, a woman goes through a bewildering series

of relationships with her husband. He is the god of love, and he is death on the top of the mountain; he is the unknown one in paradise, and he is the censor when she demands consciousness. And finally, he is the god of love at the summit of Olympus when and if she comes to her own goddesshood. All this is simply bewildering to a man. Small wonder that many a man peers around the door a little gingerly when he comes home each day to see which role is waiting for him. Add to this his own anima involvements, and it makes a complex story, but a beautiful one.

The sisters are the demand for evolution from an unexpected source. They may be Psyche's shadow. Jung described the shadow elements in a personality as those repressed or unlived sides of a person's total potentiality. Through lack of attention and development, these unlived and repressed qualities remain archaic or turn dark and threatening. These potentialities for good and evil, though repressed, remain in the unconscious, where they gather energy until finally they begin to erupt arbitrarily into our conscious lives, just as the sisters came into Psyche's life.

If we see ourselves consciously as pure loveliness and gentleness only, as Psyche apparently did, we are overlooking this dark side and it may emerge to push us out of our self-satisfied, naive paradise into new discoveries about our true depths.

Jung said that the demand for evolution in consciousness often comes from the shadow. So the sisters, those less lovely, less perfect representatives of the more ordinary, down-to-earth femininity, may be shadow elements in the Psyche myth.*

*C. S. Lewis treats this aspect of the myth—Psyche's naive identification with her own loveliness and the less lovely sisters' reaction to it—in his book *Till We Have Faces* (Grand Rapids: William B. Eerdmans Publishing Company, 1956).

5

Eros has worked as hard as he can to keep Psyche unconscious. He promised her paradise if she would not look at
him. In this way he sought to dominate her.

A woman usually lives some time during her life under
the domination of the man within her or the god within
her, the animus. Her own inner Eros keeps her, quite
without her conscious awareness, in paradise. She may not
question; she may not have a real relationship with him;
she is completely subject to his hidden domination.

It is one of the great dramas in the interior life of a
woman when she challenges the animus's supremacy and
says, "I *will* look at you." And when she looks, she sees
something beyond the human—a god or an archetype—
but in so doing she plunges herself into a loneliness that
is nearly unendurable. That is why the stalemate, the domination, the time in paradise, goes on for so long. A woman
knows intuitively that if she breaks up this state of animus
possession, it brings the most hellish kind of loneliness.

Many women experience but do not recognize the animus's autonomy over them. I remember a woman who
came to see me and related a dream in which she had made
something that was precious to her. The animus figure in

the dream said, "Give it to me." And she did. I rose straight up in the air when I heard this. I said to her, "You go back and redo that dream, and you tell him that he may not have it."

However, once a woman *sees* the animus, he can no longer be dominant in her psyche. When she knows she has an animus and she relates to him, she is no longer subservient.

The child promised to Psyche by Eros will be a god (totally unconscious) if she obeys and does as she is told —asks no questions and does not light the lamp of consciousness to see her Eros nature as it truly is. This is a possibility, and it may be that a woman will want to live in this timeless, primordial way, but she will be alien to the modern world if she does. Almost all modern women ask the questions, light the lamps, and insist on their own consciousnesses.

One of the most rewarding bits of symbolism in our story is the instruction given by the two sisters. Psyche is advised to provide herself with a light and a knife, two masculine symbols. It is exceedingly useful if a woman can understand her capacity to wield these two instruments. What does a wife do that is lamplike and what does she do that is knifelike? The sisters even tell Psyche what joint to cut through, the joint between the head and the rest of the body, to behead this terrible monster.

I think we can state it as a profound and powerful law: A woman should use the lamp, but not the knife. The knife is for private use, for discrimination, for clarity, for cutting through the fogbanks. It is for internal use. If a woman could remember to use the lamp first in the difficult times in her marriage, then she could choose whether or not to use the knife or where to use it. Usually the knife comes out first; then she gets out the lamp to see what she has done.

The knife is that devastating capacity a woman has of impaling a man with a flow of words: It is the devastating remark that skewers a man. This is also one of the ways a man's anima, his feminine side, behaves when he is in poor relationship to it. It is cutting and sarcastic; it comes with knife in hand. Our law, to use the lamp and not the knife, applies equally to the man's inner anima as well as to the outer woman.

What, then, is the lamp, and what does it show? It revealed that Eros was a god. A woman has the capacity to show the value of her man with the lamp of her consciousness. At his best, a man knows who he is, and he knows he has a god, a magnificent being, somewhere within him. But when a woman lights the lamp and sees the god in him, he feels called upon to live up to that, to be strong in his consciousness. Naturally he trembles! Yet he seems to require this feminine acknowledgment of his worth. Terrible things happen to men who are deprived of the presence of women, for apparently it is the presence of women that reminds each man of the best that is in him.

During World War II, there were isolated groups of men stationed in the Aleutians. They could not be relieved properly because of transportation problems. None of the entertainment groups went near them. More than half of these men suffered nervous breakdowns. They wouldn't shave; they wouldn't cut their hair; morale broke down entirely. Perhaps it was because there was no woman, no Psyche looking upon Eros, to remind the men of their worth.

If a man is a bit discouraged, a woman can just look at him and restore him to his sense of value. There seems to be a peculiar vacant spot in a man's psychology here. Most men get their deepest conviction of self-worth from a woman, their wife or mother, or, if they are highly conscious, from their own anima. The woman sees and shows the man his value by lighting the lamp.

I was sitting in on a family quarrel once when a woman was wielding a knife vigorously. Far down on the list of her husband's transgressions was the complaint that he got home from the office so late. He said, "Don't you understand that I stay at the office for you?" The woman collapsed. She had heard something for once. Never before had she stopped talking long enough to hear. He said, "I wouldn't go to the office except for you. I don't like the office. I work for you." There was a sudden new dimension in that marriage. The woman could have seen this if she had lit the lamp and looked.

A man depends largely on the woman for the light in the family, as he is often not very good at finding meaning for himself. Life is often dry and barren for him unless someone bestows meaning on life for him. With a few words a woman can give meaning to a whole day's struggle, and a man will be very grateful. A man knows and wants this; he will edge up to it; he will initiate little occasions so that a woman can shed some light for him. When he comes home and recounts the events of the day, he is asking her to bestow meaning on them. This is part of the light-bearing quality of a woman.

The touch of light, or acknowledgment, is a fiery thing. It often stings a man into awareness, which is partly why he fears the feminine so much. A woman, or his anima, often leads a man into new consciousness. It is almost always the woman who says, "Let's sit down and talk about where we are." A man does not often say this. The woman is the carrier of evolution for him in one way or another. She sometimes lights him into a new kind of relationship. The man is terrified of that, but he is equally terrified at the loss of it. Actually, a man greatly appreciates a woman who bears a lamp; he depends on the feminine light more deeply than most men are willing to admit.

The oil is a feminine quality. I remember someone's speaking of the old lamps that used vegetable oil and moss wicks. The oil of olive is very feminine. And we also have the phrase "to be boiled in oil." A symbol always has two sides to it. The oil supplies the light, but it also burns Eros.

Feminine light is exquisitely beautiful. There is nothing finer than the light a woman gives forth. It is a Jewish custom for the woman to light the Sabbath candles on Friday evenings. One would think it would be the man, but it is the woman. It is she who begins the Sabbath, she who provides the light.

The symbolism of the lamp in the myth points to the light-bearing capacity of women. In the Eleusinian mysteries, the women often carry torches, which shed a peculiarly feminine kind of light. A torch softly lights up the immediate surroundings, shows the practical next step to be taken. This is unlike the cosmic masculine light of the sun that lights up so much territory one is sometimes overwhelmed and lost to the immediate experience.

On the other hand, women have the knife that can wound or kill. The man is vulnerable to both of these.

Very few women understand how great is the hunger in a man to be near femininity. This should not be a burden for a woman. She doesn't have to live her whole life feminizing. For as a man discovers and gets into a good relationship to his own inner femininity, he will not rely so heavily on the outer woman to live this out for him. But if a woman wishes to give a most precious gift to a man, if she would truly feed this greatest masculine hunger (a hunger that he will seldom show but that is always there), she will be very, very feminine when her man is in a mood, so he can get his bearings and be a man again.

6

Now comes the thorniest, but most rewarding, part of the myth. First Eros pricked his finger on his own love arrows and was catapulted into falling in love with Psyche. In a way, that is what upset, or set up, the whole thing. Eros was sent to get Psyche to fall in love with a monster, with Death itself, that most hideous of beasts, but he pricked his finger on one of his own arrows and fell in love with Psyche. Then she brought forth the lamp to look at her supposedly demon husband and saw that he was the god of love. Then she accidentally pricked her finger on one of his arrows and fell in love with the god of love. This is a most puzzling thing. Psyche fell in love with love.

The quality of being in love is a superhuman quality that mankind is not yet able to bear easily. When it happens to one, one is wafted off to realms that intoxicate, to superordinate levels of consciousness that, almost without exception, are beyond one's capacity to live.

We must differentiate between *loving* and *being in love*. To try to make definitions of these takes some courage.

Loving another person is seeing that person truly and appreciating him for what he actually is: his ordinariness, his failures, and his magnificence. If one can ever cut through that fog of projections in which one lives so much of his life and can look truly at another person, that person, in his down-to-earth individuality is a magnificent creature. The trouble is that there are so many people, and we are so blinded by our own projections, we rarely see another clearly in all his depth and nobility.

Once I tried an experiment: imagining that all of the people on earth were gone except one other person and myself. I went out on the sidewalks to see if I could find that one remaining person, to see what that person would be like and how I would welcome him. I found someone. For a little while I saw the miracle of what another human being can be. There was just one, and that one became infinitely valuable. A true marvel.

Loving is something like that. It is seeing another person for the down-to-earth, practical, immediate experience that another human being is. Loving is not illusory. It is not seeing the other person in a particular role or image we have designed for him. Loving is valuing another for his personal uniqueness within the context of the ordinary world. That is durable. It stands up. It is real. If someone had told me ten or fifteen years ago that I would be equating love and durability, I would have been shocked and angry, but I suppose this is a wisdom that middle age brings.

Being in love is another matter. Being in love is an intrusion, for better or for worse, of an archetypal, a superpersonal, or a divine world. Suddenly one sees in one's beloved a god or a goddess; through him or her one sees into a superpersonal, superconscious realm of being. All this is highly explosive and inflammatory, a divine madness. The poets tell us about it in extravagant terms.

If one watches people in love looking at each other, one knows perfectly well that they are looking *through* each other. Each is in love with an idea, or an ideal, or an emotion. They are in love with love. The women are Psyche, seeing Eros in his role as the god of love rather than as a person she knows and loves for himself.

The worst thing about being in love is that it is not durable; it doesn't last. One day the bright vision of the beloved, which had previously danced with such beauty before one's eyes, seems plain and dull. The transpersonal godlike quality dims, and the personal, down-to-earth, ordinary man is revealed. This is one of the saddest and most painful experiences in life. The quality of being in love is a visitation of something divine. It is a god or a goddess on the face of the earth and does not fit at all well into human dimensions.

So what is the myth saying? The god of love himself, Eros, is pricked by one of his own arrows and falls in love with a mortal. Apparently the gods can get by with this. It is not too difficult for the god of love to be assailed by the experience of being in love because it is his nature.

Yet even the Olympians are afraid of Eros; those arrows send even the highest of the gods and goddesses into a panic. Even they are vulnerable, and the god of love himself knows the experience of being in love.

But when a mere mortal is suddenly pricked by that fatal arrow and falls in love, it is very serious. It was said that Psyche's rash look at Eros was the first time in history that a mortal has ever encountered a god or goddess and survived. Prior to this, when a mortal came into contact with a god or goddess, he was incinerated, obliterated by the power of the encounter.

Translated into psychological terms, one can say that

prior to this point in the evolution of mankind, if a man or woman actually touched an archetype, he or she was simply obliterated. The myth is telling us that henceforth, and under certain circumstances, when a mere mortal undergoes an archetypal experience, he may survive it but will be radically changed by it. I think this is what our story is teaching us. A mortal is touching something of supermortal dimensions and lives to tell the tale. Within this context, one can see what it means to be touched by the arrows of the god of being-in-love. One can see the enormity of it, the transposition of levels involved. This is the incredible, explosive experience of falling in love.

People in the Orient do not "fall in love" the way people in the West do. They approach their relationships quietly, undramatically, untouched by the arrows of Eros. Marriages are arranged. Traditionally the man doesn't see his bride until the ceremony is over and the veils are lifted from her. Then he takes her home and follows the prescribed pattern for the newly married groom with his bride.

My own Western sentiments were touched the other day when I received a letter from a twenty-year-old Indian whom I don't know well, but with whom I had set up a correspondence. He had decided that I would be the perfect husband for his eighteen-year-old sister, and he wanted to know if I would agree to this. A dowry and such things could be discussed. I went around on a cloud all day. With no effort whatsoever, without even falling in love, I could have a bride, and an eighteen-year-old one at that. It did my morale no end of good. Then I wrote back and told him that it was not possible, that I was much too old for his sister.

Our story is about a woman who was touched by something far greater than ordinary human experience. The rest of the myth tells us how to survive this divine touching.

7

At one time the experience of being touched by the gods took place in a religious context, but we moderns have relegated religion to a relative side issue in our lives. We take it lightly and leave it for Sunday, if we observe it at all. One rarely hears of a person's being profoundly touched by a religious experience. Religion has cooled in our Western culture, and we think we are too wise for it. Even the people who cling to traditional religious forms are often not greatly moved by them; they are not nourished in a profound, earthshaking way in their spiritual, inner life.

It is my contention that this profound encounter, being touched by the splendor or the power of a god, has fallen to our peculiar Western notion of falling in love. *There* we are touched.

The myth says that Psyche lights the lamp and sees that she is indeed married to a god. She pricks her finger on one of his arrows and falls in love with love. And almost immediately after, she loses him. How often this is the experience of persons when they see the godhood of another, when they fall in love!

To love is to draw close to another person, to have ties, to merge with the other person. To be in love with a person is to look right through him and thus to lose that person irrevocably. This is bad news. We do not like it and seldom comprehend what it means.

If one looks at the godhood of another person, one looks at the magnificent, transpersonal dimensions he incorporates. By definition that puts him outside the scope of one's own ordinary realm, unless one has discovered one's own godhood, which is rare. This is why being in love hurts so much. There seems to be a built-in paradox that the moment one falls in love with someone, he must acknowledge that person's utter uniqueness and thus their separateness. In such a situation we are painfully aware of the distance, the separation, and the impossibility of relationship. Also there is the terrible feeling of inferiority a woman feels when she lights the lamp and discovers that the mate whom she had presumed was a mere mortal is a god. It is a devastating, lonely feeling.

Yet the very act of being torn to bits by being in love presents its own possibility of solution. If one has the strength and courage for it, out of this dismemberment may come a new consciousness of one's own uniqueness and worth. That is a very difficult way to go, but perhaps there is no other way for some temperaments.

The best way to solve this dilemma is to stand absolutely still, and that is what Psyche finally does. Once she gets over her suicidal feelings, she sits still. If one has been dazzled out of one's wits, if one has been knocked totally out of one's orbit, it is best to keep still. One can't tell youth this; it is just not possible. This is wisdom not often heard until our more mature years.

I once had to mediate in a very awkward situation in

which two people had fallen in love with one another and were creating considerable wreckage in the close community in which they lived. My advice was to leave them alone, to put no prohibitions on them, and they would balance it themselves. And they did. This is built into the being-in-love situation. It must have its barriers and its tragedy. Tragedy means seeing a vision one cannot attain. Philosophers and poets tell us that being in love is a tragic situation. I am not talking about love. As mentioned before, loving someone is warm; it is drawing close, and it is workable. But being in love, seeing the godhood of another person, is not humanly workable.

One can translate being in love into love. This is what a successful marriage does. A marriage begins in-love and hopefully makes the transition to loving. And that, in a way, is what our story is all about. It begins as the story of a collision between a mortal and a god, between two levels of being, between humanness and a superhuman quality. We long for that superhuman quality, and then wonder that we cannot keep it. It is not humanly possible to maintain the quality of in-loveness. I remember a James Thurber cartoon in which a middle-aged couple is quarreling and he hurls back at her, "Well, who took the magic out of our marriage!"

When one has been touched by a god or a goddess, what is one to do? That question is largely unanswered in our culture. Most people suffer and endure the fading of the godlike vision of the beloved, settle down into the humdrum of middle age, and think that their vision of a superhuman quality was all a bit foolish anyway. The feminine alternative to this self-defeating and depressing end to being in love occupies us for the rest of our story.

Psyche falls back upon her elemental femininity. She

seeks out Aphrodite and is given tasks to perform that are stages of evolution in her inner development, at the end of which she is summoned to Olympus and is herself made a goddess. She is married to Eros and gives birth to her child. This is the noblest possible answer to the most perplexing question facing our society.

To be touched by a godlike experience is to become open to learning a godlike consciousness, godlike in a Greek, Olympian sense. The Greeks spoke of the archetypes as gods, which is far more poetic and adequate than our modern terms. It is both beautiful and intelligent to speak of god and goddess, Eros and Psyche, who are the great archetypes functioning within us when we have fallen in love. Once this quality has touched us, we can never return to simple, carefree, unconscious ways. Almost always, for a modern person, this touch comes to us when we fall in love with another person. History tells us of many ways men have been touched by that which is greater than themselves, but for *our* time Eros is a principle intermediary between us and the power of God.

8

To move further into the myth, we recall that, when Psyche wounds him, Eros flies home to Aphrodite and does not appear again till the end of the myth. He goes home to mother. This is precisely what almost every man does when his wife wounds him into consciousness; he takes refuge in his mother complex. He may not go home physically, but he retreats into his mother complex and disappears for a while. If a man suddenly becomes silent, is perfunctory and not available, he may have "gone home to mother," and Aphrodite reigns.

On the other hand, if we view Eros as the woman's animus, we may perhaps say that Eros held Psyche in a state of unconscious animus possession in paradise until she lighted the lamp of consciousness and then, as animus, he flew back into the inner world.

Jung said that the anima and animus function most effectively for us as mediators between the conscious and unconscious parts of the personality. When Eros returns to the inner world of Aphrodite, he is able to mediate for Psyche with Aphrodite, Zeus, and the other gods and goddesses of the inner, archetypal world. As we shall see, he is able to send Psyche help at critical times in her development by using natural, earthly elements such as the ants, the eagle, and the reeds.

One might say that for a woman to evolve, she must break the unconscious domination of her subordinate, largely unconscious, masculine component, which dictates, often negatively, her relationship to the outer world. For her to evolve, the animus, consciously recognized as such, must take up a position between the conscious ego and the unconscious inner world where it can act as mediator, an essential help to her.

A woman in a state of animus possession is not consciously aware of her animus at all. She assumes that behavior arising from the animus is her own ego-originated behavior. In actual fact, her ego is taken over in these instances by the animus. However, when a woman lights the lamp of consciousness, she sees the animus quite correctly as separate from her ego. Like Psyche, she is usually overwhelmed. The animus seems so potent and godlike, and her conscious ego self so worthless and helpless by comparison. This is a desperate and dangerous moment for a woman. But it is not the end. After she goes through the awesome shock of first truly recognizing her animus and being overwhelmed with her own seeming inadequacy in comparison, she is then equally overwhelmed by its grandeur. If one sees that one has a godlike element within, the result is an exhilarating reaction, a peak experience, much like what happens when one falls in love.

When Psyche lighted the lamp, she expected to see a beast, but she saw a god. To women, man is often either a god or a beast. When I have the courage, I can say that when one truly shows the light upon another person, he finds a god or a goddess. I do not know any greater affirmation that one can have than to be told that when one truly looks at his or her mate, one finds a god or goddess. The same is true when a woman is finally able consciously to see her animus, her inner Eros. She finds that it is godlike.

This event for Psyche is in some ways comparable to Parsifal's first sight of the Grail castle. Parsifal sees a magnificent world beyond belief, but he is not able to remain there. Likewise, Psyche loses Eros almost immediately upon discovering his true and magnificent nature as a god.

In her devastation at having seen Eros fly away, Psyche immediately wants to drown herself in a river. At each difficult point, Psyche wants to kill herself. Does this not point toward a kind of self-sacrifice—sacrificing one level of consciousness for another? Most people are repelled by this, but it is essential. If we can get back to its archetypal meaning, we can profit by it. When a woman is touched by an archetypal experience, she will collapse before it. A man loses contact with his Grail castle and sometimes spends many long years recovering it. But a woman does not leave her Grail castle, at least not for long, and it is in her collapse that she quickly recovers her archetypal connection. This may not be a happy moment for a woman, but it restores inner connections and makes a positive and helpful quality available for her assistance.

It is bewildering to a man to discover the degree to which a woman has control over her feelings, a capacity unknown to most men. A woman can enter the Grail castle almost at will; she can go to a feminine touchstone when she chooses to. And that is most beautiful. An analogous performance is much more difficult for a man to do.

A woman still must go through her tasks, but she has the help of that highly introverted, inturned quality, which is Psyche-type femininity's way of responding to the god touch she experiences.

Psyche sits and waits for a solution. A man has to pocket his knife (sword, weapon), mount his new horse (bike, car), and go out and accomplish something. The feminine way, by woman or by anima, is to wait until something in her gives her the means and the way and the courage.

An ancient Chinese story illustrates this feminine principle, which is often not understood in our Western world. A village was suffering from a severe drought; the crops would be ruined if rain did not come soon. A famous rainmaker was summoned and offered anything he needed to bring the life-giving rain. He explored the village, then asked for a straw hut by himself and five days' worth of food and water. This was quickly arranged and the people waited. On the fourth day it began to rain. The village people went in joy and gratitude to the rainmaker's hut with gifts for the saving of their village. The rainmaker blinked and explained that he had not yet done the rainmaking ceremonies. He had felt so out of tune with himself when he walked about the village that he needed time to get in touch with his own rightness. And it had rained without any further work. It is this kind of "getting right" that is the great feminine art, whether it be in a woman or in the feminine part of a man. It is clear that we are not so much talking about male and female as about masculine and feminine. This "getting right" is always accomplished in the feminine by being very still.

A woman, or the feminine principle, seems to have to go back to a very still inner center every time something happens to her; and this is a creative act. She must go back to it, but must not drown in it. She is receptive, not passive.

I remember a very wise woman I once knew who, when I would pour out all of my woes, would say, "Wait." That was terrible for me. My horse was already pawing the ground with impatience. I did not want to be told to wait, but it was right to do so, right, that is, if the problem happened to be a feminine one.

During World War II, when I worked for the American Red Cross, I went into my supervisor's office and poured out all my excitement, saying, "This has happened, and this has happened, and this has happened, and what shall I do?" She looked at me, and said quietly, "You go to lunch." She knew.

It is that feminine quality of getting back to stillness that is the sacrifice. It is observed in the Christian tradition when we say, "Here we offer and present unto Thee ourselves, . . . a living sacrifice."

Psyche makes the sacrifice. She goes to the river to give herself up, perhaps with the wrong motives, but with the right instincts.

Pan, the cloven-footed god with Echo in his lap, is sitting by the river. He sees that Psyche is about to drown herself and dissuades her. I have always read that, smiled, and gone on, but one has no right to go past anything in a myth. Why is it that Pan is the one who saves Psyche from the wrong kind of stillness?

We get the word *panic* from the god Pan. It is that feeling of being beside oneself, that wild quality, that near madness the ancients thought so highly of and we regret so bitterly when we get into it. This is the factor that helps Psyche. This myth is full of tiny observations or advice to one about what to do when one is stuck or overwhelmed. The advice at the moment is to go to Pan, the cloven-footed god. It is this god, so strange to our modern mentality, who can connect us again with earth and instinct in the right way, not in a suicidal way.

A woman's fit of weeping is a Pan reaction. Sometimes in a crisis it is a necessary and good reaction for her to have. If her husband is one who cannot stand to see a woman cry, she may simply have to put him through it anyway. Pan has something to say to her, and perhaps to him, in moments like these.

Pan tells Psyche that she must pray to the god of love, who understands when someone is inflamed by love. Here is a nice irony, that one must go to the very god who has wounded one to ask for one's relief. But it is good advice.

Being the god of love, Eros is the god of relationship. I think we can say that when a woman is in difficulty, she must turn to, must be loyal to Eros, to relationship. She must take it as her guiding principle to go the way consistent with relationship.

Psyche prays, she goes to the altars of the many goddesses instead of to Eros to ask for help, and she is rejected time after time. Each of the goddesses fears Aphrodite and will not anger her by helping Psyche.

At this stage in the Grail myth, Parsifal is Red Knighting, fighting heroic battles with all his energy. Psyche is going from altar to altar, praying. This is the same work as the man's—equal work, noble work, but differently done.

Psyche must continue to suffer until her way is clear. Fritz Kunkel once said that no one has the right to pull someone out of suffering prematurely. Psyche must go her way. If one is on the path of suffering or in one of these dry patches, sometimes one must just stay dry for a time. But if one understands the overall structure of one's suffering, a local dry patch is not so devastating or frightening.

Many of the women of the Bible had to suffer. Christ on the cross is suffering in his way, and the women at the foot of the cross are suffering in theirs.

Finally, Psyche realizes that she must go to Aphrodite herself, because it is she who holds the key to all of her difficulties. And she does.

Aphrodite gives a bitter, tyrannical speech. Psyche is reduced to nothing. She is told that she is good for nothing except to be a scullery maid, and that if there is any place in the world for her, which is doubtful, it is to be set to the lowest tasks possible, which is precisely what Aphrodite proceeds to do. The first of the four famous tasks is laid out for Psyche as a condition for her deliverance.

9

Aphrodite shows Psyche a huge pile of seeds of many different kinds mixed together and tells her she must sort these seeds before nightfall or the penalty will be death. Then Aphrodite sweeps off in grandeur to a wedding festival. Poor Psyche is left with this impossible task, which no one could conceivably do. So she sits still again and waits.

We may assume that Eros, as animus, now back in the inner world and no longer with Psyche in a state of unconscious animus possession, is able to mediate for her and to aid her in finding the strength and wisdom she needs to accomplish her tasks. We assume that it is through him that the ants hear of Psyche's dilemma and sort the seeds for her. By dusk the task is completed, and when Aphrodite comes back to check on the situation, she grudgingly allows that for such a worthless creature, Psyche has done well.

What a beautiful bit of symbolism, a pile of seeds to sort! In many of the practical matters of life, in the running of a household, for example, a woman's task is to see that form, or order, prevails. That is sorting. What household has not echoed to the cry of "Mom, where is my other sock?"

A man goes to a woman for this household sorting. The man is off to more important things, as he sees it, in the affairs of the world, and it is left to the woman to keep order in his home life. Yet a man typically does not think of a woman as being well able to sort, to discriminate, to order.

When a man makes love to a woman, he gives her seeds past comprehension, millions of seeds. She has to choose one. There, on a very rudimentary level, is the sorting. It is she who chooses, unconsciously in this case, which of these many, many seeds to develop. Nature in its excess produces so much, and the woman sorts.

In other departments of life, a woman is flooded with things to sort. When the household quiets down, a woman is left with a bewildering array of possibilities. This is hard on pure feminine nature, which has been described by Irene de Castillejo as diffused awareness, as opposed to masculine nature, which is focused consciousness. Most cultures try to solve this through custom and law by stipulating what a woman shall do to save her from having to sort. But we are a free people, and we have no such safeguards, so a woman must know how to differentiate, how to sort creatively. To do this she needs to find her ant nature, that primitive, chthonic, earthy quality that will help her. The ant nature is not of the intellect; it does not give us rules to follow. It is a primitive, instinctive, quiet quality, perhaps a masculine attribute, yet legitimately available to women.

It is profitable for a woman to gain some proficiency in this seed-sorting attribute. One might do one's tasks in a kind of geometric way, the nearest one first or the one closest to one's feeling value first. In this primitive, simple, earthy way one can break the impasse of too-muchness.

Perhaps this seed-sorting attribute is a part of woman's inner masculinity—an echo of Eros. But a woman must remember *this* basic law, that she use this cool, dry, highly discriminating function that is her animus as a connection between her conscious ego and the inner world, the collective unconscious. The animus (and anima) belong primarily in the heavens and the hells of the inner world. Animus and anima are curiously part human and part god, part personal and part transpersonal. That is why they make such excellent intermediaries between the personality and the collective unconscious. They have a foot in each world: They function best as inner spiritual guides for the conscious ego as it goes about the world.

We often depreciate the animus, but that is justified only when it is used in the wrong place. If it appears outwardly, it usually makes trouble; but it *is* a key to one's spiritual life when it functions inwardly. It is the chief connection between us as individuals and that great inner oneness, the godhead, the collective unconscious. That is where the animus truly belongs.

I think we are in trouble in our basic attitude toward sorting these days. The modern woman rebels against this act of sorting for her family, for instance, but it is a primary requirement for her development. I hasten to say that she should not have to sort things that do not belong to her. To have to sort too many objective things in the outside world is not required of all women. An amazon type (as defined in Tony Wolff's description of the four types of woman as mother, hetaera, medium, and amazon) or a businesswoman can cope with such sorting. She has a highly developed ant nature and can use her masculine component in the outer world.

Another kind of feminine sorting is not so well known

these days. I think we trip over it and come to grief with
it. The feminine in a woman, or the anima in a man, must
sort out the influx of material from the unconscious and
relate it properly and orderly to consciousness. This is, to
my mind, the great feminine function, often overlooked in
our culture.

The masculine component in personality, in man and
woman, deals primarily with the outer world, while the
feminine component deals primarily with the inner world.

A fine image of a marriage partnership is one in which
the man and woman stand back to back, he facing the
outer world where he is more at home and she the inner
world where she is more at home. But this is not a static
situation; they each hopefully move toward wholeness,
which is the total Janus-faced personality facing at once
the inner and the outer worlds.

Ideally one might imagine the man and woman as two
overlapping circles. In the beginning of their psychological development there is very little overlapping; the man
deals with and protects the family from the outer world,
while the woman deals with and protects the family from
the inner world. Gradually, as the woman and the man
each develop sufficiently their own capacities to face in
both directions, the circles move together and the overlap
is deeper.

It often happens today that both partners face toward
the outer world and neither is aware of the unconscious
or inner world. The family is left unguarded at this point.
I would urge women to take up their natural and noble
work of facing and mediating the inner world for themselves, for their husbands and families, and for society,
while helping others to learn to see the inner world for
themselves. Sorting out the influx of emotions, moods, and
archetypes for the family is a beautiful, feminine act.

10

The second of Psyche's tasks, arrogantly and insultingly set out by Aphrodite, is to go to a certain field across a river and get some of the golden fleece of the rams that are pastured there. She is to be back by nightfall on pain of death.

Psyche must be very brave (*foolhardy* is a better word, for the rams are very fierce) if she is to accomplish this dangerous task. Once more she collapses and thinks of suicide. She goes toward the river, which separates her from the field of the sun rams, intending to throw herself in. But just at the critical moment, the reeds in the river's edge speak to her and give her advice.

The reeds tell Psyche not to go near the rams during the daylight hours to get the wool—she would immediately be battered to death—but to go at dusk and take some of their wool that has been brushed off by the brambles and low-hanging boughs of a grove of trees that stand in the field and under which the rams often pass. There she will get enough of the golden fleece to satisfy Aphrodite without even attracting the attention of the rams. Psyche is told not to go directly to the rams or try to take the golden fleece by force because they are dangerous, aggressive beasts that can kill her. Some masculinity looks like this to women. Every woman needs to learn to relate with courage to the outer world, but she knows instinctively that too much of it at once is fatal, and even to go near it can be dangerous. Imagine a very feminine woman at the beginning of her lifework, looking at the modern world and knowing that she must make her way through it. She fears that she will be killed. Just walking downtown and coming home again is frightening. One can be bludgeoned to death, depersonalized by the ram nature of the patriarchal, competitive, impersonal society in which we live.

A distinction needs to be made here between rams and fleece. Perhaps we should go back briefly to the myth of the quest for the golden fleece to gain some insight about Psyche's task.

The quest for the golden fleece is one of the great masculine myths of antiquity. In it Jason and his friends prove their courage, strength, and virility. Edith Hamilton says of the quest: "Each of the finest men in Greece who came with Jason has a desire not to be left behind nursing a life without peril by his mother's side, but even at the price of death to drink with his comrades the peerless elixir of valor."

The famous golden fleece was the fleece of a ram who saved two youths, the girl Helle and the boy Phrixos, from death at the hands of their father and stepmother. He flew in at the last moment, gathered the prince and princess up, and flew away with them. Unfortunately, the girl was dropped into the sea and drowned. The boy, when he was safely set down in another kingdom, killed the ram as a sacrifice of thanksgiving. The golden fleece was then given to the king of that land by Phrixos. It was much later that Jason and the others came in search of it from Phrixos's homeland.

We can see that the ram represents a mighty power capable of saving a person from a parental situation that threatens his life. It represents a great, elemental, natural force that one can tap at times through an archetype, or it can erupt unexpectedly as an invading complex within a personality. This power is awesome and numinous. It is the burning bush; it is the vast unconscious depths that can sweep aside the frail ego if it is not in the right connection to it.

A man may have access to or be taken over by the ram force at times, but he should not identify with it. It is no accident that in the myth the girl drops into the sea and drowns. A man in the throes of a ram complex is not in relationship to his inner femininity—it is lost in the unconscious, in the sea. In the Grail myth we learned that women did not fare well while the men were Red Knighting. Ramming seems in some ways similar to Red Knighting. In either case, femininity suffers.

As mentioned above, after Phrixos was safely set down again on earth, he piously sacrificed the ram, retaining the golden fleece, which is the Logos symbol. There is as close and organic a connection between Logos and power as there is between fleece and ram. Modern Western man, using his Logos, his rational scientific mind, has found a way to tap the sources of power in his universe. By so doing, he has accrued awesome power over other men and over nature. Modern technological man has assumed a godlike quantity of power and is in danger of destroying his world with it.

How shall he manage this awesome power to his own and nature's advantage? The ancient myths tell us: Sacrifice the ram and keep the fleece, or take only that fleece which has pulled off on the bushes and cannot cause an eruption of ram madness. Or, as the modern mythmaker

Tolkien tells us, throw the ring of power back into the earth. Or, in Eastern terminology, keep a balance between Yang and Yin, between Logos and Eros. The Psyche myth says one must not try to take or use the fleece that still grows on the rams; elemental knowledge connected to elemental power is capable of destroying instantaneously.

Modern man needs to give up his godlike assumption of unnatural power over nature and the destiny of the entire world. His Logos has led him into a fixation with power, into an inflated identification with the ram, and he is not an adequate carrier of that force. Just as a person who gets too close to an archetype is obliterated, a person identifying with the ram will also be destroyed.

John Sanford observes that if a young person takes drugs before he has developed a strong enough ego to withstand the massive interior experience he may encounter, he may be obliterated. We moderns, men and women, are grasping a ram of massive proportions that may turn on us and destroy us. Should we not give up naked power plays and keep Logos in proper proportion with Eros and relatedness, relatedness to each other and to nature?

Perhaps the myth's statement of *how* much fleece and *how* much Logos speaks not only to women, but also to men. We can handle only as much Logos as will not cause an eruption of power that will destroy us personally or collectively.

There is a distinction between the masculine and the feminine way of obtaining the fleece, between the way Phrixos acquires it and the way Psyche acquires it. Phrixos must kill the ram sacrificially. Psyche need not kill the ram; she is to avoid direct contact with it and gather fleece from the branches and boughs. The idea of having to take the remnants, just the scrapings of Logos off the boughs, may sound intolerable to a modern woman. Why should a woman have to get just a little of this quality? Why can't she simply pin down the ram, take his fleece, and go with it in triumph as a man does?

Delilah accomplished her masculine need in just this way. The Psyche myth tells us that a woman can get the necessary masculinity for her purposes without a power play. Psyche's way is much gentler. If a woman wants to wield some masculine power, she need not gain it in the masculine way.

There are women who need a greater share of masculinity than the myth indicates. One is reminded of the amazons who took off their left breasts (which meant giving up a significant part of their femininity) so that they could draw a bow without the breast getting in the way of the bowstring when it was released. More masculinity may mean less femininity, and this is just the problem.

It is my feeling that Western civilization took a wrong turn some time ago, and the place of femininity is in jeopardy now. That is why this myth is so important. It talks about a right way and a wrong way for a woman to function. It is saying that a woman can get all she really needs of masculinity in a feminine way.

The myth is in no way saying that a woman may not have fleece or that she may not use her focused consciousness, her masculine component. It is saying that just as a man will only be hampered by an excess of the feminine quality, so a woman requires only a little of the fleece.

Actually, at the time the myth of Psyche emerged, the very idea that Psyche should have *any* of the fleece was novel indeed. Until that time, the quest for the golden fleece was a masculine quest, a great masculine adventure.

To obtain a bit of the golden fleece required Psyche to find and use her own courage, valor, adventuring spirit, and strength. This task was necessary for the development of women beyond the purely instinctive, unconscious feminine stage. To be sent out to gather fleece was a great advance for womankind.

And we must remember, too, that a microcosm is a macrocosm. A bit of the Logos is all of the Logos. One is reminded of the story of Christ, who was walking amidst a great crowd, jostled and touched by many people around him. Yet one woman, in a right attitude, had only to touch the hem of his garment and she was healed and made whole.

The myth tells us that the feminine need only obtain a bit of the fleece—the hem, not the whole garment—to have enough for her purposes, to be made whole.

When we talk of a woman's acquiring fleece, or masculinity, we must understand that we are not striving for an equal amount of masculinity and femininity within ourselves. Many women say they want just as much focused consciousness as a man. This is not reasonable or safe. One must be a woman with masculinity backing her up, or one must be a man with femininity backing him up. The masculinity in a woman is a minority. We all have such limits dictated by biological limits or functions. The woman who understands this can go into the business world and use her objective masculinity. She brings, along with a focused consciousness, her quietness, her touch with the source, her quality of reminding those around her of the Grail castle.

With a teenage son, a woman should be alert to this principle: She should not seek to know too much too quickly; she must not snatch the boy's world from him, take his sword away from him. A boy's masculine world is fragile and vulnerable, especially if confronted suddenly and aggressively by his mother's own masculine side.

11

Back to the myth. Aphrodite now appears and discovers that, incredibly, Psyche *has* the bit of golden fleece. In her anger she decides to really defeat Psyche. She tells the girl that she must fill a crystal goblet with water from the Styx, a river that tumbles from a high mountain, disappears into the earth, and comes back to the high mountain again. It is a circular stream, ever returning to its source, down into the depths of hell and back up to the highest crag again. This stream is guarded by dangerous monsters, and there is no place where one can set foot near enough to the stream to get even one little goblet of water from it.

True to form, Psyche collapses, but this time she is numb with defeat and cannot even cry. Then an eagle of Zeus appears.

The eagle assisted Zeus in a certain amorous episode earlier, so eagle and Zeus have a certain camaraderie. Zeus, now willing to protect his son Eros openly, asks the eagle to assist Psyche. The eagle flies to her in her distress and asks her to give him the crystal goblet. Flying to the center of the stream, he lowers the goblet into the dangerous waters, fills it for her, and brings the vessel safely back to Psyche. Her task is accomplished.

The river is the river of life; it flows high and low, from the high mountains down into the depths of the earth. The current of the river is fast-flowing and treacherous; the banks are slippery and steep. Approaching too closely, one could easily be swept off and drowned in the waters or crushed on the rocks below.

I think that this task is telling us how the feminine must relate to the vastness of life. She may take only one goblet of water. The feminine way is to do one thing and to do it well. She is not denied a second or third or tenth thing, but she must take it one goblet at a time, each in good order.

The feminine aspect of the human psyche has been described by some psychologists as unfocused consciousness. The feminine nature is flooded with the rich vastness of possibilities in life and is drawn to all of them, usually all at once. The difficulty with this is that it is impossible; one cannot do or be everything at once. Many of the possibilities open to us oppose each other, and one must choose among them. Like the eagle, who has a panoramic vision, one must look at the vast river, focus on a single spot, and then dip out a single goblet of water.

There is a heresy abroad today which states that if a little is good, more is better. Advertisements tell us to "grab all the gusto we can" in life. This will not work. It means that one is never satisfied. Even while one is engaged in one rich experience, he is looking about for other possibilities. He is never content with anything because he is always searching for something bigger and better.

Our myth tells us that a little of a quality, experienced in high consciousness, is sufficient for us. As the poet tells us, we may see the world in a grain of sand. We can focus on one aspect of life or one experience, concentrate on it, drink it in, and be satisfied. Then we can move on to whatever new experience may follow in good order.

The crystal goblet is the container in which the water is to be held. Crystal is, of course, very fragile and very precious. The human ego may be compared to the crystal goblet. It is a container for some of the vastness of the river of life. If the ego container, like the goblet, is not carefully handled in the beautiful but treacherous river, it can be shattered. One needs an eagle nature to see clearly to dip into the river at the right places and in the right manner. Perhaps, too, the ego that is attempting to raise to consciousness some of the vast unconscious depths within can be well advised to try to scoop up and contain only one goblet of water at a time lest he be overwhelmed and his ego container shattered.

The earthbound individual who approaches the river of life from the ground, from a point along its banks, from one single spot along its vast reaches, may, on the one hand, look down into a crashing, swirling confusion and feel that there is no way to sort it all out. Or, if he approaches the river from another bank at another spot, he may perhaps find a stagnant backwater with apparently no movement or life at all and see no prospect for change. An individual encountering the river of life from the narrow perspective of his own particular river bank may occasionally need to call on his eagle nature to lift his range of vision to take in more of the river, to see all the curves and turns and changes. Then he may put his own situation into better perspective and see other possibilities. We need our eagle natures, especially when we seem caught in a particularly grim bend in the river.

The advice given to us in this part of the myth is particularly appropriate for us today. Almost every woman I know has waded right out into the river and has been overwhelmed. Almost every woman I know is too busy. She is into this, studying that, driving in a car pool to this and to that, working hard on some big project, racing around until she is ragged. She needs to be quiet, to approach the vastness of life's responsibilities in a more orderly manner, to do one thing, take one crystal goblet, at a time, concentrate on it, and do it well. Then she may move on to other things.

12

Psyche's fourth task is far and away the most interesting of all, yet few women ever reach this level of development for it is beyond the range of most people's experience. Whenever I begin talking about this fourth task, I feel all the good earth of solid rationality and reason dissolving under my feet. Yet one must know these things if one is called to the last of Psyche's tasks.

Aphrodite says that Psyche must go into the underworld and obtain from the hand of Persephone herself (who reigns there) a little cask of her own beauty ointment. Psyche again collapses. This time the helper that comes to her aid is not a living being or even a natural phenomenon. A tower gives her instructions for her underworld journey.

Psyche is to take two coins in her mouth and two pieces of barley bread in her hands. She must refuse to assist a lame donkey driver who will ask her to pick up some sticks. She must pay the ferryman over the river Styx with one of the coins. She must refuse the groping hand of a dying man as he reaches up out of the water. She must refuse to assist three women who are weaving the threads of fate. She is to toss one of the pieces of barley bread to Cerberus, the three-headed dog who guards the entrance to hell, and while the three heads are quarreling over the bread, she is to go in. She is to refuse to eat anything but the simplest food in the underworld. And then she is to repeat the whole process in reverse on her way back.

A woman may not undertake the fourth task unless she has first gathered all the necessary strength from the first three. Almost always one needs a teacher or a guide, and unless one has the strength and courage, it is best not to undertake the fourth task. It is a terrible experience to be stranded partway through the underworld journey. Unless one has the coins, the barley bread, and, most important of all, the necessary information gathered from the tower, one should not begin this journey.

First one finds a proper tower, a human construction. The tower is masculine, a construct, a convention, a set of rules, a tradition, a system. Christianity is such a tower of strength and one of the best ones for us Westerners. Excellent examples of such towers are the spiritual exercises of Ignatius of Loyola, the lives of the saints, the liturgical year, and Christian retreats. Besides our own culture, there are the many systems of Yoga, Sufi mysticism, Zen, and other Oriental towers. In theory it does not matter which tower one chooses, though it is generally best for Westerners to remain with the traditions of their Western consciousness. Our own collective unconscious has patterns that are best suited to our Western ways.

The first thing that Psyche must learn is to curb her generosity, to say no to the lame man and the dying man (but only for this stage of her growth). I once had the profound experience of counseling a highly intelligent woman during this fourth stage. She nearly lost her way over this issue of feminine generosity, of having to say no to somebody. I often had to do it for her when she couldn't bear to do it herself. Somebody would phone and want something and she couldn't refuse. I had to be her tower and refuse for her. This went on for two years. It is a difficult time for a woman. During this task an old lame man drops a few sticks and asks for help to get them back on the donkey and she has to say no, or a dying man reaches up and she must say no.

Kindness and gift giving are very curious virtues. Our Western attitude toward generosity gives us almost no alternative but to be kind. When I was in India, I found a different attitude toward kindness. When I would think I was being kind to a beggar, for instance, my Indian friend would say to me, "Robert, why do you interfere in other people's lives?" I finally found an answer for him. I said, "Because I need to." "Well," he said, "if that is the case, then it's all right."

A Chinese parable speaks of the masculine and the feminine in this manner: A man stands on the mountain-top at dawn and holds forth his hands, palms up, to say the creative yes. A woman stands on the mountaintop at dawn and holds forth her hands, palms down, to say the creative no. In Chinese thought this is a way of expressing the fact that masculine and feminine each carry half of reality, the Yang and the Yin in Chinese terms, which complement each other perfectly. Each needs the other; each nourishes the other. It is the creative no with which we are concerned here, not an indifferent one. No as creation is a possibility all but lost in our modern Western world. A woman can come to a creative, limiting, form-giving no if she accomplishes this part of Psyche's journey.

This is true for a woman only in this fourth stage, only

when she has completed the other tasks. If she has not learned to be generous, this task will be poison to her. There are only certain times when the creative no is required. Then one drops it and can be generous again.

We do not have the bony hands of beggars in our society, but we have the demands on our time. The phone rings and we are asked to do a variety of things. The doorbell rings and someone wants us to give to some organization or charity. I finally decided this was not the way I wanted to give my money, but it took a lot of courage for me to say to the person at the door, "No, I have my own way."

In most primitive societies, if one does something for another, he is indebted to that person. In Africa, if one saves a man's life and that man commits a crime, the person who saved him is responsible. In India, my friend was constantly questioning me about my kindnesses to others. He would say, "Why are you doing that?" I would stutter around with such answers as "Well, it's a good thing to do" or "He touched my heart." And he would say, "That's no reason."

The myth tells us that a woman must not do good indiscriminately at this point in her life. Collective good particularly is forbidden. The reason for this is that the fourth task requires *all* of a person's energy and resources.

Ideally a woman goes through her tasks of individuation one stage at a time and incorporates the strength from one task, successfully completed, to help in the next. But practically it doesn't work exactly that way. We get all of them crowded together; all four stages impinge upon us indiscriminately. Possibly one should not even know about the fourth stage until one is actually drawn into it by necessity. Otherwise one might begin to nibble at it or to enter it a little bit. But there is no little bit to this fourth stage. Jung was adamant about this. He said, "If you are not going to see analysis through, don't begin." To make that great subterranean journey, the night sea journey, one must be prepared to carry it through. The ferryman needs his toll. One must have a sum of energy, enough energy stored up in advance to see himself across the river Styx and back.

Psyche must also say no to taking part in the weaving of fate. What woman can resist the opportunity of taking part in the weaving of the fate of the world, especially the superpersonal weaving of her children's lives, which she should not touch? A mother thinks she should guide her children, and in some respects this is true. But in other respects they are not her children; they are life's children. A mother should not stop her own life to take part in the weaving of their fate. She will serve them better by attending to her own fate.

So Psyche goes on her journey to the underworld. She was instructed not to eat very much in the underworld, so when Persephone offers her a banquet, Psyche remembers and refuses. She eats only bread and water. There is a strong suggestion here. In most cultures to eat a meal someplace is to forge permanent ties with that place, or family, or situation. Where one eats, one is somehow committed. That is why in India a Brahman will never eat in a low-caste house; it would tie him there.

Psyche gets the cask of beauty ointment and comes away, tossing the other piece of barley bread to the dog Cerberus as she quietly slips by. She finds the ferryman again, pays the second coin for her fare, and comes back.

Psyche brings the cask of beauty ointment up to the surface of the earth, past all these trials and difficulties, and then does a curious and foolish thing. She is suddenly overwhelmed by the thought that if this ointment is so precious to Aphrodite, why wouldn't it be good for her? So she opens the casket. Not beauty but a deadly sleep comes out of it and pours over her. Psyche falls to the ground as if dead.

(Let us carry the story on to the end, though we will come back to this point.)

When this happens, Eros senses or hears that his beloved is in danger, flies to Psyche, wipes the sleep off her, puts it back into the casket, closes the lid, picks Psyche up, and takes her to Olympus. (She would have died if he had not rescued her.) Eros talks with Zeus, who agrees that Psyche shall be made a goddess, to which Aphrodite raises no objections. She is apparently satisfied. The gods all agree, and Eros and Psyche are married. She gives birth to a girl, whom they name Pleasure.

13

How do we interpet Psyche's opening the beauty ointment, especially after all she had accomplished so bravely?

The beauty ointment may be a woman's preoccupation with beauty or attractiveness, with physical desirability. One can see how important this is to women throughout history, now as much as ever. A woman spends a good deal of time on her hair and her cosmetics. The masculine can never understand this.

Our society's obsession with eternal youth is in large part a demand for Persephone's beauty ointment. There are women who have opened the cask and put themselves to sleep, rendered themselves incapable of real relationships through preoccupation with externals. For a woman who is heavily made up is outside of relationship. She has on a mask, as every man knows. Sometimes such women are trying to please and rouse their inner Eros in this outer way, but in the process they lose much of their natural feminine grace.

Psyche's sleep is like a final collapse. It is the long-delayed sleep of death that was prescribed for her in the beginning by the oracle but that Eros delayed by whisking her off into his garden. Psychological death as transformation from one level of development to another is a common symbol in myths and dreams. One dies to the old self and puts on new life.

In the beginning Psyche was a lovely, innocent, feminine creature. To acquire new growth and new life she was required by the oracle, and by evolution, to die to her maidenly, perhaps narcissistic, preoccupation with her own beauty, innocence, and purity, and to become involved with life's complexities, including her dark and ugly sides and her own potentialities.

Now who could have understood all of this better than Persephone, to whom Psyche was sent for the beauty ointment? The Persephone of mythology was in the beginning herself a beautiful and innocent young maiden like Psyche, alive with youth and springtime freshness. She was preoccupied with beauty, and it was this preoccupation that drew her out of her innocence and into her destined role. She became entranced with a beautiful flower, the narcissus, created by Zeus especially for the purpose of luring her away from her friends so that Hades, the god of the underworld, could snatch her up and carry her away to the underworld to be his bride. After the rape of Persephone by Hades, and after her mother Demeter's long search and grief for her, Zeus finally permitted Persephone to come back from the underworld once each year in the spring.

Persephone had learned about beauty, its worth and its cost. She brought it yearly to the earth in the spring and summer, and she saw it wither and die with the first breath of frost as she descended again into the underworld. Yes, she knew about the fragility and desirability of beauty of any kind.

And so it is to Persephone that Psyche is sent in her final task. What better place? To whom else should the beautiful young Psyche be sent when she needed to die to her virgin, springtime preoccupation with her own narcissism, her own beauty, the narcissism that separated her from growth and from her fellow men?

Psyche had worked her way through three of the tasks, assimilating in each one progressively a more complex and more thoroughgoing conscious self-understanding. Finally, she faced the task of individuation itself, wholeness, completion. This required the deep descent into the unconscious, into the underworld, and could only be attempted after she had enough control to work at it consciously.

Curious, that having searched out in the depths of her own unconscious the secret of her problems, Psyche should regress to her former consciousness, open the casket, and die a symbolic death. When she attempts to keep and use the beauty ointment, the old consciousness, it becomes death for her.

Yet in this myth, as in most others, the death turns out to be only a sleep. For the animus, in his proper dimensions in the inner world of Olympus, is able to save the ego and arouse her again to new life on a new plane of existence. Ego and animus now have a proper, whole, complete relationship. She is his queen. The fruit of this union for her is joy and ecstasy, wholeness and divinity.

But we are not quite through with Psyche's death-sleep. Perhaps there has to be failure as well as success in order for any life to be whole. What an insufferable person Psyche would have been if she had done everything perfectly without one failure. The failure reminds her that she is human, and it reminds us of the necessity of failure in all growth.

Psyche's sleep reminds one of Christ's sleep of death in the tomb or of Jonah in the belly of the whale. This is the great sleep, the great death, the great collapse before the final victory.

We all have been trained to think that progress means success. There must, however, also be an opposite. John Sanford frequently speaks about the difference between perfection and completeness. For completeness, including failure, Psyche needed to fail here at the end of her journey. We all have our shadows, which often save us at critical moments.

When Psyche opens the lid of the casket, there is no beauty ointment in it; there is only the sleep of death. Perhaps it is the persona that Psyche has been working with. Beauty is death for her now.

Eros saves Psyche at the end of the myth, so salvation for her is a gift of wholeness, which is not earned but given by the gods. One may assume that it is Eros who has been strengthening Psyche all the time. It is Eros as animus who has appeared as ant, reed, eagle, and tower. If one takes this entirely as a woman's story, Eros is a woman's own interior animus who is being strengthened, healed, brought out of his boyish, trickster characteristics and made into a mature man worthy of being her mate. This is all done by her labor and by his cooperation. He in turn redeems her.

It is beautiful to find that some seemingly insurmountable problem has quietly worked itself out while one was busy on practical things. There is a Persian story of a young man who went up to the mountains, found a cave, and wandered in. He found a pearl of great price in the cave, but it was in the claws of a dragon so overwhelming that he knew there was no chance of getting the pearl. He went away sadly, reconciling himself to an ordinary life, which was uninspiring once he had seen the pearl. He married, had his family, worked, and then, in old age, when his children were gone and he was free again, he said, "Before I die, I will go back and look again at the pearl." He found his way back, looked inside the cave, and there was the pearl, as lovely as ever, but the dragon had shrunk to almost nothing. He picked up the pearl and carried it away. He had been fighting the dragon all of his life in the very practicalities of his daily existence.

The name of Psyche's child when it is born is translated as Pleasure. I have an intuition that it would be better to say joy or ecstasy. When a woman finally reaches her full development and discovers her own goddesshood, she gives birth to an element of pleasure, joy, or ecstasy.

I think possibly the crowning achievement of femininity is to be able to bring joy, ecstasy, pleasure into life. A man values a woman so highly because she has just this capacity or power. Men cannot find this ecstasy alone without the aid of the feminine element, so they find it either in an outer woman or in their own inner woman. Joy is a gift from the heart of woman.

It is a woman's supreme privilege and development to be a bringer of joy. In Zen Buddhism there is a tradition called the Ten Oxherding Pictures, in which the development of a man is depicted as a series of encounters with an ox or bull. Many artists have undertaken to portray the life journey of man, his spiritual development, in this fanciful way. In the first picture the man searches for his lost ox (instinct, powerful nature); in the second he finds traces of the ox; in the third he sees the ox; in the fourth he catches hold of the resisting animal; in the fifth he leads the now docile creature; in the sixth the oxherd is seated on the animal's back; the seventh shows the man meditating without the ox being near; in the eighth both man and ox have gone out of sight; in the ninth the man has returned to his beginning point in peace and tranquillity. In the tenth a sublime moment is recorded in which the man, now having his enlightenment, walks down a lane in the most ordinary way, in ordinary clothing, with nothing to mark him from any other peasant. A joy and brightness follow him, however, and all the trees burst into blossom as he passes by.

I think this is equivalent to an individual woman's final joyful state. She has and she is a beatific vision. The fruit of all her labors is joy and ecstasy.

Suggestions for
Further Reading

de Castillejo, Irene C. *Knowing Woman*. New York: G. P. Putnam's Sons (hardback). New York: Harper & Row (paperback).

Grinnell, Robert. *Alchemy in a Modern Woman*. Zurich: Spring Publications.

Harding, M. Esther. *The Way of All Women*. New York: G. P. Putnam's Sons (hardback). New York: Harper & Row (paperback).

———. *Women's Mysteries*. New York: G. P. Putnam's Sons (hardback). New York: Bantam Books (paperback).

Layard, John. *The Virgin Archetype*. Zurich: Spring Publications.

Lewis, C. S. *Till We Have Faces*. Grand Rapids: Wm. B. Eerdmans Publishing Co.

Neumann, Erich. *Amor and Psyche*. Princeton: Princeton University Press (hardback and paperback).

von Franz, Marie-Louis. *Problems of the Feminine in Fairytales*. Zurich: Spring Publications.

Weaver, Rix. *The Old Wise Woman*. New York: G. P. Putnam's Sons.

A piercing scream cut through
the air-conditioned halls . . .

This was getting old. There was enough screaming going on at Fernglen this morning to make me think I'd wandered into a haunted house attraction or teen slasher flick by mistake. Why did a gecko or garter snake elicit so much fear? Maybe, I decided, because it was out of context in a mall, unexpected. If you were gardening or hiking through a state forest, you'd be half-thinking you might see a lizard or snake, so it wouldn't startle you as much. At the mall, the scariest thing you expected to see was the total on your credit card receipt.

Following the continued screeching, I hooked a sharp left into the Dillard's wing. A young woman with a stroller stood halfway down the hall, arm outstretched and finger pointed rigidly at Diamanté's display window. Her mouth opened wide as she screamed, the sound changing to a gasping attempt at words when she saw me approaching. "It's . . . it's . . . it's . . ." she huffed.

"It's nothing to be afraid of, ma'am," I said in my most comforting voice. A peek into the stroller showed me an infant in head-to-toe pink, sleeping through her mommy's hysteria. "It's harmless. Just a—" I swiveled to look in the window, hoping to be able to say, "just an iguana," or "just a corn snake."

But it wasn't a corn snake or an iguana or even Agatha. It wasn't a reptile at all. It was a man. A naked man. A completely naked, completely dead man.

Die Buying

Laura DiSilverio

BERKLEY PRIME CRIME, NEW YORK

THE BERKLEY PUBLISHING GROUP
Published by the Penguin Group
Penguin Group (USA) Inc.
375 Hudson Street, New York, New York 10014, USA
Penguin Group (Canada), 90 Eglinton Avenue East, Suite 700, Toronto, Ontario M4P 2Y3, Canada
(a division of Pearson Penguin Canada Inc.)
Penguin Books Ltd., 80 Strand, London WC2R 0RL, England
Penguin Group Ireland, 25 St. Stephen's Green, Dublin 2, Ireland (a division of Penguin Books Ltd.)
Penguin Group (Australia), 250 Camberwell Road, Camberwell, Victoria 3124, Australia
(a division of Pearson Australia Group Pty. Ltd.)
Penguin Books India Pvt. Ltd., 11 Community Centre, Panchsheel Park, New Delhi—110 017, India
Penguin Group (NZ), 67 Apollo Drive, Rosedale, Auckland 0632, New Zealand
(a division of Pearson New Zealand Ltd.)
Penguin Books (South Africa) (Pty.) Ltd., 24 Sturdee Avenue, Rosebank, Johannesburg 2196,
South Africa

Penguin Books Ltd., Registered Offices: 80 Strand, London WC2R 0RL, England

This is a work of fiction. Names, characters, places, and incidents either are the product of the author's imagination or are used fictitiously, and any resemblance to actual persons, living or dead, business establishments, events, or locales is entirely coincidental. The publisher does not have any control over and does not assume any responsibility for author or third-party websites or their content.

DIE BUYING

A Berkley Prime Crime Book / published by arrangement with the author

PRINTING HISTORY
Berkley Prime Crime mass-market edition / August 2011

Copyright © 2011 by Laura DiSilverio.
Cover illustration by Ben Perini.
Cover design by Rita Frangie.
Interior text design by Laura K. Corless.

ISBN: 978-0-425-24273-5

BERKLEY® PRIME CRIME
Berkley Prime Crime Books are published by The Berkley Publishing Group,
a division of Penguin Group (USA) Inc.,
375 Hudson Street, New York, New York 10014.
BERKLEY® PRIME CRIME and the PRIME CRIME logo are trademarks of Penguin Group (USA)
Inc.

PRINTED IN THE UNITED STATES OF AMERICA

10   9   8   7   6   5   4   3   2   1

For all wounded warriors,
in thanks for your service and sacrifices

Acknowledgments

I owe a huge debt of gratitude to Mr. Ed Beane, director of security at Chapel Hills Mall, and his deputy, Robert Bullard, for cluing me in on what real mall cops do. Any errors in this book—procedural, operational, or otherwise—are mine, and attributable to the needs of the plot or my lack of understanding.

I also want to thank my good friend Lester Sharpless for giving me a tutorial on roller derby, a sport I'd want to try if I didn't know my aging bones and joints would make me very, very sorry.

As usual, thanks to the women who critique my writing efforts: Joan Hankins, Marie Layton, Amy Tracy, and Lin Poyer. Thanks also to my agent, Paige Wheeler, and her team at Folio Literary Management, and my editor, Michelle Vega, and all the folks at Berkley Prime Crime, especially my energetic and enthusiastic publicist, Kaitlyn Kennedy, and Ben Perini and Rita Frangie, who created this book's gorgeous cover.

My writing would not be possible, satisfying, or fun without the love and support of my beloved husband and daughters, and a host of friends full of goodwill and encouragement. Special thanks to Jill Gaebler, Cindy Stauffer, Retha Bosley (the source of Anders Helland's name), Katie Smith, Hans VonMilla, Patrick Butler, Fred and Ellen Gortler, Tim and Christy Mulligan, and Linda Major, who have gone out of their way to convince their friends, librarians, and local booksellers that my books are worth reading. I am truly blessed by your friendship.

One

. . .

It amazed me how a few hundred feet of tile floors and narrow halls amplified a scream.

With the Fernglen Galleria empty of shoppers at this early hour, the terror-stricken wail ricocheted off the tiles, so I couldn't quite tell where it was coming from. The fear in the sound got to me, though, and I pivoted my Segway, the two-wheeled electric vehicle I used to patrol miles of mall corridors and parking areas, and zoomed past the fountain, the frozen escalator by the food court, and a wing of stores with their grilles down.

"Ai-yi-yi!" came the screech again.

I turned down the narrow hall that led to the restrooms. Fernando Guzman, a member of the mall's maintenance staff, danced wildly around his wheeled gray trash can, flailing a mop this way and that. He looked like a demented warlock performing an incantation around an outsized rubber cauldron. He caught sight of me.

"EJ! *Por Díos!* Get it off me."

It was then I spotted the dragon on his head. Bearded dragon, that is. An Australian lizard. I only knew that because Kiefer, owner of the mall's reptile store, Herpetology Hut, made a point of instructing me about a different critter every time I stopped to check up on things. This bearded dragon was only about eight inches long. Gazing at me incuriously from unblinking black eyes set into a triangular head, it seemed remarkably unperturbed by Fernando's gyrations.

I got off my Segway and approached Fernando, making calming motions with my hands. "Chill, Fernando. Just hold still."

He stopped doing his impression of a broken windmill in a hurricane and stood almost still, shaking slightly. "Is it poisonous?" His eyes widened until white showed all the way around his brown irises.

"No." At least, if it was, Kiefer hadn't mentioned it. The thought made me hesitate for a second, and I tucked my hair behind my ear in a nervous gesture I'd had since childhood. I reached one hand toward the lizard.

Fernando, anxious to help, stooped down. The reptile, finding itself eye to beady eye with me, hissed and puffed out the spiny ruff under its chin. Aah, so that's why they called it a "bearded" dragon. Its fierceness gave me pause. Maybe I should call for backup, get someone to fetch Kiefer. But, no, he probably wasn't even at the store yet.

"Get it, EJ," Fernando pleaded.

It's a lizard, I admonished myself, not a camel spider. The dinner-plate-sized arachnids had creeped me out in Iraq. Just grab the damn thing. My hand flashed out and closed around the reptile. Its skin felt rough on my palm. Trying to be gentle, I lifted it away from Fernando's head, keeping a firm grip despite its wiggly attempts to free itself. It tangled its little claws in Fernando's thick, black hair, making him wince as I pulled it free.

"*Gracías, gracías!* Thank you," Fernando said fervently, straightening. He backed up a couple steps and eyed the lizard warily.

"I live to serve," I said wryly. "How'd this guy get on your head, anyway?" The lizard had gone still in my hand, its tail draped up my arm.

"I bend to pick up some trash, here." Fernando pointed to a spot under the fire extinguisher. "Next thing I know, that . . . that monster leap on my *cabeza*." He raked his fingers through his hair, as if trying to eradicate the feel of the lizard's feet on his scalp.

I brought the lizard closer to my face and stroked its back gingerly with one finger. It was kind of cute in a scaly, reptilian sort of way. "How'd you end up here, dragon? Don't you belong in a nice, secure cage at the Herpes Hut, eating insects or dandelion leaves or Purina Lizard Chow?"

The dragon hissed.

Leaving Fernando to continue his duties, I held the lizard against my chest with one hand while trying to steer the Segway with the other. I reflected that in my thirteen months as a member of the Fernglen Galleria Security Force, I'd never dealt with an animal incident. Lost kids, drug deals, shoplifting, vandalism, car theft—yes. Escaped reptiles—no. The work might not give me the adrenaline rush that patrolling the streets of Kabul or Baghdad with my military unit had, but it was still police work, of a sort, and I couldn't expect much better with a knee and lower leg mangled by shrapnel from an IED blast. The lizard nudged between the buttons of my crisp white uniform shirt, recalling my attention. I jumped and the Segway veered.

"Off-limits, buddy," I said, pulling Mr. Nosy back as his claws snagged on my bra's lace trim. I straightened out the Segway as I came around the corner into the Macy's wing where the Herpes Hut was located. Kiefer Jones ran toward me, dreadlocks flopping against his shoulders with every step. He wore a plaid flannel shirt unbuttoned over a red "My Snake Has A Reptile Dysfunction" tee shirt and jeans. His twenty-something face wore a scowl.

"EJ! You are not going to believe what's happened. I—"

"Looking for this guy?" I forestalled him by holding out the bearded dragon, who hadn't seemed to mind traveling by Segway.

"Dartagnan! Where'd you find him?" Kiefer accepted the lizard from me, and it scurried up his arm to perch on his shoulder.

"Fernando found him by the men's room."

"We've got to find the others." His dark eyes flicked to either side, as if hoping to spot . . . what?

"What others?" I asked, an ominous feeling growing within me.

"Look." Kiefer turned, flannel shirt flapping, and hurried into the Herpes Hut.

The shop looked much as always: glass terrariums lined the walls, pet food and bedding and whatnot occupied shelves running up the middle of the store, and a short counter supported a cash register about midway back. A musty wet smell hung in the air, a scent I knew came from the turtle habitats. On the surface, everything looked normal, but something didn't seem right. As I turned in a two-hundred-seventy-degree arc, I realized what was missing. No rasp of scales across rocks, or slither of heavy bodies through leaves on terrarium floors, or skritch of lizard claws on glass. The only sound was a faint humming from the fluorescent bulbs. I looked into the terrarium closest to me. No inmate. And none in the enclosures above it or on either side. My gaze met Kiefer's.

"Gone," he said bitterly. "Every single one, except the turtles. Whoever did it left this." He thrust a sheet of paper at me.

Brows arching into my bangs, I took it by one corner, careful not to smudge any possible fingerprints, although Kiefer had probably ruined them already. I read the hand-printed note. "We have liberated our opressed reptile brothers (and sisters). Sincerely, Lovers of Animal Freedom." LOAF? There was an animal rescue group that called itself LOAF?

First things first: "How many?" I asked Kiefer.

Rotating his head from side to side so his neck cracked, he said, "Twenty-one lizards, two tortoises, and fifteen snakes, including Agatha."

"Agatha?" I said with dismay.

He nodded grimly.

Great. The last thing the mall needed was a fifteen-foot python surprising customers in dressing rooms or contesting right-of-way in the food court. Agatha wasn't for sale; she was more a mascot who drew customers into the store. Kiefer had owned her for years, and I could tell by the way he shifted from foot to foot that he was worried about her.

"Anything poisonous?"

"EJ!" He looked offended.

"I had to ask." I keyed the radio and told Joel to let the other security officers know to be on the lookout for reptiles of various shapes and sizes. The Fernglen Galleria Security Force doesn't have a permanent dispatcher; one officer is assigned that duty for the day and handles the radio and any phone calls that come in. Today it was Joel Rooney.

"Come again?" Joel said incredulously, his South Carolina drawl wringing three syllables from each word.

"Reptiles," I repeated. "Lizards and turtles and snakes, oh my! There's been a mass escape at the Herpetology Hut."

I heard Joel relay the news to whoever else was in the office, and a babble of voices sounded from my radio. I sighed. The phrase "get my gun from my truck" came clearly above the chatter, and I quickly added, "None of the reptiles is poisonous—"

"Agatha just ate last week," Kiefer interjected, scrunching his face anxiously.

"—or dangerous."

Kiefer's look of relief made up for what might have been a white lie.

"Call Animal Control, too," I suggested to Joel.

"Wilco."

I turned to Kiefer. "Any idea who might have done this?" I asked, strolling past the empty terrariums lining the store's east side. It was kind of sad not to see anything scurrying around, no beady eyes staring back. I was by no means a reptile-o-phile, but I could see why people kept them as pets. "Anyone in here the last two weeks who struck you as a bit 'off'?"

"Jesus, EJ," Kiefer said, "this is a mall. The place is filled with strange people." I gave him a look and he hastened to add, "But I know what you mean. There was a couple in here last Friday—a boy and a girl, maybe eighteen, nineteen—who stuck around for the better part of an hour. They just walked up and down the aisles, looking at stuff."

"Why'd they stand out?" We had made our way to the rear of the store, and I inspected the back door, the one leading to the utility hall that ran behind the shops, as Kiefer thought. Splintered wood around the lock told me an unsophisticated bandit—someone with a crowbar rather than lock picks—had gained access this way. I snapped a couple of shots with the digital camera I kept on my utility belt.

Kiefer shrugged. "I'm not sure. They wore those camou-flaged things"—his hands brushed up and down in front of his torso—"but a lot of the kids do that." His brow wrinkled. "I guess it was the way they *didn't* talk to each other. Just walked around, looking serious. No 'Oh, look how cute,' or 'I bet that one's poisonous.' Just . . . nothing."

I straightened from my study of the door. Dartagnan had used a dreadlock like a ladder to climb atop Kiefer's head and was staring me down with an "I'm king of the moun-tain" haughtiness. Maybe he thought he'd get more lizard chow now that all his cousins had vamoosed.

After jotting down Kiefer's info, I slipped my notebook back in my pocket. "Okay. Give a holler if you think of anything else or if you see those two around. If I were you, I'd call up some buddies who aren't afraid of your merchan-dise and go reptile hunting. You've got"—I checked my watch—"fifty-one minutes until opening. After that . . ."

"Thanks, EJ," Kiefer said. "I'm on it."

Outside the Herpes Hut, I mounted the Segway and made my way to the office, waving at a few geriatric mall walkers as I sped past. Fernglen, like many malls, opened early for walkers to get in their laps before customers arrived. I debated telling them to keep an eye out for stray reptiles, but decided that might start the kind of panic the mall's management would just as soon avoid. I don't know why, but some people don't want snakes to be part of their shop-ping experience.

Fernglen Galleria sat just outside Vernonville, Virginia, halfway between D.C. and Richmond, about five miles west of I-95. It's laid out in a big X, with the food court located on the ground floor where the four wings come together. Department stores—Macy's, Dillard's, Nordstrom, and Sears—anchored each wing, and kiosks selling everything from sunglasses to calendars to skin potions sprouted in the middle of the wide halls like mushrooms after rain. Lots of glass in the roof gave the mall a light, airy feel and encouraged the luxuriant hostas and ferns and other greenery planted in huge stone boxes that inspired the mall's name. I couldn't help but think the junglelike growths might attract some of the escapees. I peered into the planters as I passed, but didn't spot anything with scales.

The security office was tucked down a side hall off the left spoke, the Sears wing, like something shameful to be kept out of sight. The mall's administrative offices sat across the hall from us, and as I slowed down, Curtis Quigley, director of mall operations, the grand poo-bah in charge of making sure the retail space stayed rented, tenants' issues got resolved, customers streamed into Fernglen, and the mall made beaucoup bucks for its investors, pushed through the glass door. He was clearly headed for the security office, but when he spotted me, he changed direction. Uh-oh. He hurried toward me with that "I'm holding a quarter between my cheeks" walk that Joel could imitate to great comic effect.

In his early fifties, I guessed, Curtis Quigley affected European-style suits tailored to hug his tall, narrow frame, and regimental ties. Sandy blond hair was slicked back from his forehead and tucked behind his ears, brushing his collar. He always wore starched white shirts with French cuffs and had a set of cufflinks for every day of the week. Today being Monday, oval cat's eye stones glinted at his wrist.

"Officer Ferris." Quigley summoned me with an uplifted hand.

I glided up to him and got off the Segway.

"What's this I hear about a reptile invasion?" Quigley spoke with a faint British accent; rumor had it he'd picked it up during a college semester in London and hung onto it ever after, believing it made him sound cosmopolitan.

"It's not an invasion," I said. "The reptiles from the Herpes Hut are gone and—"

He scrunched his eyes closed as if in pain. "I wish you wouldn't call it that. So déclassé."

Repressing the urge to roll my eyes, I said, "Sorry. The Herpetology Hut. For all we know, the thieves took the reptiles with them." We could always hope. Maybe Dartagnan the Bearded Dragon was wilier than his brethren and had escaped from the bandits. Yeah, I liked that hypothesis. It would make my life much easier if there weren't reptiles loose in—

"OhsweetJesusit'sasnake! Killitkillitkillitkillit!"

The garbled screech came from behind me and around the corner. "Excuse me," I said to Quigley, and darted back the way I'd come, feeling the jolt of every step in my stupid knee. I rounded the corner to see two elderly women I recognized as dedicated mall walkers slamming their outsized purses down on the tile floor. *Wham! Wham!* I didn't know what they had in their bags, but it sounded like maybe a toaster and a ten-pound dumbbell.

"Ladies!" I said, as a plump woman in pink reared back, preparing to whack her purse down again. "What's the problem?" I surreptitiously scanned the floor nearby but didn't spot a flattened reptile. However . . . was that a tail peeking out from behind the concrete urn dripping English ivy? The tail twitched and slithered farther behind the urn. I moved so my body blocked the women's view.

"A snake!" the rounder one in the pink velour tracksuit

said. She had improbable red hair and big-framed glasses like Dustin Hoffman wore in *Tootsie*. "I'm pretty sure it was a rattler." She nodded for emphasis.

"Don't be silly, Pearl; it was just a little garter snake or some such," the taller woman said. "If it isn't just like you to overreact."

"Like you weren't just as scared as I was!" Pearl replied hotly, looking like she might take her handbag to her walking buddy.

It took me five minutes to calm them and explain the situation. When I suggested Kiefer might be offering rewards to people who found and returned his reptiles *unharmed*, they got all excited and went to round up some of their friends for a snake hunt. I took a deep breath and blew it out forcefully, checking behind the urn—the snake had made good its escape—before returning to the security office. Curtis Quigley was gone—thank goodness—but I walked smack into Captain Woskowicz.

At least six-two, with bulging muscles I suspected came from steroids, a shaved head, and a lumpy nose, Woskowicz decked his uniform with enough epaulettes, badges, and medals to be mistaken for a Middle Eastern dictator or the head of a South American junta. None of them were military medals or insignia I recognized; they looked like he'd found them in Cracker Jack boxes. He had the personality and paranoia to go with the look. He rattled a box of breath mints in one meaty paw.

"Ferris," he barked. "Why haven't you given me a report on the break-in? Quigley was here wanting to know the details."

"I was just coming to fill you in," I said. I didn't add the "sir" I knew he expected. In my book, you got a "sir" or "ma'am" until you proved you didn't deserve it; Woskowicz had supplied that proof within thirty minutes of my signing on at Fernglen.

"Well, I'm sure a military hotshot like you, a commando or special forces killer or whatever you call yourself, could have this wrapped up in no time," he sneered. He dumped half a dozen Tic Tacs straight from the container into his mouth and crunched down on them.

"I was with the security police," I told him for the nine thousandth time. Woskowicz had never been a sworn officer of any description—military, city police, sheriff's deputy—so he'd had it in for me ever since I got hired on after my convalescence and medical retirement from the air force.

"Well, you're not a real cop anymore, are you? You're a mall cop like the rest of us. So get on the horn to the Vernonville PD"—he jerked his thumb toward the phone—"and get a patrolman out here to make a report. We'll need it for insurance purposes." He stomped back toward his office where he spent most of the day playing computer poker, I suspected, and guzzling from the bottle of Maker's Mark I'd seen once in his lowest desk drawer.

"I already called them," Joel said as soon as Woskowicz was out of earshot. "Although I know you could investigate as good as they could. Better. Just look how you figured out what was going on at the Hat Factory."

"Thanks." I smiled and sank into the rolling chair across from his desk. Joel was our newest hire, an eager twenty-three-year-old with curly brown hair, puppy-dog eyes, and residual baby fat padding his large frame. He managed to make the security officer uniform we all wore—crisp white shirt with insignia, black slacks, and black "Smokey the Bear" type hat—look rumpled and comfortable instead of stiff and official. He had, for some reason, decided to hero-worship me just a little bit, although I was less than ten years his senior. I had to admit that it was gratifying, but a little embarrassing, as well. Lord knows, I was no hero, not with a bum knee that kept me from getting a job with any of the eighteen police departments I'd applied to, and not with the nightmares from that last firefight that kept haunting me. I massaged my knee for a moment, then stood. "Guess I'd better get back on snake patrol."

Joel grinned, digging dimples into his chubby cheeks. A smear of cream cheese glistened on his chin. "I'll let you know when the Vernonville cop shows up."

"Great. You missed a spot," I said, pointing at my chin, and left as he reached for a napkin.

Although there were still ten minutes until official mall opening time, the place felt busier than usual with Kiefer and a herd of his employees and pals, armed with long-handled nets, combing through the planters looking for escaped merchandise, and the usual morning walkers—moms with strollers and the geriatric contingent—getting in on the act. Word had apparently spread. When I bumped into him in the Nordstrom wing, Kiefer said they'd recovered eight animals already. His burnished mahogany face shone with hope. "Maybe we'll have 'em all rounded up before lunch."

And maybe I'd win the lottery. "Great," I said. "Agatha?"

"Not yet," he said, flipping his dreads over his shoulder. "You wouldn't think it'd be so easy for a fifteen-foot snake to disappear, would you?"

A piercing scream cut through our conversation. I raised my brows. "Sounds like maybe someone found her," I said. "I'll let you know." Giving Kiefer a two-fingered salute, I turned the Segway and purred down the hall toward the sound.

This was getting old. There was enough screaming going

on at Fernglen this morning to make me think I'd wandered into a haunted house attraction or teen slasher flick by mistake. Why did a gecko or garter snake elicit so much fear? Maybe, I decided, because it was out of context in a mall, unexpected. If you were gardening or hiking through a state forest, you'd be half thinking you might see a lizard or snake, so it wouldn't startle you as much. At the mall, the scariest thing you expected to see was the total on your credit card receipt.

Following the continued screeching, I hooked a sharp left into the Dillard's wing. A young woman with a stroller stood halfway down the hall, arm outstretched and finger pointed rigidly at Diamanté's display window. Her mouth yawned wide as she screamed, the sound changing to a gasping attempt at words when she saw me approaching. "It's . . . it's . . . it's . . ." she huffed.

"It's nothing to be afraid of, ma'am," I said in my most comforting voice. A peek in the stroller showed me an infant in head-to-toe pink sleeping through her mommy's hysteria. "It's harmless. Just a—" I swiveled to look in the window, hoping to be able to say, "just an iguana" or "just a corn snake."

But it wasn't a corn snake or an iguana or even Agatha. It wasn't a reptile at all. It was a man. A naked man. A completely naked, completely dead man.

Two

...

I got the woman to stop screaming by telling her she'd scare the baby, radioed Joel to tell him we had a "potato" (our code word for a really, really bad situation) at Diamanté, and asked him to call the Vernonville PD—again. "The situation's contained and there's no threat," I said so he wouldn't prod the Vernonville cops into sending the SWAT guys, "but they'll want to send a detective." Maybe four or five. And a crime scene team. And at least a sergeant, if not a lieutenant.

"Roger," Joel said. "What've you got, EJ?"

I sighed, making a mental note to talk to him about radio discipline. "A potato," I emphasized. "A hot potato."

"Aah, you don't want to say on the radio." His voice conveyed his belated comprehension. "Do you want Tracy or Harold?"

They were the other two Fernglen officers on duty this morning. "Send them both," I said. I'd put them on crowd control when they arrived, have them block off the whole wing. The store owners would whine, but it couldn't be helped. "And you'd better tell Woskowicz."

I studied the scene in the window more carefully after scanning the floor in front of it for footprints or evidence of any kind. Nothing. Diamanté was an upscale clothing boutique, and the display featured a pool scene meant to show off the latest in cruise swimwear. Mannequins wore bikinis that cost more than a week's pay, a shimmer of blue cellophane represented the water, and the naked man sat on a webbed lounger, his head slumped toward his right shoulder. Wiry gray and black hairs matted his chest and sprouted in ones and twos along his shoulders and upper arms. Sunglasses covered his eyes but did nothing to hide the bullet hole dead center in his forehead. He was posed so his left arm lay along the arm of the chair and his hand cupped a pink acrylic glass with a tiny cocktail umbrella poking out. I didn't see any other injuries or a gun. Noting the lack of blood in the display, I took a few photos and then turned back to the witness.

No more than twenty-two or -three, she sat stiffly on the bench, hands clasped in her lap, gaze fastened on the baby. She wore low-cut jeans, a yellow tank top layered over a lime green one, and orange Crocs. I introduced myself and got a whispered "Gina Kissell" in return.

"That's a darling baby," I said, hoping to set her at ease. "What's her name?"

"Kaycee," she said. She pushed the stroller back and forth with one foot.

"How old?"

"Two months tomorrow." Gina looked up at me, and a faint smile flickered around her lips before disappearing when her gaze fell on the Diamanté window. "Is that man really dead?"

"Yes," I said.

"Was he . . . murdered?" Horror fought with fascination in her voice.

Undoubtedly. I didn't see any way he could have shot himself, disposed of the gun, and wiped up any spilled blood before dying in the lounger. "There'll be an investigation," I said. "Can you tell me what happened?"

"I don't know," she said, alarmed.

"How did you come to discover the body?" I clarified.

"Oh. Well, my mother's been after me to lose some weight—it's so hard after a baby, even though I only gained twenty-one pounds with the pregnancy—and so I've been walking here three times a week. Usually I come with Dawn, my sister-in-law, but she wasn't feeling well this morning." Gina twisted a tendril of straight black hair around her forefinger. "So, anyway, I brought Kaycee, and we hadn't done one whole loop when I noticed . . ." She pointed at the store window. "At first, I thought it was a joke, you know, someone putting a naked mannequin in the window for a laugh. But then, when I looked again, I saw that it wasn't . . . that he didn't . . ." She stuttered to a stop.

"It's okay," I said, patting her shoulder. "Did you see anyone?"

"Just other walkers," she said.

"Near here?"

"No, out in the main hall. There wasn't anyone here but me and Kaycee. Can I go?"

"Not yet," I said. The homicide detectives would want to interview her when they arrived. I didn't tell Gina, but she could well be here until lunchtime. Baby Kaycee let out a squawk, and Gina bent to pick her up as the other two security officers on the day shift came around the corner.

I asked Tracy to make sure no one came into the wing.

She nodded and headed off a couple of shop employees. I looked at my watch. Damn. Opening time. I motioned the other officer toward me, and he loped over, eager to see what was going on. Harold Wasserman was a retired engineer in his sixties who'd come to work for the Fernglen Galleria Security Office so he'd have a good excuse not to babysit his four-year-old grandsons. Twins. Short and slim with gray hair, he looked professional in the uniform, but I'd never seen him display much initiative.

"Hey, EJ, what's going on?"

I briefed him quickly, motioning toward the body in the window, and asked him to make sure no one entered the wing from the Dillard's at the far end. I also told him to ask any shop managers and employees on the wing to stay put until the police had done their investigating.

"They're not going to like that," he said, shaking his head. A whiff of cigarette smoke floated off him. Damn. I'd lost the pool. Thirty-nine days ago, he'd quit for the sixth time since I'd known him; the longest he'd made it had been sixty-two days. My bet this time had been fifty-five days.

"I don't give a flip if they like it," I said. "Just make sure they don't come looky-looing, messing up the scene."

As he trailed off, voices and the scuffing of several pairs of heavy shoes heralded the arrival of the police. Two uniformed police came around the corner with a tall, blond man in a gray suit. He scanned the corridor and immediately told one of the uniforms to call for more patrol officers. The other uniform started slinging yellow and black crime scene tape across the entrance to the wing. I walked to meet the detective.

He towered over my five-six, and I figured he must be at least six-three or six-four. Slim and in his midthirties, he had eyes that hovered between blue and gray, and a strong nose and jaw. Almost white-blond hair advertised his Nordic ancestry, and the cut of his gray suit and polish on his wingtips made him look more like the VP of a medium-sized company than a cop.

I held out my hand and said, "I'm EJ Ferris. Let me fill you in on what's happened."

His gaze slid over me, and I got the feeling he cataloged all the essentials in that two second glance: wavy chestnut hair with bangs, dark blue eyes, pale Irish complexion with a smattering of freckles, medium height and build with curves in the right places, limp in left leg. He'd be able to pick me out of a lineup.

"Detective Sergeant Anders Helland," he said with no discernible accent. His handshake was warm and strong. "And I'll decide what's happened here."

With that, he brushed past me, headed for Diamanté and the body. I stared after him, anger rising as heat in my face. Chill, I told myself. Be professional. I took long strides to catch up, not wanting to look like I was scurrying after him. From memory, I told him, "Gina Kissell"—I nodded toward the witness rocking Kaycee in her arms—"discovered the body at approximately nine fifty. She was here for exercise and saw no one in the vicinity. The lack of blood around the body makes me think he was shot elsewhere and brought here after he was dead. There are no signs—"

"Did you disturb the scene?" he asked, looking down his long nose at me. His brows, several shades darker than his hair, twitched together, and his eyes went as icy as a fjord in January.

"No. No one's been in there since the body was discovered." I glared at him.

"Well, thank God for small favors. At least you knew enough not to trample all over the scene."

"I used to be—"

But he was turning away again, examining the scene in the display window, before I could tell him I'd been a cop. A real one, not just a mall security officer. I knew my anger was way out of proportion to the slight, knew that most of my coworkers wouldn't have a clue about how to handle a murder scene and that Helland had lumped me in with them, but still his response stung.

More cops arrived, including a fortyish woman in a tan pantsuit who carried large cups in each hand. Steam and the smell of coffee escaped from the vents in the lids. "Wow, that's effin' creative," she said, gazing at the body in the window and handing a cup to Helland. "What's up with that, do you suppose?"

"Thanks." Helland pried off the lid and blew on his coffee. "I'd say our murderer has a sick sense of humor."

"Or he or she was really pissed at the vic," I put in.

They both turned to stare at me, the woman's brows arching as she looked from me to Helland. About my height, she wore sensible pumps and a chartreuse blouse with her pantsuit and a round-faced Mickey Mouse watch on her left wrist. Reddish brown hair corkscrewed around her face. When it became clear Helland wasn't going to introduce us, I said, "EJ Ferris. I'm with the Fernglen Security Force."

"Blythe Livingston," she said with a smile. "Detective, Vernonville Police Department, by way of Boston PD."

As if I couldn't tell by her accent. I returned her smile and we shook hands.

"Let me have your key to the store." Helland held out a peremptory hand.

"No."

His eyebrows soared. "No?"

I could tell he wasn't used to hearing that word. "No.

None of the security staff or mall administration has keys. Only the tenants do. For liability reasons—the mall doesn't want its security officers or staff vulnerable to accusations of theft. I'll have to call the store's owner and get her to let you in."

"Do it." Helland stepped to the grille and bent to examine the lock that bolted it to the floor. "Is there another door?" he asked, straightening.

"Around there," I said, pointing to the small hallway to the left of Diamanté. It led to the restrooms, a janitor's closet, an outside door for deliveries, and the service hallway that ran behind all the stores on this side of the wing.

Without a word, Helland disappeared down the hall.

Blythe Livingston made a "what can you do?" grimace behind her partner's back and followed him.

I radioed Joel and asked him to get Finola Craig's phone number and address. "Wait. Never mind," I said, catching sight of the platinum-haired Finola apparently arguing with the cop blocking access to the corridor. A crowd of interested shoppers had gathered behind her and were craning their necks to see down the hall. No sign of reporters yet, but I knew they'd be along shortly.

I hurried over and convinced the patrol officer to let Finola in.

"Oh, my God, EJ, what's going on? He said something happened at Diamanté?" Anxiety pinched her pale face with its heavy but tasteful makeup. Her eyes searched mine for some clue to what was happening.

"Opening time was twenty minutes ago," I said, putting a hand on her forearm to keep her from dashing toward her store. "Where've you been?"

She flapped a harried hand. "Monica was supposed to open today, but she called at quarter to ten to say she was throwing up and couldn't come in. It took me this long to cancel my dentist appointment, throw some clothes on, and drive over here."

Finola never looked like she "threw" her clothes on. Today's pearl gray suit with a sapphire cami and clutter of chains and pearls around her neck was typical of her usual attire and of the clothes she carried at Diamanté.

"Monica?" I asked.

"Monica Goudge. She's new. I hired her last week."

I made notes.

"Was there a break-in?" Finola persisted. "I hope they didn't vandalize the shop. You read about people doing such gross things when—. I've got to call my insurance company." She pulled a tiny cell phone from her clutch bag just as Helland and Livingston emerged from the hallway. Spotting them, Finola dropped the phone back in her purse and broke away from me. She trotted toward the detectives as fast as she could in three-inch heels and a pencil skirt. "Hello! Are you the officers in charge? I'm going to need your report for—" She broke off as she came even with the display window.

"What in—?" She stared incredulously and took a step toward the window. "Jackson! Oh my God!" She stood as stiffly frozen as the mannequins in her display window.

"Ma'am, can you ID the victim?" Blythe Livingston asked, drawing Finola away.

"It's Jackson," Finola said. A shudder rippled through her. "Jackson Porter."

"Your husband? Boyfriend?" Helland asked, observing her narrowly.

"No!" She turned a shocked face toward him. "Nothing like that. He was a customer. A good customer. I need to sit down." She tottered toward the bench where Gina Kissell still sat, but Livingston led her toward a bench farther down the hall. Helland headed toward Gina and the baby.

"You should know—" I started to say, but Helland stopped me before I could tell him about the snakes and lizards colonizing the mall.

"We can take it from here," he said. "You can go back to patrolling the halls or helping shoppers find their cars or whatever it is you do. We'll be in touch if we need anything."

His casual dismissal sent a ripple of icy anger through me. What a supercilious jerk! He didn't want to hear what I had to say? Fine! I hoped he tripped over Agatha and she strangled him.

Unfortunately, I tripped over Captain Woskowicz before I could get away from the scene. He ambushed me outside the police tape just as I was climbing onto my Segway. Grabbing my upper arm, he leaned in close so the ever-growing crowd couldn't hear what he was saying.

"Ferris! What the hell is going on here and why wasn't I briefed? I am the director of security, after all. I need to know what's going on in *my* mall." His nostrils flared, and he breathed minty bourbon fumes on me.

Stone-faced, I filled him in on what I knew. "The police have it in hand," I said. "They don't want our help."

"Of course they don't. Why should they?" He stared at me a moment, and then a mean smile curled his lips. "Hurt your feelings, did they? Didn't want assistance from a broken-down war hero?"

I folded my lips in to keep from saying anything. The fact that he read me that easily made me wince, but I was determined not to show it. I caught sight of a TV camera over his shoulder. For once, I was glad to see a journalist. "There's a reporter. She probably wants to interview you."

"Where?" He jerked his head around, spied the reporter,

and started toward her, fixing an oily smile on his face. Woskowicz wallowed in publicity like a warthog in mud. I'd once heard him tell someone that "the babes are hot for TV personalities." Since he had the personality of a wolverine, I didn't figure any amount of TV exposure would turn him into a babe magnet. Although, he had three ex-wives, so you just never know.

Massaging my arm where he'd grabbed it, more to rub off his cooties than because it hurt, I made my getaway on the Segway. I decided I deserved a quick break after coping with escaped reptiles and a murder, so I radioed Joel to tell him I'd be at Merlin's Cave, my friend Kyra's shop, for a fifteen-minute coffee break.

"I thought you might check in here," Joel said, a pout in his voice. "I got bagels with that cinnamon cream cheese you like."

Poor Joel. He was clearly desperate to get the scoop on the activities at Diamanté. "I'll swing by before lunch," I promised him.

Smiling at the shoppers I passed, I almost made it to Merlin's Cave before a woman with an anxious expression flagged me down. I slowed reluctantly. "Do you need help, ma'am?"

"Oh, yes," she said. She was matronly looking, with salt-and-pepper hair, a plump figure, and two shopping bags hooked over her elbow. "I think a man is following me!" She cast a flustered look over her shoulder. "He was behind me at Macy's, and I spotted him again when I stopped for a pretzel and now there he is *again*! Do you think he's a thief, that he's after my purchases?"

Since her bags were from a lingerie boutique and a cookware shop, not a jewelry store or an electronics place, I doubted he was interested in stealing her merchandise.

Probably some innocent shmoe, doing his shopping, who happened to cross paths with this woman once too often. "Which man is it, ma'am?"

"He took a photo of me, too," she said indignantly. "At least, I think he did. Do you think he's a pervert? That's him, over there." She jerked her head three times, trying to be discreet but failing miserably, at a man standing with his back toward us, staring into the window of a card shop. He was tall, slightly stoop-shouldered, and seemed to have white hair under a navy beret.

I studied his back and felt my ire rising. I'd accomplished nothing all morning, but this I could deal with. "You go on, ma'am," I told the woman. "I'll make sure he doesn't follow you. Let me take care of it."

"Oh, thank you," she whispered. "I'll go to my car now. I'm supposed to meet my daughter for lunch."

She bustled away, looking back two or three times and hugging her bags close to her body, as I left the Segway and stalked toward the man.

I tapped his shoulder, and he gave a realistic start. "Don't pretend you didn't see me coming," I said sternly. "I know you were watching my reflection in the window."

He turned, showing me the seamed face of a man in his eighties, but with bright blue eyes that seemed much younger. They twinkled as he smiled and held up his hands at shoulder height. "I guess you caught me. Damn! I must be losing my touch."

I sighed heavily. "Grandpa, how many times do I have to tell you not to spy on the mall customers?"

Three

• • •

"I've got to keep my hand in, Emma-Joy," he said with a cajoling smile. "Where else am I supposed to practice? You know what happened when I tailed that man downtown."

The man, whom Grandpa Atherton was convinced was casing a jewelry store for a heist, had ambushed Grandpa and decked him with a right hook, kicking him and breaking a few ribs for good measure before running off. Grandpa had spent a night in the hospital, and I'd gotten long-distance grief from my mom for letting Grandpa put himself at risk. As if he listened to anything anyone said. It was rumored that he had defied Wild Bill Donovan, the founder of the Office of Strategic Services, which later became the Central Intelligence Agency, on more than one occasion.

"You *don't* need to keep in practice," I told him, knowing it was a waste of breath. "The CIA was a long time ago. You're retired. Why don't you take up golf or bocce ball or

stamp collecting like other people your—" I'd been about
to say "your age," but Grandpa was vain about his age,
insisting he didn't look a day over seventy, so I changed it
to "—like other retirees?"

He flapped a dismissive hand. "Boring. I still have my
wits and my health. Just because the Cold War's over doesn't
mean we're secure. Spies are everywhere. More countries
than ever are out to learn our secrets. I can still serve this
country by—"

"By terrorizing suburban housewives picking up a new
vegetable scraper at Williams-Sonoma?" I asked dryly.

"Emma-Joy!" He tried to sound hurt.

"Don't 'Emma-Joy' me," I said. "I'm responsible for the
well-being and safety of the mall's customers and—"

"I didn't hurt her," he said. "Having an attractive man
follow her is probably the most exciting thing that's happened
to her all year. She'll tell all her friends about it at bunco
tonight." He tipped his beret to a rakish angle and winked.

A smile slipped across my face before I could stop it.
"Go home," I said as sternly as I could. "Or, if you insist on
hanging around, make yourself useful by finding a few
snakes and lizards." I explained about the reptile liberation.
"Don't you have an infrared gadget or something that can
find their heat signatures in the planters?" Grandpa was gaga
for gadgets, combing the Internet and hitting up spy buddies
and God-knows-who for techno-gadgets that detected,
photographed, surveilled, recorded, and, for all I knew,
made Belgian waffles while videotaping a target. Maybe if
he were occupied with the reptiles, he wouldn't hear about
the murder until after the cops left the mall. I didn't want
him trying to spy on the murder investigation, antagonizing
Detective Helland and his crowd. They had guns.

Grandpa brightened. "I have something I can try . . . but

a reptile should be roughly the same temperature as its environment, right?" He crinkled his brow. "That's a challenge. But maybe—" Without another word, he strode away from me, mentally sorting through his extensive collection of gadgets to find one to help with reptile roundup.

Dealing with Grandpa had used up my break time, so I phoned Kyra to let her know I wouldn't be by. She reminded me of her bout that evening, and we agreed to have dinner afterwards. I swung the Segway around and headed for the office, hoping Captain Woskowicz was still tied up with the reporter. He wouldn't want me investigating the murder, would insist it was the cops' job. Maybe it was, but that didn't mean I had to close my eyes and ears, did it? And if I happened to do a little research on the victim, whom Finola had obligingly identified, and discovered something relevant, well, then, maybe the look-down-his-nose Detective Helland would be grateful when I turned the information over to him.

Joel was the only one in the office when I got back, and he shook his head when I raised my eyebrows and nodded toward Woskowicz's office. "Still out."

"Good." I plopped myself down across from Joel and smeared cinnamon cream cheese on the bagel he pushed toward me. "Thanks." I swallowed the first bite and then gave in to the pleading in Joel's brown eyes. "Oh, all right." I filled him in on the murder scene. "The cops are going to want the video. Why don't you burn them a CD? We'll look at it before we hand it over."

"Okay," he said, making a note. "Then what?"

"If this was our case to solve, we'd interview Finola; research the vic's background and interview his family, friends, and coworkers; work the scene and get the autopsy results; talk to all the employees on the Dillard's wing; do a timeline of the vic's movements . . . and that's just for start-ers. But it's not our case. So we do nothing." I swiveled the chair around to face the computer.

"So why are you typing in 'Jackson Porter'?" Joel asked.

"Curiosity."

The key words "Jackson Porter" and "Vernonville" brought up a surprising number of documents and articles. I skimmed them, learning that Jackson Porter was fifty-three, that he had a wife named Elena (an attractive blonde with suspiciously unlined skin and plump lips), a son named Robbie, twenty-two, and a house about ten miles outside of Vernonville proper. If the photos of Porter shmoozing at charity events, glad-handing council members, and wielding a shovel at ground breakings were anything to go by, he was a mover and a shaker in the community. A developer, it looked like. I tried to concentrate with Joel breathing onion-bagel breath over my shoulder.

"I know who killed him," Joel announced a moment later. His voice buzzed with excitement.

Skeptical, I swung around to face him. "You do?"

He nodded, excited. "For sure. He's the guy behind Olympus, the golf course and hotel they're going to build behind Fernglen." He gestured toward the north. " 'A vaca-tion fit for a god.' "

I'd heard the slogan before and knew about the golf course going in behind us, but I hadn't connected it with Porter. "So who killed him?"

"One of the independent merchants here in the mall," Joel said. "They were all ready to murder him. They figured that the shopping center he was putting in at the resort would undercut their business. Some of them would go under. Especially specialty clothing stores. Stores like Diamanté." He gave me a meaningful look.

"You think Finola did it?" I had trouble envisioning the petite, immaculate Finola endangering her manicure by hauling a dead body around her shop, but stranger things had happened.

"Absolutely." He nodded like a bobble-head.

"Finola Craig weighs maybe a hundred and five pounds," I pointed out. "Porter looked like a solid two-twenty." I let him do the math.

That only stopped him for a second. "She shot him, right? You don't need to be a linebacker to shoot someone." He jumped into a Weaver stance, arms extended as if holding a gun. "Pow."

"No blood at the scene." At Joel's blank look, I explained. "He wasn't shot in the window. The murderer shot him somewhere else and moved him."

"Oh." Joel's disappointment showed in his eyes. He returned to his chair and slumped into it, his broad thighs stretching the fabric of the black uniform pants. "Well, she could still have done it."

"Sure she could," I agreed cheerfully. "And so could a dozen or two dozen other people. In police investigations, we like to rely on a little thing called 'evidence.'"

"Excuse me."

Detective Anders Helland filled the doorway, all broad shoulders, sharp suit, and patrician features. Joel jumped to his feet; Helland had that kind of presence. With an effort, I remained seated. "Yes?"

"That idiot Woskowicz isn't here, is he?" Helland said it like he didn't give a damn if Woskowicz was listening from the next room.

Against my will, my opinion of the detective went up a few notches; anyone who could zero in on Woskowicz's idiocy within minutes of meeting him deserved some respect. Although, Woskowicz's intellectual failings weren't exactly hard to suss out. "No."

"The cretin actually walked right into my crime scene. No gloves, no booties, no common sense. God knows what evidence he destroyed or corrupted." Ignoring Joel, Helland focused on me, his pale gray eyes assessing. "I need a liaison here at the mall. You're it."

"I don't wa—"

"For starters, I'll need blueprints of the mall, names of all employees with contact data, video from any cameras that would have line of sight on either the interior or exterior entrance to Diamanté, and a corned beef sandwich with extra mustard. Think you can handle that?"

"Yes, sir!" Joel piped up before I could tell the man what to do with his corned beef sandwich. "EJ already got me started—"

"I'll have the documents and video to you within the hour," I said, keeping my tone professional.

But Helland was already out the door and I doubted if he heard me.

A little browbeating got me the blueprints from the mall manager's office in record time. But the personnel list was another matter. They didn't have one. Each of the stores maintained their own list of employees; no central list existed. Quigley's office maintained personnel records only on the mall's direct hires: janitorial staff, security staff, and mall administration. I accepted the list of those employees, knowing it wouldn't satisfy Helland, and crossed back to the security office where Joel had finished transferring the camera data to a CD. We sat side by side in front of his computer monitor, fast-forwarding through a whole lot of nothing, looking for a murderer hauling a body into Diamanté. Detective Helland was going to be disappointed by the video evidence, I suspected. Although the mall had approximately one hundred cameras, only about a third of them were actually hooked up. The rest were for show, to scare crooks away from shoplifting or vandalism, the video equivalent of "This house protected by So-and-So Security" stickers on the windows of a house with no alarm system. A flicker of movement on the screen caught my eye and I paused the CD.

"Weasel," Joel said.

He was right; it was only Billy Wedzel, the midshift officer responsible for mall security from eleven at night to seven in the morning. The camera had caught activity near the movie theater until the last film let out at just past midnight, but nothing after that. A couple of fuzzy cars entered the north garage at just after two a.m., moving with the stuttering motion that not enough frames per second produced. I wished Helland and crew good luck in getting a license plate number. The cars were on the opposite side of the mall from Diamanté, anyway, and probably had no connection with the murder.

"Well, that wasn't worth wasting a CD on," Joel observed, disappointed.

I popped the CD out and slid it into a case. "Maybe the murder will get management to upgrade the camera system," I said, not believing it. Cost cutting was the order of the day at Fernglen, and it would take a terrorist attack or an alien invasion, I figured, to get Quigley to allocate more money to security. Taking the blueprints, the abbreviated personnel list, and the CD, I glided back toward Diamanté.

Crime scene tape still roped off the area, but the crowd had diminished. The body was gone from the display window, I noted with a glance, and Gina Kissell and her baby had left. The lone cop standing at the entrance to the wing

looked over at Detective Blythe Livingston when I told him
I had documents requested by Detective Helland. She stood
talking to a crime scene technician who was stooped over,
removing his blue paper booties, and she nodded permission
for me to enter. The uniformed officer had me sign in on a
clipboard before letting me pass.

Feeling a bit like an interloper, and hating it, I approached
Detective Livingston. "I've got the CD from the security
cameras and some of the data Detective Helland asked for,"
I said.

"Some?" she asked with an appraising look from shrewd
brown eyes.

I tucked my hair behind my ear. "The mall doesn't have
a consolidated list of all employees—they're hired by the
individual stores." I thrust the documents and CD toward
her, but she put her hands up, palms out, refusing to take
them.

"I'm due in court in thirty minutes, so I'm out of here.
He's in the store." Noting my hesitation, she added, "We've
processed it. It's okay to go in." On the words, she headed
away from me with brisk click-clacks from her pumps.

Armed with her permission, I crossed the threshold of
Diamanté, automatically cataloging what I saw. Other than
in the display window, where three mannequins lay in a
tangle of stiff limbs and vacant stares, probably pushed aside
so the coroner's team could remove the body, nothing looked
out of place. No footprints, mud, blood, or other marks
marred the marble-tile floor. Widely spaced racks of clothing, many glistening with the sheen of silk or the sparkle of
sequins, stood undisturbed, waiting for a wealthy socialite
to spin them and make a selection. The glossy red doors that
led to three fitting rooms were all discreetly closed. The
scent of a lavender air freshener overlay the faint, sweet odor

of decay. Breathing shallowly through my mouth, I moved further into the store.

A cash register sat unattended on a glass-topped counter filled with jewelry. No smudges. Finola and her staff clearly did a better job with cleaning than I did; my glass-topped coffee table showed fingerprints, dust motes, and cat hairs mere seconds after I Windexed it. Voices came from the open door of an office tucked behind the counter, and I approached quietly, willing to eavesdrop to learn what the early investigation had turned up. However, as I neared the door, Finola Craig emerged, saying, "I'm perfectly certain nothing's missing." Her slender fingers toyed with the chains dangling from her neck, making them clink. "With the exception of that"—she waved toward the window—"everything is as it should be. I closed up myself last night: reconciled the register, cleaned the counters, vacuumed, straightened the stock. Oh, hi, EJ." She looked startled, but not unhappy, to see me.

Detective Helland came out of the office. "About time," he said, spotting the folders I held. He stepped toward me and stretched out an imperious hand. Slapping the folders into his left hand, I noted the breadth of his palm and his long fingers. No ring. My eyes met his, and I dared him to mention the sandwich.

"Thanks. I'll let you know when we need something else. Don't worry about forgetting my sandwich," he added blandly. "One of the uniforms picked one up for me." He nodded toward a deli bag I hadn't noticed on the far side of the register.

The man was infuriating. Reluctantly, I let professionalism win out over my irritation. "The security officer on duty last night was—"

"I'll go through this," Helland interrupted, waving the

folder, "and let you know who I need to interview. You can set them up." Without a "thanks" or a "good-bye," he strode from the store, leaving fluttering fabrics in his wake.

I gave Finola Craig a speculative look, wondering what she'd told Helland, but decided to talk to her later. Helland might pop back in, and I was damned sure he wouldn't be happy about me interviewing one of his possible suspects. Not that I cared about his happiness or planned to let his anticipated ire stop me from interviewing anyone I wanted to, but I didn't want him to catch me. Besides which, I needed to get back on patrol. "Are you holding up okay?" I asked Finola as we moved toward the door.

"It's horrid," she said, blinking rapidly. Blotches of darker gray blossomed on the breast of her pearl gray jacket. "Nothing like this has ever—I can't believe that Jack is—" Pulling a lace-edged hanky from her skirt pocket, she hurried away from me in the direction of the restrooms. I stared after her for a moment. Yes, having someone murdered in your boutique was an ugly thing, but she seemed overly distraught to me. She'd referred to the vic as "Jack." Pretty cozy way to talk about a casual customer. What, exactly, had her relationship with the dead developer been?

Swinging by the Herpetology Hut, I was hoping for an update from Kiefer, but the store was locked and he wasn't there. Probably still out corralling his stock. As far as I knew, the Vernonville PD hadn't sent anyone to take his statement yet, and there'd been no sign of anyone from Animal Control. Sigh.

"Miss! Officer!" A man hurried toward me, suit jacket flapping, fleshy face reddened by anger or exertion.

I stopped the Segway. "How can I help you, sir?"

"My car! Some criminal spray painted my Beemer. In broad daylight!"

"Show me," I said, dismounting from the Segway. Unfortunately, I had a pretty good idea of what he was going to show me; we'd been having trouble since Christmas with cars getting spray painted by kids—it felt like teens to me—clever enough to avoid our surveillance cameras. They tagged one car a day, always at different times. I walked beside the incensed man to the wall of doors giving access to the north parking lot. On the way, I got his name—Kenneth Downs—and his address. It wasn't hard to spot his car once we emerged into the weak February sun. It was the only black BMW in the lot with "Jesus Is Ur Savior" written in orange across the hood and driver's-side panels. The "i" in "Savior" was dotted with a smiley face. Downs gobbled at the sight. "It's . . . it's sacrilege!" he finally spat.

I didn't think he intended the irony. Without replying, I took photos of the graffiti and jotted notes for my report. "You'll need to inform your insurance company," I told Downs, giving him my card. "You can have them call me."

"Aren't you going to fingerprint it or something?" he asked, walking around the car, head bent looking for other damage. "Maybe I should call the real cops."

"There won't be fingerprints," I told him, having taken it upon myself to dust the first couple of graffitied cars we'd found in December. "The taggers wear gloves. And you're certainly welcome to call the Vernonville PD, but I can tell you they won't send an officer out for property damage of this sort. They'll just file a report."

"I pay taxes!" Downs grumbled. "For what?" He yanked open the car door and it bounced off him, leaving a smear of orange on his slacks. "Damn it!" He slid into the car, slammed the door, and ground the gears as he pulled out, narrowly missing a woman pushing a baby stroller.

"You're welcome," I said to his rapidly disappearing

bumper. The woman with the stroller gave him the finger, and I felt like high-fiving her. Throughout my law enforcement career, from the time I'd enlisted in the air force and gone to Lackland Air Force Base in San Antonio for training, my biggest challenge had been remaining polite and even sympathetic in the face of crass rudeness. I forced myself to remember that citizens weren't used to confronting violence—attacks on their persons or property—and that they felt violated. Still, I had to bite my tongue sometimes when people acted entitled or abusive. In many ways, dealing with criminals or enemy soldiers was an easier proposition. And wasn't that a sad statement, I thought, returning to the mall.

Four

. . .

I walked back into the security office at three, the end of my shift (I was on days this week, which ran seven to three), after a couple hours of patrolling. I'd reassured two shoppers who'd encountered lizards (and returned the little geckos to Kiefer), discouraged a teenager from riding his skateboard down the escalator, and helped an elderly gentleman find his car. Routine. The kind of humdrum policing I did most days. All the while, the murder played in the back of my mind, and I made a mental list of the things I'd follow up on . . . if it were my case, which it wasn't.

As I pushed through the glass doors to the office, I heard an unwelcome voice apparently finishing up a joke. Weasel. Billy Wedzel, actually, but "Weasel" fit better. He followed the punch line with nasty laughter, the kind of Beavis and Butthead sniggering adolescent boys have perfected. "Get it?" he said in his nasal voice. "Her ta-tas—"

"I got it," Joel said in a long-suffering tone. "I just didn't think it was funny."

"Well, who asked you, asswipe?"

I stepped far enough into the office that they spotted me. "Well, look who's here. General Ferris." Weasel gave me a mock salute, touching his middle finger to his brow. He had sunken cheeks, a sharp nose, and dishwater blond hair that fell lankly across his brow. He slouched back in a chair, his booted feet propped on a desk near his expensive cell phone. His white uniform shirt showed yellow patches under the arms as he laced his fingers behind his head. "I hear tell you found a dead body today."

"A customer did," I said. "I was curious about how Mr. Porter ended up in a display window on your shift, Weasel." Weasel was permanently on the midnight shift, eleven p.m. to seven a.m. The rest of us worked staggered, rotating shifts, but Weasel had a deal of some sorts with Woskowicz and always worked mids. No one complained because no one else wanted that shift.

Joel shot me a warning glance, but I ignored him. I knew Weasel was meaner than a feral hog, that he was in tight with Woskowicz, but I didn't give a damn. He was, at best, lazy, and, more likely, a thief.

He scowled. "I didn't see nothing."

"There's a surprise. Just like you don't see anything when merchandise marches out of Macy's on the midshift or cars get boosted from the parking garage. You should see an ophthalmologist," I said with spurious concern. Crossing to my desk, I flipped through the couple of message slips on the blotter. Nothing urgent.

"Now you just wait a minute," Weasel said, sitting forward and bringing his feet to the floor with a thud. "Are you calling me a crook?"

"Did I say that?" I gave Joel a wide-eyed, questioning look, and he obligingly shook his head. "I just expressed concern for your vision problems. Like last night . . . what did you see? Anything unusual go down?"

Not having access to the autopsy and forensic reports, I had no idea what time Helland and his team thought the body had been arranged in the window. The mall closed at five on Sundays, and dark came shortly thereafter at this time of year, so I figured it could have been anywhere between six p.m. and four thirty a.m. Probably not any later than that since commuters would have been zooming by on their way to spend a fulfilling day in their cubicles.

"It was a quiet night," Weasel said. His cell phone rang and he glanced at it, then ignored it. "I didn't see anything on my rounds. It was quieter than a NASCAR track on Christmas Day." His eyes shifted away from mine, and I knew he was lying. Trouble was, I didn't know what he was lying about. He could have spent the whole night holed up in the office with a magazine and a six-pack, or he could have been engaged in something nefarious that had nothing to do with the murder, or—

"Is there a problem here? Aren't you off shift, Ferris? What are you still doing here?"

Woskowicz was back, and although his words were rough, his expression spoke of self-satisfaction. I looked closer to see if canary feathers dangled from his lips. "Be sure to watch the five o'clock newscast tonight," he said, sticking his thumbs in his belt and puffing out his chest. "They'll show my interview with that hot reporter. She was really into me. We're hooking up later this week for a drink."

"Way to go, boss," Weasel said, leering. "You ready to go to lunch?" His phone rang again, and this time he picked it up, covering his mouth as he muttered into it.

Joel rolled his eyes at me.

"I'm on my way out," I said, knowing I'd get nothing more from Weasel with Woskowicz standing there. And it wasn't my job to interrogate Weasel, I reminded myself. Helland and crew would get onto Weasel, probably by tomorrow, and they'd dig out whatever nuggets he had to offer. I hauled my gym bag from under my desk and slung it over my shoulder, giving the room a generalized "Bye" as I walked out, already thinking ahead to the pool and how good it would feel to swim half a mile, let the water ease away the day's worries and frustrations.

On my way to the south lot where I'd left my car, I passed Tombino's, the combination bar and restaurant that had been a fixture in Fernglen since the mall first opened. Through the smoked glass window, I caught sight of Finola Craig sitting at a table in the bar, staring morosely into a tall glass. My footsteps slowed. She looked like she could use a shoulder to cry on. But if I went in and had a drink with her, I probably wouldn't make it to the pool. Finola was a big girl; she could share her woes with the bartender and call a cab to get home. I marched past Tombino's and actually had my hand on the exit door when I spun with a little growl and walked back to the restaurant.

Tombino's was dim, even in the middle of the afternoon, and deserted except for Finola, a bartender swabbing a beer glass with a rag, and a kid running a vacuum in the restaurant. It smelled like tomato sauce and garlic. The lunch special was always "Pasta Your Way," where for $6.99 you could have all-you-can-eat pasta topped with marinara, pesto, or Alfredo sauces. Finola didn't look as though she'd bothered with lunch—she'd gone straight to cocktail hour, judging by the three sword-shaped plastic skewers at her elbow. A fourth held a wedge of pineapple and a cherry in her drink. She sat with one elbow on the table, cheek on her hand, the other hand loosely cupped around the base of her glass. Her usually immaculate blond hair had straggled loose from her French braid, and she'd tossed her gray suit jacket onto the back of her bar stool; it had fallen in a crumpled heap to the floor.

"Hey, Finola," I said, retrieving the jacket and laying it on the next table. Sliding onto a stool, I scooted it closer to the high, round table. "How're you holding up?"

She lolled her head to one side and looked at me from glassy eyes. "Jus' great."

"Would you like a drink?" The bartender interrupted us.

"Club soda." It might be the end of my workday, but I couldn't see downing a beer at this hour. I turned back to Finola.

"Have the police told you anything?"

She shook her head, nearly rocking herself off the stool. She clutched at the table. "Not a damn thing. Oh, except that I can't open the ssstore until Friday at the earliest. D'you know what no revenue for a week will do to me?"

I didn't know, but I didn't imagine it could be good. "No."

"I'll be down the crapper." She made a flushing motion with one hand and a noise like running water. Then she giggled.

I didn't think I'd ever heard the elegant, reserved Finola giggle. "I hope it's not that bad," I said. "Maybe you'll get a really big crowd this weekend." I didn't say it out loud, but widely publicized murders—as I was sure this would be— frequently attracted crowds of looky-loos wanting to inspect the site of violent death. Their reasoning eluded me, but I'd seen it happen time and again.

She shrugged, sending the blue camisole's strap sagging down her arm. She pulled it up. She peered at me as if trying to focus on my face. "Maybe. Maybe not. There's not much margin in retail, you know, and now with that damned Olympush going up—" She seemed to lose her train of thought, her eyes drifting to the side. With an effort, she brought them back to my face. "Hey! Maybe now that Jack is dead—" She stopped again and lifted her glass, taking a long swallow.

"Now that Jack is dead—" I prompted.

"Poor Jack." Tears filled her eyes.

"Were you good friends?"

"You could say that." A wistful smile curved her lips.

The bartender chose that moment to plunk down my club soda and I could've strangled him. By the time he sponged up a damp circle from Finola's glass, she had recovered herself a bit.

"Customer," she said, nodding. "Jack was a good customer."

"But you sell ladies' clothes."

"Um-hm." A tiny frown appeared between her brows. "Jack liked ladies."

I wasn't sure which way to take this conversation. I didn't think I was going to get anything else out of her about her relationship with Jackson Porter, so I went with, "When was the last time he bought something from you?"

"Saturday. Cocktail dress. A tangerine number by Tadashi Shoji." She fluttered her hands in the air, seeming to indicate ruffles or a floaty material like chiffon.

"For his wife?"

She blew an un-ladylike raspberry. "Elena's not a size two! I need another drink." She signaled to the bartender, but I shook my head at him. "Hey!" She glared at me.

"Let me take you home, Finola," I said, slipping off the bar stool to help her stand.

"Got my car," she mumbled, her chin falling toward her chest.

"I don't think so." I draped her arm over my shoulders and wrapped my arm around her waist. Thankfully, she was a skinny thing, probably a size two, unlike Elena. The helpful bartender, probably hoping I'd get her out of his bar before she upchucked, found Finola's purse and hooked it over my forearm.

"Thanks," he said. "I was getting worried about her. Your drink's on me."

Wow, a free club soda. I gave him a "just doing my job" shrug and nudged Finola toward the door. Luckily, my car was parked close by because she was leaning heavily on me by the time we got there. I propped her against the side of my bronze Miata and opened the passenger door. Thank goodness the temps were in the low fifties instead of the icy teens we'd experienced last week. A woman shepherding two toddlers gave me an odd look and crossed to the far side of the row. I maneuvered Finola into the front seat and handed her a shoe box from the backseat after dumping out the strappy silver sandals I'd bought last week in a moment of madness. Who was I kidding? I couldn't wear heels like that anymore. The shoes were in the car so I could return them.

"Here." I put the box in Finola's lap when she showed no inclination to hold it. "Use this if you feel sick." I buckled her in, closed the door, and went around to the driver's side. Once settled, I asked, "Where do you live?"

A gentle snore was my only answer. I looked at her slumped against the window, the harsh sun illuminating the lines around her lips and the crepey skin on her bare arms that the dim light in Tombino's had camouflaged. She was in her midfifties, I figured, not her forties, as I'd always thought. With a sigh, I dug through her purse, finding her wallet and her driver's license.

I drove to the modest townhome some fifteen minutes from Fernglen, found Finola's keys, and opened the front door, then returned to the car to lug the groggy boutique owner into her house. I guided her back to her bedroom and located some aspirin in the medicine cabinet, noting fluffy taupe bath sheets and an array of expensive-looking lotions on the counter. She took the aspirin as docilely as a child and promptly passed out on the bed. Propping two pillows under her head and turning her head sideways so she wouldn't choke if she threw up, I left her keys and purse on the granite counter by the coffeepot—sure to be her first stop when she awoke with a massive hangover—and left, turning the lock in the knob as I closed the door.

Back in the car, I checked the time: four thirty. Damn. I could still work in a swim before Kyra's bout, if I kept it short, but the pool would be crowded now with after-work exercisers. I liked to swim more or less alone, still uncomfortable with the gawping that my leg injuries received. In desperate need of exercise, I headed reluctantly to the YMCA just two miles from my patio home. In the locker room, redolent of wet metal and antiperspirant—someone must have sprayed herself lavishly—I stripped quickly, keeping my back to the room, and pulled on my orange swimsuit with the racer back. Wrapping my hibiscus-print beach towel around my waist so it draped to my ankles, I headed for the showers and the pool entrance, wondering for the thousandth time why they needed so many mirrors. From the waist up, I looked okay, maybe better than okay, with glossy chestnut hair and long-lashed eyes, a bustline that was a happy medium between Keira Knightley and Dolly Parton, and strong arms and shoulders from the swimming.

Below the waist . . . I hustled past all the mirrors, rinsed off, and headed to the pool.

Several lap swimmers were crawling and breast-stroking in the lanes, and a rowdy group of eight-year-olds had assembled for a lesson at the far end. Sitting on the pool's edge, I quickly unwrapped the towel and slid into the water in one smooth movement, turning to place the towel on the deck. A surreptitious look around discovered no stares or pointing; no one had noticed. Adjusting my goggles, I struck out for the far end of the Olympic-sized pool, letting the exertion and the water strip away the stress that had built up in my body. I didn't know how nonexercisers made it through the day without killing someone.

Hair still damp, I arrived at the city auditorium just as the roller derby bout was getting underway. On a Monday night there wasn't much of a crowd, and I got a seat on the bleachers near the front without any trouble. The oval track was laid out at a slight angle to the long axis of the hardwood floor with rope under the tape to give the skaters a tactile indicator when they were going out of bounds. A computer-driven projector showed the score and the time remaining on a screen over the stage at the south end. Big speakers on the stage shrieked a guitar riff from a song I didn't know, undoubtedly by a band I'd never heard of. The league had padded the hard edges of risky wall corners and stationed volunteers—grinning young men—at two side entryways as "girl catchers" to stop errant skaters from sliding out of sight and into possible harm.

I spotted Kyra right away—not hard to do since she's a six-foot-tall black woman and was wearing the purple uniform and helmet of the Vernonville Vengeance, the roller derby team she'd skated with for over two years. Her long hair frizzed from beneath the helmet to midback, much

longer than when we'd first met, when I was eleven and she
was twelve. My folks had brought us to Vernonville to visit
with Gran and Grandpa Atherton in the big Colonial home
they'd lived in before Gran died. Kyra had skated by the
house one morning when I was sitting on the porch, sulking
about how boring it was going to be with no one but my
brother Clint to play with. We'd hit it off immediately, and
I cried when it was time to go back to California. Kyra and I
called each other weekly during the school year, and I had
looked forward to returning to Gran and Grandpa's each
summer after that. Kyra had even visited us in California a
couple of times before graduating high school a year ahead
of me and going off to Duke. A college track and field athlete, she had won a silver medal in the hurdles at the Olym-
pics. She started skating because running on a treadmill
during the gloomy winter months was "too damned boring."

I'd been skeptical about roller derby, but it wasn't what
I'd expected. The women ranged in age from about twenty
to almost forty and, like Kyra, were into it for the fun of
skating and being part of a competitive team. Some of the
women were muscle-bound, some were almost waiflike.
Some sported tattoos, some didn't. As the women whizzed
around the track, with the jammers trying to lap the other
team, I admired the way they worked together, the way a
skater would scramble up if knocked down. There was definitely no crying in roller derby, not even when a nose got
bloodied, a finger got jammed, or a hip got bruised in a fall.

I yelled along with the crowd, urging the Vengeance to
pulverize the visitors, the Morganville Morgue. The Vengeance won, 147 to 113. Kyra celebrated with her team, then
skated over to me and plunked down on the bleacher, gym
bag in hand. She was breathing hard and had a smell of clean
sweat about her.

"I'm going to be sore tomorrow," she said, unlacing her skates.

"You say that every time."

"Yeah, well, it's true every time. And it gets truer every year. We're not getting any younger." She threw a Blue Devils sweatshirt over her tank top, pulled on matching sweatpants, and slipped on flip-flops decorated with beads and yarn wrapped around the straps. She wiggled her strong toes with their purple-polished nails as if glad to be out of the confining skates.

"It's forty-two degrees out," I said.

"I know."

"Where to?"

We made a swing through the deli at the Giant, collecting an eclectic mix of sushi, tortilla soup, curried chicken salad, and mini éclairs, and headed back to my house. One story of brick front with forest green trim in a community that boasted a pool, lush landscaping, and quiet neighbors—my house might not be my parents' California spread, but it was all mine. I'd bought the small ranch house, part of a planned "village" of similar homes, when I moved here just over a year ago. When the military medically retired me, I didn't know where I wanted to live, although I knew I didn't want to return to L.A. and be near my folks. The thought of Mom and Dad trying to coddle me, and my former friends politely not asking about my leg, convinced me I wanted to live as far away as possible. When Grandpa Atherton mentioned that a friend of his was selling the rancher that he'd used as a rental property, I drove out from Walter Reed—the military hospital in D.C. where I was doing my rehab—to view it. My mom had begged me to buy the house and move to Vernonville to "keep an eye on" Grandpa. I suspected she was likewise urging him to keep an eye on me, worried about my knee and my mind-set; being forced out of the military and discovering I couldn't work as a cop had depressed me for a while.

Being offered the job at Fernglen Galleria sealed the deal. Having Kyra nearby was a huge bonus. I bought the house, even though it was a bit of a fixer-upper. The last renter had done some damage—I suspected he was either a rock star wannabe practicing Keith Richards's hotel-room-trashing techniques, or had eight children or a pack of wolves. I'm not patient enough to be the do-it-yourself type; the "measure eight times, cut once" philosophy of construction, plus the need to make fourteen trips to the home improvement store in the middle of every project, drive me batty. So, I was hiring the work done as my mall paycheck allowed. The project currently underway was tiling the kitchen floor, since the renter had managed, in some never explained way, to scorch and burn several spots in the linoleum.

"I see progress," Kyra said, surveying the tiled but ungrouted area in the breakfast nook that had expanded by several feet since she'd last visited. My current handyman, a flaky college kid trying to earn money for spring break, had left a wet saw pushed up against the butcher-block table, and the untiled portion of the floor was nothing but raw plywood. I hadn't laid eyes on him in almost a week and he wasn't returning my calls.

"Yeah, I expect *House Beautiful* to show up any day now," I said. The clutter of trowels, buckets, and pallets of tile annoyed me, so I pulled some of Gran's Noritake china from the cupboards and some Molson from the fridge, and led the way into my family room so we could watch *Dancing with the Stars*, our Monday-night ritual.

"So, what's with the murder?" Kyra asked during the first commercial break. She popped a piece of sushi into her mouth, having started with the éclairs.

I told her what I knew about Jackson Porter's death, which wasn't much. "Had you heard any talk about his development, Olympus?" I asked. "Among the mall merchants, I mean?"

"Some. I wasn't worried about it."

"You run a magic store," I pointed out. "I doubt Olympus was going to cut into your business."

"Exactly." She relaxed back against the terra cotta–colored leather sofa and took a swallow of beer.

"So who was worried?"

She slanted me a glance from her long, narrow eyes. "Mostly the clothing boutique owners and the sporting goods people. Finola Craig, Terrence Chou of the Upper Limit, Colin at Pete's Sporting Goods. She was trying to get an injunction or a stay of execution or whatever you call it to stop the construction. She was working with Dyson Harding at the university, the archeologist who was against the resort because it was being built on Native American burial grounds, or something like that."

"I vaguely remember reading about that," I said. I had to admit I paid more attention to the international news, especially updates on the military's progress in the Middle East, than the local news.

A growling noise came from behind us, and Kyra and I looked over our shoulders to where a giant rust-colored cat sat behind the sofa, twitching his truncated tail. Fubar. I'd adopted him as a young stray a year ago when I'd been released from the hospital. He had a mangled ear and a shortened tail, and I didn't know if he'd tangled with a coyote, a car, or an abusive owner. After our first month together, when I'd imprisoned him indoors in order to keep him safe, we'd come to an agreement: we could each come and go as we pleased. To that end, I installed a cat door and he stopped flaying the furniture. Now, he blinked his golden eyes at me, demanding applause. A dead mouse dangled from his mouth.

"I hope you found that outside, Fubar," Kyra said, eyeing the rodent with distaste.

"Of course he did," I said with more certainty than I felt. Fetching a roll of paper towels from the kitchen, I persuaded Fubar to give up his trophy by bribing him with some hamburger. I was pretty sure Fubar only bothered to hunt in order to coerce me into upgrading his menu. I quickly shrouded the little victim in Brawny and put him in the outside trash. When I returned, Fubar had settled on Kyra's lap and was purring loudly as she provided commentary on the samba talents of an Olympic javelin thrower.

"You could shake your booty better than that," she told the cat. "I don't know why they've never had a roller skater on the show."

"The show is called *Dancing with the Stars*," I said, emphasizing the last word.

"Oh, please. Like you ever heard of that guy who was in a boy band two decades ago. Or that reality 'star' whose only source of protein is insects."

"Call up the producer. Maybe they'll book you."

"Nah. I couldn't be away from the store that long. How about your dad?"

I choked on a bit of curried chicken. "Please, don't give him any ideas." The idea of being confronted with my father's latest face-lift on TV every Monday was enough to ruin my appetite. I glared at Kyra.

Laughing, she changed the subject. "So, have you met the new cookie man? He is hotter than a snickerdoodle straight out of the oven." She flashed a lascivious grin.

"Cookie man?"

"The guy who bought the cookie franchise in the food court," Kyra said impatiently. "Jay Callahan. I introduced myself today. We're going out Thursday night."

"Fast work." I dragged the conversation back to the murder. "If you hear anyone talking about Porter or the resort, can you let me know?"

"You want me to spy for you?"

"Not exactly. Just fill me in on the gossip. People say things in front of you that they don't mention to me. It's the uniform."

"Are you supposed to be investigating this murder?" Kyra asked, keeping her gaze on the television where a soap opera star who should have had more dignity, despite her character's thirteen marriages, four illegitimate children, amnesia, and stint as a circus aerialist, writhed on the floor as her professional partner hopped over her. "I'd think Captain Was-a-bitch would rather have you ticketing litterbugs."

"Maybe. But the detective in charge of the case has made me his 'mall liaison,' so I'm going to do as much liaisoning as I can get away with, Woskowicz be damned."

Five

. . .

When Tuesday morning rolled around, I found myself more eager to get to the mall than I had been in months. I knew it was the challenge of the murder drawing me in. That, and the opportunity to round up more reptiles, of course. Feeling generous, I bought Joel a huge cinnamon bun at the coffee place where I got my first cup of caffeine. I put it on his desk with a flourish and he beamed. "Thanks, EJ!"

"It's about time," Weasel growled, dark stubble shadowing his jawline. "Let's do the turnover briefing so I can get out of here."

"I'm twenty minutes early," I pointed out, shoving my gym bag under my desk.

"Yeah, well, ya want a medal?" He rolled his chair over beside me, and I leaned away from his funk, a mix of sweat, cigarette smoke, and old beer. Either the man never washed his uniforms—completely possible—or he'd been boozing it up on duty—also possible. "Nothing much happened last night," Weasel said, not referring to any notes. "Those stupid-ass kids tagged another car about oh-one-hundred hours."

"What'd they write this time?" Joel asked around a mouthful of sticky bun.

"'Love the Lord Ur God With All Ur Heart,'" Weasel sneered, making a heart shape in the air for the last word.

"'And with all your soul and all your mind.' Matthew 22:37," Joel supplied. "What?" he asked when Weasel and I stared at him. "I paid attention in Sunday school."

"Yeah, well, I don't think the owner of that Jaguar XKE is liking the Bible very much right now," Weasel said with a laugh that turned into a phlegmy cough.

"Anything else?" I asked.

"Nah," Weasel said. "Quiet as a tomb." He shoved to his feet, checking his cell phone. "I'm outta here. When the boss comes in, tell him I'll see him at Rauncho's at the usual time."

"Sure thing, Weasel," Joel said, making a note.

When Weasel had plodded out, carrying a rank-smelling cooler, I turned to Joel. "Doesn't the concept of a Christian graffiti gang seem like an oxymoron? I mean, isn't there something in the Bible about thou shalt not deface your neighbor's property?"

Joel pretended to consider it, licking sugar from his lips. "Nope. Don't think so. The only thing about writing I remember in the Bible is Moses with the stone tablets, and I don't think the Ten Commandments count as graffiti."

"Hello?"

We turned to see a woman pushing through the glass door. She brought to mind the word "puffy." Puffy blond hair, the kind I associate with Texas debutantes, poofed high on the crown of her head and flipped out slightly at jaw length. A puffy face and slightly red nose spoke to overindulgence last night or a cold, and she wore a puffy white quilted jacket with gold metal zippers scoring it in half a dozen places. White leggings and velvet mules trimmed with marabou finished a look that might have worked on a teenager but not on the fifty-something she appeared to be. "I'm Elena Porter," she said through coral-lipsticked, collagened (puffy) lips. "The police told me EJ Ferris found my husband yesterday. I'd like to talk to him, if he's here?" She looked at Joel.

"I'm Emma-Joy Ferris," I said, rising to shake her hand. "I'm sorry for your loss, Mrs. Porter."

She pulled a tissue from her jacket pocket, dislodging a glove. "Yes, well, I'm just getting used to the idea. It hasn't really hit me yet." She dabbed at her eyes.

Stooping to pick up her glove, I asked, "What can I do for you?"

"Can we talk in private?" she asked. "And I could really use some coffee." She fixed her eyes on my cup like a vampire staring at a pint of O-positive.

"Sure. Let's walk down to the Bean Bonanza kiosk. It's the only thing open right now. Suzie makes a lot of money from the mall walkers." I kept up a flow of meaningless prattle as we walked to the Bean Bonanza and bought our coffee from the energetic young entrepreneur who seemed to run the kiosk eighteen hours a day by herself. I'd often wondered how she managed potty breaks. Mrs. Porter didn't say much until we'd settled on a bench in front of the bookstore and she'd had several sips from her cup.

"I'm not usually so out of it," she apologized. "But what with my maid quitting yesterday, on top of the news about Jackson, and I haven't even been able to find Robbie to tell him . . ." She blinked back tears.

"Robbie?"

"Our son. He's . . . difficult. He had a fight with Jackson two weeks ago, and we haven't heard from him since. I'm so afraid . . ." She cut herself off with another glug of coffee. "But that's not why I came. I was hoping you could tell me about finding Jackson."

"Excuse me?"

"The police just said he was found at Diamanté, that he'd been shot. They didn't give me any details." She looked at me expectantly.

I wasn't sure what to tell her. "A young woman discovered Mr. Porter's body," I said. "One of the mall walkers. She screamed and I responded. I could tell immediately that he was dead, Mrs. Porter, that he'd been dead for a while. There was nothing I could do."

An elderly couple walked by, arms pumping, his fish-belly legs displayed by navy shorts, hers covered in blue sweats.

"Surely there's more to it than that."

I sensed a tension in her I didn't understand. Was she looking for signs of negligence, thinking that I could have saved Jackson Porter if I'd responded more quickly, administered first aid or something? If so, that turkey wouldn't fly; the autopsy would bear out that he'd been dead for hours before I came on the scene. "Not really," I said. "That was about it. I called the police, and they responded very quickly."

"No, no." She brushed aside the police with a flick of her hand. "I mean, how did he look?"

Ah, I thought I understood what she wanted. "He looked peaceful, Mrs. Porter," I said. In truth, he hadn't looked much of anything other than dead, but she seemed to want to hear he hadn't suffered. "I'm sure death was instantaneous."

"It hurts me to think of him suffering," she said, sniffing.

Her eyes tracked a young man pushing a jog stroller with a laughing baby in it. "Did you take photos?"

The question caught me off guard. "I'm sure the police have all the photos they need," I said, not quite sure why I didn't want to own up to snapping some pictures. It was something about Mrs. Porter's moist mouth and avid eyes that put me off.

"You did." She stated it as a fact and put her coffee cup on the bench between us. "Let me see them."

"Mrs. Porter, I really think—"

"I have a right to see them. He was my husband." Her agitated voice attracted attention from the salesclerk hefting up the grille at the teen clothing store. The girl, decked out with multiple piercings, stared at us for a moment, then ducked under the metal bar and rattled it back down. "Jackson's last moments are important to me."

I didn't point out that his "last moments" had occurred well before I took the photos. "Ma'am, I think you'd do better to remember your husband as he was the last time you saw him alive. There's no point to dwelling on—"

"Have you ever had a husband murdered?" she asked, pushing to her feet and stumbling a bit as the kitten-heeled mule slipped out from under her foot. Without giving me time to answer—I guess she went with the odds—she added, "So don't tell me what I should dwell on. I want to talk to your boss. I should have started with him in the first place." She took off, a great ball of puffiness, headed back to the security office.

I caught up with her even though trotting made my knee ache. No way was I going to tag along behind her. She stiff-armed the office door and blew through just as Captain Woskowicz dropped a sheaf of papers on Joel's desk. He was wearing sunglasses this morning and looked like a caricature of the crooked cinema cop who gets blown away by Clint Eastwood or Charles Bronson by the movie's end. Mrs. Porter was clearly impressed.

"Ooh," she breathed. "I'm sure you can help me."

"I'd be pleased to, ma'am," he said, obviously admiring. He removed his sunglasses, revealing bloodshot eyes.

"This . . . your . . . she found my husband's body yesterday and took photos, but she won't let me see them."

From her accusatory tone, you'd think I'd shot Porter myself. "Mrs. Porter, Captain Woskowicz." I made the introductions, resigned.

"Elena," she said, holding out her hand.

Woskowicz took it, but his gaze shifted to me. "Do you have photos of Mr. Porter, Ferris?"

"Yes."

"Then share them with Mrs. Porter." He made a "what's the big deal?" gesture.

"I don't think the police—"

"Did you take them while on duty?" At my tiny nod, a glint of triumph lit his eyes. "Then they're mall property. Let's see 'em."

Reluctantly, I pulled my camera from its pouch on my utility belt. Without speaking, I clicked until the first photo of Jackson Porter, sprawled on the lounger, came up. I handed the camera to Woskowicz, who shifted it from side to side to avoid the glare as he and Elena Porter looked at it. Tears filled the woman's eyes and left tracks down her cheeks, and she put a tentative finger on the screen. "But he's naked!" she gasped. "They didn't tell me." And with her hands at her mouth, she spun on her kitten heel and hurried out of the office.

"Good going, Ferris," Woskowicz said, tossing the camera at me and striding back to his office.

"He's a total a-hole," Joel said, echoing my thoughts. The look in his eyes said he clearly wanted to see the photos, too, so I laid the camera on his desk and swiped the last bite of the cinnamon bun.

"Did you see the news reports this morning on the murder?" Joel asked without looking up from the camera's tiny screen.

"No. What'd they say?"

For answer, he turned his computer screen so I could read it. "Local Developer Murdered," the headlines blared. In smaller type, it read: "Councilman Questioned." Now that was interesting. I scanned the article, learning that a number of witnesses had seen Porter Sunday afternoon lunching with Councilman Earl Gatchel, at Tombino's of all places, and that Gatchel had been questioned extensively at police headquarters yesterday. "Sources indicate," the article went on, "that Gatchel was under investigation for improperly influencing council members in favor of Jackson Porter's development projects. Insider reports on his finances indicate that during weeks when the Vernonville council voted on zoning or other measures related to Porter's projects, large sums of money flowed into and out of an account that has been traced to Gatchel. When contacted by this reporter, Gatchel had no comment."

"What do you think?" I asked Joel, looking up from the screen to see him watching me.

"Gatchel did it," he said positively. "They had lunch, Porter said something to set him off—maybe he offered to cooperate with whoever was investigating Gatchel to save his own hide—and Gatchel offed him."

"I thought Finola was your front runner."

He squirmed a little under my teasing. "You were right—she's too small."

"So why'd Gatchel pose Porter in Diamanté's window?"

"Who knows?" Joel shrugged, obviously not considering it important. "Maybe to warn off other people who might be in a position to testify against him."

"You make him sound like a mob boss, instead of a penny-ante local politician with a flair for bribery," I said.

"Even penny-ante local politicians want to protect their asses," he said.

"Good point," I said, and he blushed.

Tracy Jensen and Harold Wasserman came in just then, and we exchanged greetings and speculation about the murder. After ten minutes, I left to begin my rounds; it was close on nine o'clock and merchants were beginning to filter in. My first stop on the Segway was the Herpetology Hut; I wanted to check in with Kiefer and see how many critters he'd recovered. Kiefer wasn't there, but a girl who could have been his sister, his girlfriend, or a new employee was chopping lettuce and carrots on a cutting block beside the cash register. She told me he was in the food court. A glance in Agatha's enclosure told me the python was still missing.

I waved to Fernando as I entered the food court and looked around for Kiefer. Weak sunlight poured through the glass panes in the ceiling, and the scents of coffee, tomato sauce, and stale grease permeated the air. White-topped tables with chrome legs awaited the customers who would trickle in around midmorning. I liked their clean shine at this time of day, before they got spattered with ketchup, streaked with hamburger grease, and dotted with crumbs. I spotted Kiefer, dreads draped over his shoulders, talking to a man I didn't know at the Legendary Lola Cookies stand. He held a large cookie. As I motored closer, Kiefer saw me and beckoned me over. He wore the same flannel shirt as yesterday, over a purple tee shirt that read, "My python is smarter than your fifth-grader." He smiled.

"Hey, EJ," he said, "we rounded up thirty-three animals yesterday. One old dude found fifteen of them all by himself. He had some sort of motion detector gadget—it was bitchin'."

Let's hear it for Grandpa Atherton.

"We're only missing four now. Two lizards, one snake, one tortoise, and Agatha. I guess that's five."

"That's what I came over to find out," I said, dismounting. "Are they okay?"

"One skink lost a tail, but other than that they're cool. I wish I could get my hands on those dumbass LOAFers who turned them loose. Don't they know reptiles need controlled temperatures and a special diet? They're not rodents: they can't make it on garbage and cookie crumbs. No offense, Jay."

The man behind the counter smiled. "None taken."

My first thought was that he didn't eat much of his product. He was average height, about five feet ten, and lean in an athletic way, with strong biceps showing beneath the short sleeves of his orange "Legendary Lola Cookies" tee shirt. Wavy, dark red hair grazed his collar, and hazel eyes showed a gleam of humor. I could see why Kyra thought he was hot even though he was shorter than she was. His gaze flicked between me and Kiefer, and I got the feeling he noticed a lot. He looked more like a firefighter or a soldier—someone active, used to making decisions—than a baker, and my cop antennae went up.

"You must be the new Lola," I said, offering my hand.

"Oops, sorry," Kiefer said. "EJ, this is Jay Callahan. Jay, EJ Ferris, our own supercop."

"Nice to meet you," Jay said with a strong handshake.

"What brings you to Fernglen?" I asked.

"A good business opportunity," Jay said, gesturing at the display case filled with a dozen kinds of cookies. The glass-fronted oven behind him showed multiple tins of browning cookies, and the smell of vanilla and cinnamon made me realize my breakfast had consisted of nothing more than a stolen bite of sticky bun.

"Have you been in the cookie business a long time?"

"Long enough."

Was he deliberately dodging my questions, or was he just taciturn? I couldn't decide. I turned back to Kiefer just as he bit into the huge chocolate chip cookie.

"Did the Vernonville cop ever show up?"

Kiefer swallowed and flashed a crumby grin. "Yeah. Dude showed up about closing. Bought a corn snake from me."

I rolled my eyes. "Did he do anything more useful than that?"

Kiefer shrugged. "Wrote it up. Gave me a report for my insurance."

"Well, I'll keep my eyes peeled for the rest of the escapees, especially Agatha."

A worried look clouded Kiefer's brow. "I just don't know where she could be."

My mind flashed to the *Harry Potter* movie where the basilisk lives in the plumbing at Hogwarts; there were miles of ductwork and pipes in the mall. I hoped Agatha hadn't found her way into them. "I'm sure she'll turn up," I said optimistically. "She's probably found some place nice and cozy to curl up."

Waving good-bye to the two men, I resumed my patrol, making a mental note to see what I could find out about Mr. Jay Callahan, cookie-meister. I followed my usual route but found myself in front of Diamanté a few minutes earlier than usual. The grille was down, and yellow crime scene tape was threaded through it. The mannequins still sprawled where they had fallen, a poor advertisement for the expensive swimsuits they wore. They looked like co-eds who'd overindulged on a spring-break spree and collapsed in a drunken stupor. Poor Finola.

I was just debating whether to call Finola to see how she was doing, and maybe see if she knew the name of the woman Jackson Porter bought the cocktail dress for, when Grandpa Atherton came around the corner wearing a gray tracksuit and sneakers. An Orioles baseball cap partly covered his snowy hair.

"Emma-Joy!" he hailed me. "You didn't tell me about the murder."

"Good morning to you, too, Grandpa," I said.

He waved aside the niceties. "You weren't trying to keep me away from the action by sending me off on that lizard hunt yesterday, were you?" His sharp gaze fixed on my face.

I concentrated on looking innocent and added a soupçon of affront for good measure. "Of course not. But the police have that case well in hand. Kiefer tells me you did a fabulous job finding his stock."

"Nothing to it with the right equipment. Fill me in on the murder."

Accepting the inevitable, I gave Grandpa a brief rundown on the Porter case. "The police have a viable suspect," I finished. "And they don't want anything from us except access to personnel records and the security-camera data."

Grandpa snorted. He didn't have a high opinion of Fernglen's security technology. "The dpi on your cameras is so poor, you'd be lucky if you could tell a sumo wrestler from a burlesque dancer."

"Well, I don't think the cameras showed any wrestlers, dancers, or murderers," I said.

"An inside job," Grandpa said immediately. "They knew how to avoid the cameras."

I'd already thought of that. "It could be," I admitted, "but it could also be that someone scoped the place out beforehand. It's not that hard to spot the cameras if you know what you're looking for." I pointed at the camera lens clearly visible above the storefront we were passing. "The mall *wants* people to know about the cameras. They're meant to discourage theft more than to ID criminals after the fact."

"Tell you what, Emma-Joy," Grandpa said with the air of a monarch conveying a boon, "I'll tail this Gatchel fellow for you, find out what he's up to."

"That's not necessary, Grandpa," I said, meaning "don't." The chicken part of me said that at least if Gatchel spotted him and complained, it wouldn't be in my mall. "There's nothing in this case related to spying. Why do you want to pursue it?"

"Got to keep my hand in," he said with a grin that deepened the wrinkles around his eyes and mouth. "The tradecraft of investigation is a lot like what they taught us at the Farm. Besides, I don't have anything pressing on the national security front right now, so I'm free to help my favorite granddaughter."

"I'm your only granddaughter," I pointed out, passing up the chance to argue about his definition of "help."

He tweaked my cheek between his thumb and the side of his forefinger and jiggled it. "You'd still be my favorite if I had a dozen granddaughters," he said.

"Popping out a dozen children would've landed Mom in the nearest looney bin," I said.

He laughed loud enough to cause a pair of women to turn and stare. "Brenda never did have much fortitude," he said.

"And you've got to admit your brother Clint was a rare handful."

"Still is," I muttered, thinking of the postcard I'd gotten last week from Burma or Myanmar or whatever it was called these days. Clint (named after Dad's hero, Eastwood) had ended up as an investigative journalist, clearly inheriting a large dose of Grandpa's nosiness and liking for cloak-and-dagger activities. The postcard promised me a ruby when Clint got back to the States. "Did you know ruby and sapphire are the same mineral?" he'd written.

Clint collected stray facts the way belly buttons collect lint. I'd emailed to say that my paycheck didn't run to gemstones so the relationship of rubies and sapphires had never concerned me. I figured there was a fifty-fifty chance Clint would actually show up with a ruby. Or, he might show up with a political dissident he'd helped escape from the ruling junta. You never knew what you were going to get with my brother.

My radio squawked; it was Joel summoning me back to the office. "Got to go, Grandpa," I said. "Stay out of trouble." I stood on tiptoe to kiss his cheek.

He waggled his white brows at me. "Can you doubt it?"

Oh, yeah.

Six

. . .

Back at the office, I spotted Detective Helland before I pushed through the doors. He had his hands clasped at the small of his back and he was pacing back and forth, Joel watching anxiously from behind his desk. He wore an elegant navy blue suit today with a tie patterned with yellow and blue ovals. When Helland saw me, he frowned. "Did you take photos of the murder scene?" he asked without preamble.

What was it with the photos today? "Yes."

He nodded, as if I'd confirmed something he suspected. "Do you have any idea how much damage you may have done to our case? I thought you were more professional than that."

His biting tone caught me off-guard. "Excuse me? How does taking photos damage your case? It's standard crime scene procedure."

"Don't play dumb. Your posting them on the Internet

could make catching the killer a hundred times more difficult. At the very least, it'll make weeding out the attention seekers who confess to the murder almost impossible."

Clenching my fists at my sides, I looked him straight in his icy gray eyes. "I did not post any photos on the Internet."

"Really?" His brows arched. "Then how did these get online?" He swung Joel's computer screen around so I could see photos of Porter's body displayed in the Diamanté window. "You were the first one on the scene, and I'll swear none of my team leaked these."

For a moment, the photos fogged my mind so I couldn't think straight. They looked almost exactly like the ones I'd taken. Then, my brain snapped into gear. "I can think of two possibilities off the bat," I said. "Gina Kissell—the mom who found the body—might have taken photos. I admit she didn't seem like the type, but she might've done it. Everyone has a camera in their cell phone these days. Or, it could've been the murderer." Before he could respond, I yanked my camera out of its pocket. "Here. Have your experts compare my photos to these." I gestured at the computer. "They won't be the same. You can apologize later."

I spun on my heel, stumbling when my knee buckled, and stalked out of the office. Climbing on the Segway, I headed for Kyra's shop to vent. I felt vaguely guilty about leaving Joel to cope with Helland's anger, but Helland wasn't angry with him. I'd have punched the man if I'd stayed in the office two seconds longer. How dare he accuse me of sabotaging his case?

Kyra was with a customer when I parked the Segway outside Merlin's Cave and stalked in, so I amused myself by looking around. A fountain splashed in one corner, emitting a dry-ice mist, and gentle music played from invisible speakers. The store was dimly lit, to resemble the cave it was named after, I supposed, and was cooler than the mall corridors. The stock consisted of an eclectic mix of magic tricks; New Age crystals and incense and tarot decks; videos and nonfiction books having to do with magic, myth, mysticism, religion, ESP, and the like; a large selection of fantasy fiction for kids and adults; and some Native American art and dream catchers. Kyra was absolutely the last person you'd expect to find running a store like this since she was an agnostic and far more interested in the here-and-now than in the afterlife or parallel universes or anything else that couldn't be proven with a petri dish and a Bunsen burner. But her aunt Harmony (her real name) was on a yearlong sabbatical to Tibet, and she had persuaded Kyra to take over the store in her absence. In her real life, after she'd won the silver, Kyra became a software whiz who wrote programs with coaching applications. She'd made enough on the sale of some program for scheduling sporting events that she could afford to take a year off to help her aunt by running Merlin's Cave.

The customer left, a bag tucked under one arm, and Kyra turned to me with a grimace. "She just asked if I'd like to join her coven. Do I look like a witch to you?"

"What does a witch look like?" I asked, already feeling less angry than when I'd walked in.

"Green skin, pointy hat—didn't you see *Wicked*?" Kyra asked. She smoothed the colorful silk of her long skirt against her hip. Her real taste in clothes ran more to slacks and stark, modern lines, but she'd quickly figured out that looking like an Indian mystic or wise herbalist resulted in more sales. "What brings you here looking like you want to borrow my lance"—she had a real lance near a display of King Arthur books—"and run someone through?"

"Not a bad idea," I said, envisioning myself on a strong

white steed, galloping toward Detective Helland, lance held level. I told Kyra about Helland's accusations.

"He's really gotten under your skin, hasn't he?"

"He treats me like I'm an incompetent boob," I said. "Of course that pisses me off." I pinged a wind chime hanging near me, and it made brassy tinkling noises.

"Of course."

"What's that supposed to mean?" I peered at her suspiciously.

"Nothing."

I could tell by the way she was trying not to smile that she meant something, but I didn't pursue it. "I met your cookie man," I said instead.

"And?"

"And he's pretty hot. But I'm not sure about him. He was evasive when I asked a few questions about his background."

Kyra laughed. "Girl, just because someone doesn't want to trot out their resumé and their psych profile within two seconds of meeting you doesn't make them a suspicious character. Get out of 'cop mode' on occasion and go with the flow. Loosen up." She opened her arms and swayed. "Buy some lavender oil to calm you down or get a massage to open up your chakras or something."

"You wouldn't know a chakra from a chocolate chip," I accused, having no idea myself.

"Sure I do. She sang that song 'Through the Fire.'" Kyra hummed.

"That was *Chaka* Khan," I said, laughing despite myself. "I've got to get back to patrolling."

I'd only gone past eight storefronts when I spotted a young boy—maybe three—lugging what looked like an old army helmet toward his mother. On closer inspection, I realized it wasn't a helmet but a tortoise with the tip of its head just peeking out of the khaki-colored shell. I guided the Segway close and got off.

"Did you find that tortoise here in the mall?" I asked the boy.

Wearing a striped shirt under denim overalls, he looked at me from big, unblinking brown eyes. "Turtle."

His mother hustled back from where she was inspecting lingerie in a display window. She was young and skinny and dressed in tight denim. She put a protective hand on her son's shoulder. "Is there a problem?"

I introduced myself and explained about the animals being released from the Herpetology Hut on Monday. "I think that tortoise is probably one of the animals that was turned loose, and I'd like to return it. Or I can tell you where the store is if you'd like to take it back."

The little boy's eyes had flicked back and forth from his mom to me during our conversation. Now, he hugged the tortoise to his chest. "Mine." His lower lip poked out in an ominous way.

"Of course it's yours, Jimmy," the mother said. She shot me a triumphant look and said, "Finders keepers."

A great child-rearing message. I sighed, knowing I couldn't prove the tortoise was one of Kiefer's. "You're very lucky, Jimmy," I said, squatting down to his level, despite my knee's complaining. "My mommy wouldn't even let me have a turtle."

Curiosity overcame suspicion. "Why not?"

"Because they need a big, expensive kind of home called a terrarium with a heat lamp, and they need special food, and because of salmonella."

I sensed the mother listening.

"What's sal—What's that?" Jimmy asked.

The tortoise waved its feet and craned its neck, attempting to run away in midair.

"It's a sickness that makes you throw up. I hate throwing up, don't you? Yuck. It's not the turtle's fault, though."

"I trew up at Brynn's birfday party," he volunteered.

The mother gnawed on a cuticle and said, "Jimmy, give the lady back her turtle."

Obedient to the pressure of her hand on his shoulder, he thrust the tortoise toward me, and I took it gingerly, holding it on either side like a huge hamburger bun. "Thank you," I told him. "You took good care of the turtle, and I'll make sure it gets back to its home. Tell you what, do you like books?"

Jimmy nodded tentatively, clearly rating books considerably below pets.

"If you go by the Herpetology Hut, I'm sure my friend Kiefer would be happy to give you a book about turtles and snakes for taking such good care of this tortoise." I told the mom where to find Kiefer's store and got on the Segway, setting the tortoise between my feet.

"I wanna snake," Jimmy was telling his mother as I glided away.

I delivered the tortoise to a grateful Kiefer and explained about promising Jimmy a book.

"Happy to do it," Kiefer said. "Hey, a woman came in and said she saw an anaconda in the fountain, and I went down there, but there was no sign of Agatha. Now that word's gotten around, I'm afraid people will be seeing snakes everywhere."

"Great." Just what we needed: hysterical shoppers thinking a copperhead lurked behind every clothes rack or a mamba slithered in every planter.

I left the Herpes Hut and swung by the fountain, just for the hell of it, not because I thought I'd see Agatha sunning herself on a rock. The fountain consisted of an attractive pile of rocks and plants with water tumbling into a tiled basin with a wide rim that kids liked to walk on. It splashed at the juncture where the arms of the X came together on the ground floor. Tiered planters surrounded it on three sides, making the space feel like a leafy glade; it certainly offered enough dense foliage to hide Agatha, but I didn't spot any movement in the greenery. Taking the elevator up to the second level, I was zipping down the corridor toward the office when I glanced down the Dillard's wing and spotted a familiar figure outside Diamanté, crouched as if trying to raise the grille. Finola Craig. What was she doing here when the store was still off-limits as a crime scene?

I veered down the hall, and she rose to greet me, moving in slow motion, like an octogenarian afraid of falling or a woman who'd had three too many cosmopolitans the night before. She wore a black pantsuit today, in a heavy raw silk, with a white cowl-necked blouse. Mourning attire? Her bloodshot eyes had dark circles beneath them, and the way she winced every time someone walked by made me suspect she could give Woskowicz a run for the title of "Most Hungover Mall Employee."

"Hi, EJ," she greeted me. Her platinum hair was pulled back extra tight into a bun, as if to make up for its waywardness last night.

I nodded at the store. "You weren't trying to get in, were you?" It looked to me like the crime scene tape was askew. I realized I didn't know if she'd been trying to *un*lock the grille, or if she was locking it again after having been in the store.

She hesitated. "Did you take me home last night?"

I nodded, letting her dodge my question. "Yes. I didn't think you should be driving."

She laughed without humor. "I doubt I could've found

my car in the condition I was in. I had to take a taxi over here this morning. Thank you."

"You're welcome."

"I don't get like that too often," she said, clearly embarrassed. "I think the last time was my twentieth college reunion, and that wasn't yesterday."

"You'd had a tough day."

"Yes, well." She shifted the large tote on her shoulder, and I wondered what was in it. Had she removed something from the store? I had no reason to think that, but the idea nagged at me. Six or eight shoppers passed by as I thought, their steps slowing as they stared at Diamanté's windows, perhaps hoping to spot another body.

"You mentioned last night that Jackson Porter was in the habit of buying stuff for a woman who wasn't his wife."

"I did?" She looked aghast. "I'm not normally so indiscreet. I keep customers' purchases confidential. Please don't mention it to anyone."

I didn't make her any promises. "Can you tell me who?"

She squirmed and her fingers played with the zipper on the tote. Finally, she said, "Velma Maldonado."

"Do the police know about Ms. Maldonado?"

"They have copies of all my records." She didn't sound happy about it.

Ah, but a receipt would only say that Porter had bought a dress or other item, not who he bought it *for*. Finola had a slippery way with words; I'd have to remember that. I tingled at the idea that I had uncovered a piece of information the police might not have.

"Look," Finola said, "I've got an appointment with my insurance adjustor. I've got to go. See you around, okay?" And she hurried off toward the Dillard's, clutching the tote tightly against her side.

Leaning forward, I put the Segway in motion, pondering Finola's presence. In all probability it was completely innocent: she wanted to look at the window and see what kind of damage she was dealing with, or she needed inventory records or something and didn't think there'd be any harm in slipping past the police tape to pick them up. Still—

A man stepped directly into my path, and I braked to avoid hitting him. When I saw it was Detective Helland, I wished my reflexes hadn't been so quick. His thick blond hair glinted in a shaft of sunlight, and his eyes seemed a warmer shade of gray than earlier. I stared at him stonily, not dismounting, but not running him down, either.

"I'm sorry."

The words hung between us. They sounded sincere. I felt myself thaw an infinitesimal bit.

"The lab examined the crime scene photos on your camera. They're not the same as the ones on the Internet."

"I know."

"You're not going to make this any easier for me, are you?" The corner of his mouth slanted up ruefully.

I just stared at him, inviting him to continue.

"The kid in the security office—he told me you used to be a military cop?"

Joel needed to learn to keep his mouth shut. "So?"

"Thank you for your service. Twelve years is a long time to give your country." His gray eyes, fringed with dark lashes, met mine.

I almost reared back in astonishment. His thanks seemed heartfelt. "I loved it," I blurted, then clamped my lips closed. I didn't want to share anything about myself with the arrogant detective.

"Let me buy you a cup of coffee."

I had no good reason to refuse. "Okay." I parked the

Segway by the wall and walked beside him to the food court. My head just topped his shoulder. A few moments later, cups of coffee in hand, we strolled to the huge picture window that looked out on the south parking lot and the fields beyond. The food court noises of patrons talking, grills hissing, and chairs scraping back drifted around us. The view from the window was restful, green and bucolic, including a couple of cows grazing placidly by a small stream.

"Porter was going to turn that into a golf course," I said, gesturing with my coffee cup. "I'd guess he made a few enemies with that plan." I slanted a look at Detective Helland.

"More than a few," he admitted. "If you're asking about suspects, there's no shortage of those."

I decided to take advantage of his more forthcoming mood. "What about his wife? She came by this morning."

Helland blew on his coffee. "According to Porter's lawyer, she and the son are to split the inheritance and a healthy chunk of life insurance, but she's got an alibi. Rock solid."

Hm. In my experience alibis weren't "rock solid" unless the suspect had been in prison or on life support during the pertinent time. "What was it?"

He ignored my question, as I figured he might. Propping his shoulders against the window, he looked down his aquiline nose at me. "How come you're a mall cop? Why didn't you sign on with a police department when you separated from the military? PTSD?"

I could ignore questions as well as he could. "Did you know Jackson Porter bought a cocktail dress for his girlfriend on Saturday? Her name is Velma Maldonado."

A faint crease appeared between his brows and was gone. He didn't gratify me by pulling out a notebook to write down the name, but I knew he'd memorized it. "If you read the paper this morning, you know we've got a 'person of interest' that we're focusing on."

"Gatchel."

He nodded.

"Even if he and Porter were involved in some sort of political shenanigans or bribery, why would he take the risk of lugging Porter's body into the display window?"

"Good question. What can you tell me about the guard who was on duty Sunday night, Billy Wedzel? Is he a stand-up guy?"

"Have you talked to him?" At his nod, I said, "Well, then, you know. I suspect he spends more time in the office playing computer solitaire or watching movies than patrolling, but I don't know that for a fact." Although I'd found a DVD of *Reservoir Dogs* in the computer drive one morning. "So it's entirely possible he didn't see or hear anything useful Sunday night. And I wouldn't be surprised if—" I cut myself off. I couldn't accuse Weasel of theft without a shred of proof.

"—if he might be helping himself to merchandise on occasion?" Helland sounded as though I'd confirmed his suspicions. "He's got a sheet."

"He does?" That surprised me. How the hell had he gotten a job as a mall security officer if he'd been arrested before? His buddy Woskowicz. "Any convictions?"

Helland shook his head. "Weaseled out of all of them."

Maybe that's where his nickname came from. I pondered this news while Helland drained his coffee. He pulled a folded sheet of paper from an inside jacket pocket and handed it to me. It was a mug shot of a man in his early twenties, white, with limp brown hair and a defeated look in his eyes.

"We haven't located Robbie Porter yet, the victim's son.

We understand he hangs out here on occasion, maybe dealing."

"Is that what he was arrested for?"

"Cocaine."

Great. As if escaped reptiles and a murder weren't enough, now I had a resident drug dealer to contend with. I studied the photo again, but I was sure I'd never seen him.

"Can you keep an eye out for him, maybe ask around?" He gestured to the food stands and the shops beyond. "I don't have enough manpower to put someone on this full-time, but since you're here all day . . ."

I suddenly saw the motive behind his new approachability. "So, I help you locate a suspect and feed you info about Porter's purchasing history, and you give me nada?"

He had the audacity to smile, showing straight, white teeth. "That's the way it works in a police investigation. Citizens give information to the police, not vice versa."

"Sounds like the Gestapo," I observed. I plucked the photo of Robbie Porter from his hand.

"Don't try to apprehend him if you spot him," Helland cautioned. "Just give me a call."

Not trusting myself to respond to that blatantly insulting remark, I bit out, "Thanks for the coffee," and strode away, being careful to keep my steps even and not limp. Several of the food court owners and workers waved or said "hi" as I passed, and I acknowledged them on autopilot, more deter-mined than ever to show the supercilious Detective Helland with his "we're the police, you're just lowly citizens" attitude that an ex-military cop could detect as well as he could. Better.

Seven

. . .

I actually found myself wishing for Grandpa Atherton as I did my last patrol of the day, keeping an eye out for Robbie Porter. I figured Grandpa might have some good ideas about how to locate the young drug dealer. I wondered what he knew about facial recognition software and whether or not we could use it with our cameras to scan for Robbie Porter's face. Probably not, given the lousy picture quality. I called Grandpa's cell phone, but he didn't answer. Presumably, he was following Earl Gatchel around. After doing my turnover briefing and logging out, I hit the Y on the way home for a good swim, pleased to have the pool entirely to myself.

Fubar greeted me on the front sidewalk when I arrived home. No dead rodents in evidence. I stroked his rust-colored head as he butted my calf. "What's the great hunter been up to today?" I asked, unlocking my door and stepping over the mail to enter the hallway.

Without answering, he dashed past me and ran for his food bowl, as if expecting steak tartare to have appeared since he last checked it. Disappointed with his kibble, he gave me a long-suffering look.

Picking up the mail, I tossed catalogs and grocery store flyers into the trash can I kept near the door for that purpose, and found myself left with a utility bill and an envelope whose return address was the Fredericksburg Police Department. Hardly daring to hope that they were responding favorably to my application, I took the letter into the kitchen and pulled a pomegranate-flavored water from the fridge. Only after I'd twisted off the cap and taken a long swallow did I slit the envelope with a paring knife.

Thank you for submitting your application to the
Fredericksburg Police Department. We regret

I quit reading and crumpled the page into a ball, which I fired across the room. Fubar promptly pounced on it, batting it between his paws. "Kill it, Fubar. Tear it up," I encouraged him in a lackluster voice. He disappeared beneath the table with it and came out a moment later, a tiny scrap of paper decorating a whisker.

"Good kitty." I sank down onto the floor and patted my leg, thinking that cuddling with my cat might make me feel a little better after rejection number nineteen. Fubar galloped past me as if a pack of Rottweilers were in pursuit and pushed through the cat door. "You can be replaced," I called after his disappearing tail. This was why people had dogs, I told myself, pushing awkwardly to my feet.

I decided to distract myself from my disappointment by making a cheese soufflé for dinner. The recipe required enough concentration that I couldn't dwell on how another police department had decided against hiring me. Separating yolks from egg whites and whisking melted butter and flour together helped me push down the disappointment. I put the Broadway cast recording of *A Little Night Music* in my stereo and sang along. Just as I eased the soufflé into the preheated oven, the phone rang.

Caller ID told me it was my folks. I sighed and picked up the phone.

"Sweetheart! Have we got a wonderful surprise for you."

Dad. And his surprises were frequently less than wonderful. Downright embarrassing or awful at times. Like the pink Versace dress he'd bought for me to wear to the Oscars with him the year before I joined the air force. I was only seventeen, but the plunging neckline, skintight fit, and ruffly mermaid flare made me look like a cross between Britney Spears and Ariel before she got her legs. I was pretty sure "Versace" was Italian for "bimbo." Of course, there was the time he brought a fleet of limos to my fifth-grade class and took us all to the zoo, which he'd reserved just for our use that day. That'd been embarrassing, but in a good way.

"I need to spend about six months in the D.C. area for my new project, so your mom and I have rented a little place in Alexandria"—probably something the size of Mount Vernon with a staff—"to live in this spring. We'll be able to see so much more of you. I don't understand why you never make it out to California," he said, and I could hear the pout in his voice.

"I have a job," I said, taking the phone out onto my tiny back patio. Twilight hazed the sky, and a pair of cardinals argued near the boxwood hedge that separated my ten-by-ten patch of lawn from the neighbor's. I shivered in the chilly air. "I can't just pick up and leave whenever you and Mom throw a party or host a charity event or something."

"You don't have to work."

"Yes, I do." For my sanity. To feel like I was making a contribution to the world. To not turn into a vapid party girl with nothing to think about other than what trendy night spot to be seen in or how to end up on someone's best-dressed list. My father and I had had this conversation roughly six hundred twenty-seven times; I knew what came next: "Honey, if money's an issue—"

"Hon, if money's an issue, you know I'm more than happy to—"

"Did you read about the murder in my mall?" I changed our script.

"A murder?" Concern and surprise sounded in Dad's crisp voice.

I told him about the case, pleased by his interest, even though I knew he was mentally sorting through the story elements, testing them for inclusion in a script. "Have you apprehended the perp yet?" he asked.

I sighed, irritated as always by his lame attempts at cop lingo, a habit he'd picked up when his first series, *Roll Call*, was such a success. "Nope. And I won't get to," I said. "The Vernonville PD's got this case."

"The stiff in the display window would make a great opening shot," he mused, "but I don't think we want him nude. That would pull an 'R' rating for sure. Maybe if wardrobe could dress him in a woman's bathing suit . . . Oh, your mom wants to talk to you."

"Hi, Mom," I greeted her.

"Oh, poor baby, did you get turned down by another police department?" Her soothing voice flowed over me, and I pictured her on the lanai at their Malibu house, expertly dyed blond hair slicked back under a sun hat, relaxing on the poolside lounger.

"Yep." I'd given up long ago trying to figure out how she could know what was happening in my life based on a single word like "hi." Must be some kind of mom ESP. Maybe Kyra had a book about it. "But I don't want to talk about it."

"Of course not." So we chatted about their upcoming visit to Virginia, my brother's work—"I think he's in Malaysia, now," Mom said. "I do hope he's careful if he's interviewing terrorists again"—and her charity work. Mom might look like a typical Hollywood spouse—blond, sleek, and fashionable—and she might come across as a bit ditzy, but she could mobilize volunteers like no one else and had raised hundreds of millions for cancer research over the years after her mother died of ovarian cancer.

"How's your grandfather?" she asked with a bit of trepidation. "I hope he's been behaving himself."

"He's great," I said. "And of course he's behaving." I crossed my fingers.

"Well, that's good," she said doubtfully. "It would be nice if we could get him interested in bridge, or maybe bird-watching. A nice, quiet hobby." One that didn't get you beaten up. Or land you in jail. Or require the purchase and use of deadly weapons. She left all that unsaid, but I heard it in her voice.

Yeah, good luck with that.

We said our good-byes, and I ate my soufflé in front of the television with a bottle of Potowmack Ale. Afterwards, I strummed on my guitar for a while, practicing the Rodrigo *Fantasia* I'd been working on for some weeks. I concentrated ferociously enough to push all thought of the murder from my head. Fubar still hadn't returned when I was ready for bed, but that wasn't unusual. I left a light on in the hallway for him—yeah, I know cats can see in the dark, but it just seemed friendlier—and went to bed. Some time later—my clock said almost midnight—I was awakened by a thump. Caught in the throes of my recurring nightmare, with the whump of the armored Humvee next to mine exploding as it rolled over an IED in Aghanistan, it took me a moment to orient myself. The thumping came again—definitely not part of my dream. I sat up in bed. "Fubar?"

Thump-thump-thump! I recognized it as knocking. Pulling a robe on over my nightgown and easing my Beretta nine-millimeter from my bedside table, I headed for the front door, only to realize the knocking was coming from the back. Stranger and stranger. I cut through the kitchen, leaving the lights off so I didn't silhouette myself as a target. Skirting the pallet of tile on the floor, I flicked on the patio light and illuminated a tall figure pressed up against the window. Hastily, I set my weapon on the counter and unlocked the door. Grandpa Atherton stumbled in, almost tripping over Fubar, who shot past him, eager to be in on the unusual midnight activity.

"Hello, Emma-Joy. Hope I didn't wake you." He gave me a smile that turned into a wince and pressed a hand to his forehead.

A cut on his forehead was dripping blood, so I grabbed a paper towel, dampened it, and pressed it to the wound as I led him to the kitchen table. "Grandpa! What on earth—?"

"The operation didn't go exactly as planned," he said.

I shushed him while I cleaned the cut—not very deep—on his forehead, swiped it with antibiotic ointment, and stuck a Band-Aid on it. "There. I think you'll live."

"Thank you," he said. He leaned back in the chair, looking tired and old. His all black clothes—windbreaker, turtleneck, and slacks—drained the color from his skin. "Could I bother you for a spot of whiskey?"

Pulling a bottle of Jim Beam, which Clint had left when

he visited six months ago, from the cabinet over the stove, I poured a healthy slug into a juice glass. "Chin-chin," he said, knocking back half of the amber liquid. His hand was shaking slightly, and I looked away, pretending I hadn't noticed.

Fubar leaped onto the table and sniffed at the glass, wrinkling his muzzle with distaste. I shoved the cat off the table and sat beside Grandpa, my arms crossed on the table. "Now, would you like to tell me what's happened?"

"You know the target was Earl Gatchel," he said, recovering a bit as he told his story. "Address: 1338 Churchill Place. Divorced. Two grown kids. No pets. A million-four plus change in his checking account."

"Suspicious," I said, not wanting to know how he'd come by that piece of data.

"Especially considering his salary as a councilman wouldn't pay for the gas in his Mercedes, and his flooring business has been losing money for three years." Grandpa took another sip of his whiskey. His hand was steady now. He might be aging, but he was still sharp as a tack; he didn't once refer to notes while reciting Gatchel's activities. "I picked him up at his council office, where he argued with a woman, another council member, and then left with a box he placed in his trunk. I followed him to his home, where he spent most of the afternoon making phone calls to his ex-wife, his sons, the bank, a couple of friends, and a restaurant."

"You tapped his phone?" I asked incredulously. I held up a hand. "No, don't tell me."

Grandpa just smiled. "At nineteen thirty he left the house to have dinner with his lawyer at the Shrimp Factory. I followed him there and then returned to his house."

"You broke in. Oh my God." I reached for the whiskey

bottle and poured myself a shot. I knocked it back and coughed. Nasty stuff. Give me a good beer any day.

"Child's play," he bragged, clearly pleased with himself. "The alarm system—well, never mind that. I had just about finished downloading files from his computer"—he held up a thumb drive—"when I heard the garage door opening. Apparently, he didn't sample the Shrimp Factory's crème brûlée or stay for an after-dinner drink. In short, he returned much sooner than I had anticipated. Perhaps he received bad news from his lawyer and it ruined his appetite. At any rate, I was trapped upstairs.

"I'm getting on in years, you know," Grandpa said with the air of someone sharing a confidence, "and my bones are a bit brittle for a jump from the second story. So I hid in a closet. It reminded me of that time in Bratislava—but that was a woman, not business. Anyway, I'd been up there an hour and seven minutes, getting stiff, when I heard a gun go off. I knew immediately what had happened."

"A gunshot?" My eyes widened. "Please tell me the police didn't find you."

He frowned at me. "Really, Emma-Joy, give me a little credit. I ran downstairs and discovered that Gatchel had, as I suspected, killed himself. He'd blown his brains out in front of the television. There was nothing I could do for him. So I left the same way I came in, unfortunately bumping my head on the window frame." He touched the bandage gingerly.

"Did you disturb the scene at all?" I leaned forward and searched his lined face. "Fingerprints? Shoe prints? Did anyone see you?"

"No one saw me," he said testily. "I wore gloves"—he pulled a pair of latex gloves from his pocket and dropped them on the table—"and I didn't contaminate the scene; it was clear from the doorway that Gatchel was dead. You know," he said, "it's been a damn long time since I saw a body. At least, one that wasn't laid out in a four-thousand-dollar coffin and surrounded with lilies and carnations. East Berlin, 1982." He lapsed into silence.

The outline of his skull showed beneath his skin, the dent where his temple curved in, the line of his nose that seemed sharper now than it had a few years back. Grandpa Atherton was getting old and I didn't like it. I also didn't like the way I felt protective toward him, like I needed to take care of him. He was the grandpa and I was the granddaughter, damn it—grandpas take care of grandkids, not vice versa. When I realized I was the catalyst, if not the reason, for him being at risk, I couldn't sit still. I rose to pour him a glass of water.

"Here." I put the glass in front of him. "You can stay here tonight. I'll drop you at your place in the morning. Grandpa—"

"Oh, don't be a worrywart. I haven't had this much fun in decades."

The impish smile he gave me almost persuaded me that housebreaking might be a better way to stave off old age dementia than crossword puzzles and sudoku.

I slept fitfully the rest of the night, waiting for the police to knock on the door and demand that I turn over Grandpa. Nothing of the sort happened, however, and I dropped Grandpa at his cottage in the Serendipity Heights retirement community Wednesday before reporting to work. He was none the worse for his night's adventures; in fact, he was scrambling me some eggs and toasting a bagel when I got up. He promised to sift through the data from Gatchel's computer and let me know if anything interesting turned up.

"Anything interesting in the news?" I asked Joel when I got to the office. I didn't get a paper delivered and hadn't had time to check online. I sincerely hoped Grandpa hadn't made the headlines.

"Well, there's a short article about snakes being loose in the mall."

Just what we needed. Quigley would be livid if our customer traffic went down.

"And Earl Gatchel was killed last night," Joel said, his brown eyes avid. "Maybe someone offed him to keep him from spilling the beans. Maybe it was the same person who snuffed Porter."

"What beans? Didn't you think Gatchel killed Porter?"

"Well, yeah, but what if the conspiracy is bigger than the two of them?"

"Unlikely," I said, trying to discourage Joel's theorizing. "It's more likely Gatchel committed suicide."

"Yeah, that's what the reports say," Joel admitted, scrolling down with his mouse. " 'Probable suicide . . . pending autopsy . . . no note . . . distraught over financial reversals and his role as central figure in murder investigation' . . . yada-yada." He rolled back from his desk, lacing his hands over his stomach. "So, I guess that's it for our murder. Case closed." Disappointment sat heavily on his young face.

"Case closed?" I asked, surprised. "Why would you say that?"

Joel shrugged. "It seems obvious. Whatever bribery or kickback scheme Porter and Gatchel had going, it was about to blow up in their faces. Gatchel killed Porter to keep him from testifying about it and then shot himself when it looked like the police were closing in."

I was about to point out that his scenario didn't explain how Gatchel got access to Diamanté or why he left the body in the window, when Detective Blythe Livingston walked in. Her rust-colored suit jacket blended with the hair corkscrewing to her shoulders. Medium-heeled boots peeked from beneath her slacks. Her face was makeup free, but her strong brows and naturally reddish lips stood out. "Good morning," she said, "I suppose you heard the news?"

We nodded. Pushing a curl off her face, she said, "Fernglen's on my way to the PD, so I thought I'd stop in and let you know we're releasing the boutique today; the owner can get back in and do her thing."

"Finola will be glad to hear that," I said. "Thanks."

"Gatchel's death wraps the whole thing up, so we won't be doing anything more with the scene."

"You're closing the case?" I asked, avoiding Joel's triumphant look.

"Ya gotta like it when the perp saves the state the cost of trying him," she said, winking.

"But . . . if it was Gatchel, how'd he get into Diamanté? Did he even own a gun?"

She gave me a look that made it plain she was humoring me, but said, "Gatchel's firm had the flooring contract for Fernglen. He might have had a key left from that installment. As to the gun, he owned a nine-millimeter, but since we don't know where he killed Porter, we don't have a bullet for ballistics comparison. There's always a few loose ends."

In my humble opinion, there were enough loose ends to weave a rug with, but I only said, "So you figure Gatchel committed suicide because his lawyer passed along some bad news?"

Her eyes narrowed. "How'd you know he met his lawyer last night?"

Oops. "I didn't," I said as coolly as I could. "But anyone in his position would be in touch with a lawyer."

She seemed to buy it. "Well, you're right. His lawyer told him the DA had gotten an indictment. Gatchel was supposed to turn himself in today. He called his family to say good-bye and then"—she shaped her thumb and forefinger into a gun and held it to her temple—"lights out."

"Did he leave a note confessing to Porter's murder?" I asked, wondering if maybe Gatchel had fallen on the note when he died, hiding it from Grandpa.

Annoyance creased Livingston's brow. "No. Like I said, there are always loose ends." She looked at Mickey's face and raised a hand in farewell. "I've gotta run. Nice working with you."

"You, too," Joel and I chorused as she pushed through the glass doors.

"Back to business as usual, I guess," Joel said.

"Mm," I said noncommittally, mentally laying out the steps I'd take to find out who really killed Jackson Porter. The police might be satisfied that they'd solved their case, tied it up with a big bow marked "Rest in Peace," but I just didn't buy it.

Eight

. . .

The phone rang as I was getting ready to leave on patrol and Joel picked it up, holding it a couple inches from his ear when yelling poured out of it. "Quigley," he said to me when the shouting stopped. "Wants to see you ASAP. Want to bet someone parked in his slot again?"

"No bet." Picking a white fuzzy off my black uniform slacks, I strolled across the hall to the mall operations office. It had the same gray-green carpet as the security office, and identical cherry-veneer desks and rolling chairs. Prints from the mall's frame shop decorated the walls, discreet price tags tucked into the corners.

"Go on back," the young receptionist said. "He's waiting for you."

Tapping on Quigley's half-open door, I entered when he called, "Come in."

He leaped to his feet when he saw me, nostrils flaring. "This has gone too far," he announced. Today's suit was navy pinstripe, offset by a yellow shirt with a white collar. I sneaked a peak at his cuffs as he ran a hand through his hair—yep, the gold and citrine cufflinks.

"What has?" I asked.

"These . . . these vandals! They defaced my Karmann Ghia." He looked truly distraught. I knew he loved his classic car and frequently took it to car shows in the tristate area. "They are thumbing their noses at us." He flung up a hand. "My spot is clearly marked 'Mall Manager.' " He said it as if the words provided a magic force field that should have protected his ride. " 'Do unto others . . .!' I'll do unto them when you catch them!' " His usually mild, slightly harried expression was replaced with a fierceness I'd never seen in him before. I felt sorry for him.

"We'll find out who's doing this, Mr. Quigley," I said. "It might help if we had a little more in the budget for cameras in the parking lot or overtime so we could do some surveillance."

"Whatever it costs," he said, reaching into his jacket pocket as if to pull out his checkbook and write a check on the spot. His hand emerged with a snowy hanky. Blotting his forehead, he returned it to his pocket. "Thank you, EJ. I want this to be your number-one priority. Now that the police have resolved that incident at Diamanté—"

What, someone was going to wash his mouth out with soap if he said "murder"?

"—you can concentrate on these graffiti artists. Artists—hah! They're nothing but common delinquents."

"Common" was the worst thing Quigley could think of to call someone. "I'll get right on it," I promised, slipping out of the office.

I made a mental to-do list as I mounted the Segway: (1) Find humongous python before film crews arrive to film reality movie called *Snakes in the Mall*. (2) Trap spray-painting Christians and let Quigley feed them to the lions. (3) Solve murder case and deliver culprit to arrogant detective, graciously accepting his thanks and apologies.

I got on the phone to Grandpa for help with items one and two. He said he felt fine and would bring some gadgets down to the mall around lunchtime. Then I started on my rounds, keeping an eye out for Agatha. Kiefer, when I went by the Herpes Hut, was worried that the news report might bring out a bunch of Agatha-hunting psychos. I reassured him as much as I could and continued down the corridor, stopping to chat with Fernando for a moment when he pulled his big, gray trash bin out of the men's room near Nordstrom. He said he hadn't seen any reptiles since Dartagnan colonized his head, and seemed to think he should be congratulated. I checked in with Joel—nothing happening—and was poking around in the large planter near the fountain, hoping to roust Agatha, when Kyra strolled by, deep in conversation with a man I didn't know.

She spotted me at the same time I saw her and beckoned me over. "Hey, girlfriend, come meet Dyson Harding. He's a professor at the Vernonville Colonial College, just up the road."

"*Dr.* Dyson Harding," he said, shaking my hand. "PhD, of course, not MD." He was medium height and ten to fifteen pounds overweight with the kind of soul patch Apolo Ohno had made popular, and horn-rimmed glasses and jacket with leather elbow patches that he must have bought in the "absent-minded professor" section of his local clothing store.

"EJ Ferris. What brings you to Fernglen?" I looked from him to Kyra.

Kyra spoke first. "He's an archeologist. He's concerned

that the Olympus development is being built on a pre-Clovis settlement." She said the last words awkwardly, like a foreign language.

"Many items of huge archeological interest will be lost if the development goes through," Harding said earnestly.

My brow wrinkled. "But . . . didn't Jackson Porter's death put the kibosh on Olympus?"

"Maybe temporarily," Harding said, "but I want to make sure the development is deader than Porter. I'm trying to enlist the help of independent stores owners"—he nodded at Kyra—"in lobbying against the development. The city council can afford to ignore the merchants or the archaeology community if we stand alone. But if we band together"—he clasped his hands tightly—"then we're a force to be reckoned with."

Once more into the breach . . . Into the valley of death . . . Damn the torpedoes, full speed ahead . . . I expected him to spout one of the great rallying cries.

Instead, he blinked and looked hopefully at Kyra. "I've got a petition." He lifted a clipboard I hadn't noticed. "Can you get signatures from the mall merchants? And it'd be great if a Fernglen contingent came to the council meeting next week. They'll have to pay attention to us. We'll show them that we are not to be ignored!" He leaned over to kiss Kyra on the cheek, murmured, "Catch you later, Ky," and strode away, jacket flapping.

I wondered if he knew his "won't be ignored" line was perilously close to the phrase the psycho bunny stabber in *Fatal Attraction* used. I'm not sure the association was a good one. "How'd he latch on to you?" I asked Kyra.

She sighed. "We were at Duke together. Don't say anything, but we went out once or twice."

I choked back a laugh. "Well, I'm sure he'll set the world

on fire with his petition. If the council members don't vote his way, he can bonk them over the head with his clipboard."

Kyra didn't laugh as I'd expected. "Don't underestimate Dyson. He's always been something of an activist. At Duke, he started a petition to get rid of a tenured ecology professor who was a consultant for a pesticide manufacturer. Dy called it a conflict of interest. When the petition got no results, he researched every article and book the guy ever wrote and found some sections that could be considered plagiarism. And then photos of the prof snuggling with a woman other than his wife showed up in the newspaper. The prof swore that he didn't know the woman, that she'd flung herself at him unexpectedly, but the damage was done."

"Really?" I stared in the direction Dyson Harding had taken. It might not be a waste of time to dig up a little more background on him and find out what he'd been doing Sunday night.

Kyra headed back to Merlin's Cave, and I started toward Diamanté, only to be stopped by a middle-aged woman wearing an "I need to complain" look on her face. Dressed in a long navy skirt, an olive-colored twinset, and low-heeled boots, she had the aura of an office manager or church volunteer coordinator.

"Officer," she said when I asked if I could help, "there's a situation that needs your attention." Her slightly bugged-out eyes fixed on my face, wanting me to betray alarm.

"Yes? What is it?"

She lowered her voice to a whisper. "That woman on the bench back there, behind me, is nursing a baby. In public!" From her tone, you'd think someone was conducting satanic rituals involving rodent entrails in the mall corridor.

I didn't say what I wanted to: Really? Feeding a baby?

Horrors! Instead, I said, "I'll take care of it, ma'am. Thank you for letting me know."

Satisfied that she'd done her public duty, the woman gave a triumphant sniff and headed toward Dillard's. Sighing, I glided toward the nursing mother. Only two weeks ago we'd received an operating directive on nursing mothers from the company that owned Fernglen and several other malls. It told us to direct nursing mothers, especially those who weren't discreetly covered up, to the room set aside for them. This was not a part of the job I liked, but I amused myself by thinking how Joel or Harold would feel about having to deal with a nursing mother.

The mother in question was in her late thirties and had a shawl draped over her shoulder and torso. I couldn't see anything of the baby except blue-bootied feet. Nevertheless, I followed the directive and informed her about the nursing room.

"Really?" she said, a pleasantly surprised expression on her face. "I didn't know you had one. We're about done here"—she nodded at the baby—"but I'll use it next time. You should publicize it more."

"You're right," I agreed. Wishing the mother a pleasant shopping experience, I putt-putted toward Diamanté, wondering if Finola was back in business.

She was. The crime scene tape was gone, and a new display graced the window. This one featured mannequins posed with tennis rackets, wearing the latest in expensive tennis gear. Leaving the Segway outside, I pushed through the door, unconsciously holding my breath. Realizing what I was doing, I breathed in cautiously, relieved to sniff no hint of death. It had been obliterated by an efficient cleaning team and a woodsy air freshener.

Finola came out of the office at the chime from the opening door and paused when she recognized me. "Hello, EJ," she said. She was back to her usual soignée, pulled-together self in an emerald green jacket over a copper-colored shell and black slacks. Makeup covered any lingering traces of grief or hangover, and her hair looked newly blonded and styled.

"Back in business, I see."

"Finally." She exhaled deeply. "It was a huge relief when the detective called to say they were closing the case. I hadn't realized how much it was hanging over me until I talked to her."

"Had you ever met Earl Gatchel?" I asked. "The man they think killed Porter?"

Small white teeth bit at her lower lip. "Not that I know of. The police asked me the same thing. His wife has been in here a few times, though. I checked my records and found credit card payments from Rhonda Gatchel."

"His ex-wife."

She shrugged. "I wouldn't know her to see her."

It seemed like a really thin connection to me. Why had Gatchel—if he did indeed kill Porter—left the body in Diamanté? Why not in Macy's or at the movie theater? Or why not wherever he killed him? That one was easy: the murder site was incriminating, would point a finger to the murderer. Maybe—

The door chimed behind me and two women walked in. One I recognized immediately as Elena Porter, looking far less puffy than the day before, dressed in a maroon suit belted at the waist and knee-high black boots with outrageous heels. I didn't know the other woman. She was taller than Elena by a good six inches and had black hair that hung to her shoulders. The same vintage as her friend—midfifties—she wore high-waisted wool slacks that emphasized her leanness and a white silk blouse under a black leather jacket. A tiny gasp escaped Finola before she moved forward to greet them.

"Mrs. Porter, I am so sorry for your loss," she said stiffly.

"Thank you."

An awkward silence descended until the tall woman said in an attractive alto, "We're here to find something for the funeral. Poor Elena doesn't have anything suitable."

Elena sniffed and dabbed a tissue at her eyes. "We're burying my dear Jackson on Thursday. I expect hundreds of people to attend the service. Will you be there?"

"Um, I thought—" Finola started.

"Because I don't think it'd be appropriate, under the circumstances," Elena continued as if Finola hadn't spoken.

"The circumstances?" Finola's voice betrayed bewilderment and a hint of fear.

Elena opened her pale blue eyes wide. "Why, Jackson's body being found here. I've been in touch with my lawyer about your liability."

"Where will the service be?" I intervened, giving Finola time to recover herself. I was relatively certain she couldn't be sued for having a murder victim turn up in her store. Unless, of course, it turned out she killed him.

Both women looked at me as if I were a mannequin who had suddenly burst into speech.

"So I can let the mall employees who might have known Mr. Porter know," I said. "I understand he shopped and lunched here frequently. I'm sure some of them will want to pay their respects."

"Oh. Durbane's Funeral Home," Elena said. "At ten o'clock."

"They do a lovely job," the other woman put in. "It's where we had the memorial for my poor Wilfred three years ago now. We met here, you know, shortly before his daughter's wedding. This mall has been around a long time." She looked around reminiscently. "So many changes."

"I'll say," Elena said. "I remember bringing Robbie to skate when there was an ice rink where that big sporting goods store is now."

The women drifted into memory-lane mode, apparently forgetting their funeral-attire-buying mission.

"I'm EJ Ferris," I said, offering my hand to Elena's friend.

"Catherine Lang." Her handshake was firm, her hand bony but warm.

"Catherine's my best friend," Elena said with a fond look for the other woman. "I don't know how I would have made it through this dreadful, dreadful time without her support." Her gaze flicked to me. "She found Jackson . . . his body," Elena said, giving me a not too friendly look.

Catherine Lang's dark brows arched slightly. "How awful for you. But I suppose you're used to it. Being in law enforcement, I mean."

I appreciated her characterization of mall security work as "law enforcement." I said, "You never get used to it." I didn't point out that the mall wasn't exactly awash with bodies. "I'm sure you've got a lot to do; I'll let you get to your shopping. Again, I'm sorry for your loss, Mrs. Porter." Nodding at Finola, who had recovered herself and was ready to shepherd her customers toward suitable (expensive) funeral attire, I left the shop.

My mind whirled. Why in the world would a widow shop for funeral duds at the store where her murdered husband's body had been found? And what was the byplay with Finola about her not being welcome at the funeral? I'd already had suspicions about the nature of Finola's relationship with Jackson Porter and now they resurfaced. But if she'd had an affair with the man, why was Elena shopping in Diamanté?

My cell phone vibrated and I answered. Grandpa Atherton said, "I need a cookie. You're buying."

Nine

...

I spotted Grandpa's tall figure and white head as soon as I reached the food court. He wore a white cable-knit sweater over a blue shirt and tan slacks. He was at Legendary Lola Cookies, chatting with Jay Callahan.

"EJ," he said as I approached, "this is—"

"We've met," I said. "Hi."

Callahan smiled. A dimple appeared in his chin, making him look younger. "Let me guess: you're a chocolate chip person." He reached for a cookie. "With nuts."

"What do you want, Grandpa?" I asked, pulling out my wallet.

"I think he's a gingerbread kind of man," Callahan said.

I stared at him. "What? Are they teaching some kind of mystic cookie divination at baking school now?"

Grandpa laughed. "I already told him what I want," he said.

Callahan grinned, handing over the cookies with a

flourish. A timer dinged and he turned to pull a tray from the oven. As he bent over, the fabric of his slacks tightened against the line of his leg, seeming to bulge just above his ankle. Was he carrying a gun? Surely not.

I added a coffee to my order and forked over the money, assessing Jay Callahan. He smiled in a friendly way and turned to help a customer with three small children. Escorting Grandpa to a table where we couldn't be overheard easily, I asked him how he was feeling.

"I'm an octogenarian, not an invalid," he said. "I'm fine, EJ. All in a day's—or night's—work. I've often thought that if Donovan hadn't recruited me, I would've made a good second-story man."

"It's never too late to reinvent yourself," I said, breaking off a chunk of my cookie. "All the women's magazines say so."

"You should consider it," he said.

I stared at him.

"Come on. Being a mall cop isn't for you, EJ. Where's the challenge?"

"It's temporary," I said. "Until I get on with a police department."

"That's not going to happen." He tempered the brutal comment by reaching for my hand. I pulled it away. "You've got to face up to the fact that your injury has disqualified you for police work. It's stupid, but there it is."

"I love being a cop," I said. "Loved."

"Even if you're not willing to give up that dream, you could do something else in the interim. You've got too much on the ball, EJ, to molder away in this mall."

"Maybe not," I said with a feeble attempt at humor. "I'm having to call you in as a contractor to catch a bunch of teenage graffiti artists." I explained about the cars getting tagged—one per day—at different times and different places around the mall. "They got Quigley's beloved Karmann Ghia this morning," I said, "so I've been told to shut them down, cost no object. I was thinking that a few of your mini-cameras, something they wouldn't spot . . ."

"I have just the thing," Grandpa said enthusiastically. "Tiny devices no bigger than a ladybug. I can mount them on car antennas, on light posts, and other places where no one will spot them. A friend of mine who's still in the business on the contract side says that a couple of these babies were planted on . . . well, let's just say they gave us a lot of intelligence about Saddam's inner circle. I'll scout for likely locations this afternoon. Can you get me a diagram showing where and when cars got spray painted?"

I'd already done one up, hoping to spot a pattern (I hadn't), and I pulled the page out of my pocket, handing it to Grandpa. "Thanks," I said. "I really appreciate this. While you're doing that, I'm going to see if I can't get a lead on Robbie Porter, the murder vic's son. He apparently peddles drugs here at Fernglen on occasion; the police haven't caught up with him since Porter died, and they've asked me to help track him down." I showed Grandpa the mug shot.

"Loser," he said trenchantly, studying the photo. "Suspicious, too, that he hasn't come forward since his father's death. Unless he's living under a rock, he must've heard about it."

"You're right." I hadn't considered that. "Of course, if he partakes of his product, he may *be* living under a rock, or his brain may be fried so badly he doesn't remember his own name." I tucked the photo away.

"Make me a copy of that, too," Grandpa said, using the table to push himself upright, "and I'll come in early and survey the mall walkers. There's an attractive young woman of about seventy I've been wanting to get to know. This will give me the perfect excuse for chatting her up." With a wink, he headed for the escalator.

I shook my head, brushed the cookie crumbs off the table into a napkin, and dropped it into the trash can. As I started for my Segway, Jay Callahan waved me over to his counter.

"I couldn't help overhearing part of what you were saying," he said, leaning forward, his forearms on the counter. A sprinkling of light red hairs dusted his sinewy forearms. "Is there much of a drug problem at Fernglen?" His hazel eyes met mine. Despite his serious expression, I didn't get the feeling that he was tremendously worried. When I didn't immediately respond, he added, "I've put most of my savings into this business, but I can still back out of the deal. If this mall has a reputation as a spot for drug deals, it'll chase away my customers."

"You seem like a savvy guy . . . didn't you check out the mall before you bought Lola's?" I asked.

He seemed taken aback by my question. "Of course."

"You didn't hear anything about Fernglen being a haven for the drug crowd, did you?" He shook his head. "Well, there's your answer. By the way, is that why you've got a gun? Because you're nervous about the drug element?"

He stilled and his eyes became watchful. "Who says I've got a gun?"

I nodded toward his feet. "Ankle holster. Left leg."

Without conceding that he had a gun, he asked, "How long have you worked in mall security?"

"About a year," I said. "Why?"

"And what did you do before that?"

"What is this—a job interview? I'm not looking to trade up to cookie selling."

"Humor me."

I couldn't see a reason not to tell him. Lots of people knew. "I was in the military. Air force."

He nodded, as if I'd confirmed his suspicions. "Staff sergeant? Tech?"

This guy knew a lot more about the military than your average mall merchant. "I made E-7," I said, "and then I went to OTS—Officer Training School—and got commissioned. I retired as a first lieutenant."

"Retired? You're too damn young."

I didn't feel the need to fill him in on my medical situation. "So, I guess you have a relative in the military?"

Jay grinned, showing lots of white teeth and the chin dimple. "My brother and my sister. He's army, she's navy. You don't want to be around our house during the annual Army-Navy football game."

"And what branch were you in?"

I slung the question at him, hoping to take him by surprise, but he only laughed and rubbed at a spot on the glass with a rag. "Me? I'm just a cookie entrepreneur."

I gave him a "sure you are" look and turned away, aware that I was behind schedule with my patrols.

Three people stopped me in the next hour to tell me they'd seen Agatha. They didn't say "Agatha," of course. They called her "a honkin' big snake," "a giant python," and "a snake big enough to swallow my little brother." She was in a dressing room at Macy's, under a Dodge Caravan in the parking garage, and in the back row of one of the movie theaters . . . pretty much simultaneously, if I believed all my informants. I had to follow up on each of their leads—none of which panned out—and I was more than ready to hide out in the office with a sandwich come lunchtime.

Scanning the twelve camera screens when I came in, I saw nothing of interest. Apparently Joel didn't either, because he was playing computer solitaire. He started guilt-ily when I came in.

"Woskowicz not around?" I asked.

"Said he had a meeting to go to," Joel said.

Hm. Woskowicz usually hung around the office more, making life miserable for all of us. What could he be up to with his frequent absences in the past couple of days? Maybe nothing more than sleeping off hangovers or romancing his new reporter friend. Whatever it was, I was in favor of it.

I had managed two bites of my turkey sandwich and a swallow of peach-flavored water when the phone rang. Joel answered with, "Fernglen Galleria Security, Officer Rooney speaking." He took a couple of notes and slid the page across to me when he hung up. "Shoplifter," he said. "Rock Star Accessories. She left the store with a pair of earrings she didn't pay for, heading toward the exit near Macy's."

"What about Tracy or Harold?" I asked, waving my sand-wich at him. "Can't they take this one?"

"Harold's helping a guy in a wheelchair change a tire on his van, and Tracy called in sick today."

"Great," I grumbled, chewing quickly.

Joel scanned the camera screens. "There," he said, point-ing at a young teenager in patterned tights, with a long blond ponytail. "That's her."

I studied the slim figure weaving her way toward the exit near the movie theaters. "I'm on it. Have the Rock Star associate meet us back here."

I hopped onto the Segway and sent it gliding toward the movie theaters in the next corridor, wishing I had lights and a siren, not because I needed them, but because they were fun. Nothing like responding Code Blue to a situation. The girl was walking quickly when I spotted her, her short, blue skirt flipping with every step. Passing her, I curved the Segway around to block her path. "Miss?" I said, stepping down. "Let's chat."

Only fourteen or fifteen—why wasn't she in school?—she had a smattering of freckles across a pert nose and light brown eyes fringed with mascaraed lashes. Blond bangs hung to her brows. About my height, she looked like a cheerleader or a soccer midfielder: athletic, clean-cut, from a middle-class background. But if I had learned only one thing during my time at Fernglen, it was that shoplifters came in all shapes and sizes and from all economic backgrounds. Her gaze flicked past me to the doors that opened temptingly to the parking lot. She edged forward, as if gathering herself to run, and I took a step toward her.

"I'm not in school because it's a teacher workday," she said with a "gosh, aren't I precious" smile. Maybe it worked better on her parents than it did on me. "In fact, my mom's waiting for me in the parking lot."

She made as if to move again, but I put out an arm. "That's great. Then you can have her join us in the security office."

"What!" Her mouth dropped open, showing expensive orthodontia. "Why?"

"Or, you could just show me what's in that Rock Star bag"—I pointed at the pink plastic bag she clutched in one hand—"and the receipt."

"Are you accusing me—?"

"The salesclerk at Rock Star saw you put some earrings in your bag," I said. "You have two choices: come with me now and see if you can persuade them it was an accident, or wait with me while I call the police."

She weighed her options for thirty seconds, and then her shoulder slumped. "Can I ride that?" She gestured at the Segway.

"No."

We arrived at the security office as the clerk from Rock Star hurried up. I thought her name was Carrie or Casey. Long, brown hair framed a narrow face. A black tunic with a scalloped neckline fell to midthigh over a pair of red leggings. Unfortunately, she wore far too much of the Rock Star stock to look pulled together; several pairs of earrings dangled from her lobes, two metallic belts wrapped her waist, a variety of barrettes and hair combs restrained her long hair. Bracelets and necklaces jingled with every step. "That's her," she said, nodding.

"Jerk," the girl by my elbow muttered.

"Let's go in and talk this over," I said, motioning to the security office. "What's your name?"

"Julia," the girl said, trying to hold onto her bravado. "It was no big deal."

"We want to prosecute," the Rock Star clerk said. "I've already called the police."

I wasn't surprised. Rock Star always pressed charges. Along with the music/DVD store, Rock Star Accessories suffered more losses than almost any other merchant, probably because they attracted the tween and teen clientele who mostly didn't have a lot of money to spend and who thought it was "cool" to shoplift. Also, their merchandise was eminently "liftable," unlike, say, a coffee table from the Macy's home store.

"The police!" Julia looked as though she'd just realized the consequences of shoplifting might not be pleasant. "But I didn't mean to take them. Here, you can have them back." She plunged her hand into the bag and pulled out a pair of chandelier earrings that probably cost all of $4.99. She thrust them at the clerk, who put her hands behind her back and shook her head.

"Our policy is to prosecute," she said snippily.

Julia looked wildly from the clerk to me, ponytail swishing across her shoulders. "Look," she said, "if you can overlook this just this once—I swear I've never done anything like this before—I can tell you who killed that guy in Diamanté."

I worked on keeping my expression neutral. Joel was less successful; his brows soared toward his hairline.

"The police have closed that case," I said.

"Well, they've got the wrong guy," the girl replied. She crossed her arms over her chest.

I didn't mention that they didn't "have" anyone, that their suspect had killed himself. "What makes you think so?"

"Will you let me go?"

I sent a glance to the Rock Star clerk, who was listening avidly. She shook her head. "No way."

"We'll see," I said, beginning to dislike Miss Rock Star. Holding people to standards is one thing, being rigidly inflexible another.

"Depends on what you know about the murder," I told Julia. I seriously doubted that she knew anything—what connection could she possibly have with Jackson Porter?— and was making a desperate bid for freedom.

Sensing that my "we'll see" was the best she was going to do, Julia said, "It was my mom." She promptly burst into tears.

Ten

. . .

Reactions to Julia's accusation were mixed.

"That is the lamest thing I ever heard," said Miss Rock Star with a sniff.

"You would rat out your mom?" This came from Joel.

I thought she sounded just scared enough and tragic enough to be telling the truth. Or, at least what she thought was the truth.

Julia sobbed on, mascara beginning to track down her face.

"Why don't you call your mom?" I suggested, handing her a box of tissues.

"Uh-uh," she managed between sobs. "I can't."

"Let me see your cell phone." I held out my hand.

Swiping the back of one hand across her cheeks, Julia pulled the phone from her pocket and handed it to me. I found "Home" in her call list and pushed the button.

"No, don't!" the teenager said, realizing what I was doing. She lunged for the phone, but I held it above her reach.

"Sit," I ordered.

A voice said, "Hello. Hello?" from the phone, and I lowered it to my ear.

"Hello, ma'am," I said, then introduced myself. "We have a situation involving Julia here at Fernglen Galleria, and we need you to come by. You know where the security office is? On the second floor, near Sears."

After a moment's stunned silence, she said, "I'll be right there."

I gave her big points for not sputtering, arguing, or chewing me out. Handing the phone back to Julia, I asked, "What makes you think your mom had anything to do with Jackson Porter's death?"

"She hated him," Julia said. Her tears had dried up and sullenness had taken their place. "Him and that development he was building. I thought it would be cool to have new shops and a resort with a pool right around the corner, but it turned my mom into a raging bitch."

"That's no way to talk about your—" Joel started, his southern sensibilities affronted, but I stopped him with a glance.

"Maybe you could walk Cassie here—"

"Carrie," Miss Rock Star said.

"—back to her store and get her statement. I'll keep an eye on the screens and get the phone," I said.

"Sure thing," Joel agreed.

I waited until they had left the office before turning back to Julia. "So you live near here?"

"Across the way. The hotel's gonna back up to practically against our fence. I'm sure my mom wouldn't have been so pissed off if we'd been gonna end up on one of the golf fairways," she said cynically. She scraped at chipping blue polish on her thumbnail, not meeting my eyes. "She organized the whole neighborhood to protest the development and get a court order to stop it. Had a meeting with that Mr. Porter and everything."

"Really?" I let her momentum, and what I suspected was typical teenage-daughter resentment of her mom, carry her on.

"Yeah, he even came to the house. I heard her say that if he were dead there wouldn't be an Olympus to ruin our property value."

"And that's what makes you think she killed him?"

"No. It was the blood."

Now she had my attention. "What blood, Julia?" For the first time, I was glad I wasn't a cop. If I had been, I'd've been obligated to make sure one of Julia's parents was present, and to jump through a lot of other hoops before questioning the girl. As it was, we were just two private citizens having a conversation.

"In the backyard.. He was at our house on Sunday afternoon, and then he was dead on Monday and there was a whole lot of blood in our backyard." Tears trembled in her voice again.

"Did you hear a gunshot?"

She shook her head. "No, but I spent the night at Taylor's house."

I thought for a moment as Julia watched me anxiously. "Do your folks own a gun?"

She nodded, ponytail bobbing. "Yes. My dad gave it to my mom when they got divorced."

What a thoughtful guy. Before I could ask anything else, Julia volunteered, "The blood's not there anymore. I saw it Monday morning when I came home to get ready for school. When I got home that afternoon, it was gone. I mentioned it to Mom at dinner and she got all edgy, told me not to worry about it. Do you think she did it?" she finished in a whisper.

"Did what?"

The question came from a woman who bore a striking resemblance to Julia. She had the same blond hair and high cheekbones and the same basic build, although she had a bit more padding at bust and hips than her daughter did. She wore a zip-up fuzzy vest over mom jeans and looked like she could make corporate purchasing decisions, coach a kids' soccer team, do the family taxes, and still have dinner on the table by seven o'clock. She was accompanied by a pin-striped-suited man with a briefcase who had "lawyer" stamped all over him. How had she rounded him up so quickly?

"Did what, Julia?" She looked searchingly at her daughter, who evaded her gaze.

"I'm EJ Ferris," I said, stepping forward with my hand out.

"Marcia Cleaton," she said, with a firm shake. "And this is—"

"Denny Snodgrass," the lawyer said. "I'm Marcia's lawyer."

"Boyfriend," Julia muttered.

"What seems to be the problem here?" Snodgrass asked, ignoring Julia.

"The clerk at Rock Star Accessories observed Julia leaving with merchandise she hadn't paid for," I said.

Marcia Cleaton gasped. "You were shoplifting?"

"Why do you always assume the worst, Mom?" Julia snarled, conveniently forgetting that she had, in fact, shoplifted.

"I'm sure it's just a misunderstanding," Snodgrass put in unctuously. "I'm sure the mall doesn't wish to press charges in this kind of case." He looked at me.

I wasn't sure what he meant by "this kind of case." Were we not supposed to press charges when the perp was a cute teenager? When the perp's parents were (presumably) upstanding members of the community? Or when we were confronted by the might of the legal system as represented by one Denny Snodgrass? "It's not up to me," I said. "I believe Rock Star has already called the police. The store will make the decision to press charges or not."

As I said it, Joel slipped back into the office and quietly resumed his seat.

"I'm sure we can reason with them," Denny said as Marcia Cleaton crossed to her daughter and tried to hug her. Julia shrugged out from under her mother's arm.

"I can't believe you shoplifted," Marcia Cleaton said again, staring at her daughter as if at a stranger. "Your father and I taught you better than that. You get a reasonable allowance. You make money babysitting. Why—"

"At least I didn't kill anyone!"

Marcia Cleaton reared back as if slapped. "What the *hell* is that supposed to mean?" Her voice went from puzzled mother to pissed-off corporate honcho in a heartbeat.

Having spat out her accusation, Julia stood, like a burden had lifted from her shoulders. "Come off it, Mom. I saw the blood." She strode toward Snodgrass and the door. "C'mon, Denny."

"The blood? Are you talking about—"

"I'm talking about Jackson Porter, okay?"

Marcia paled.

Little-girl bravado and a too-grown-up desire to inflict hurt shone on Julia's pert face, mixed with a teaspoon of satisfaction at her mother's reaction. I'd never felt a yearning for children—it wasn't like I was set against the idea with the right guy, but I'd never felt incomplete without them—

but watching this byplay was convincing me that parenting Fubar was the closest I wanted to come to the real thing. I could cope with a dead rodent or two and the occasional hairball yakked up onto the carpet. This ugliness was something else entirely.

"Don't say anything, Marcia," Snodgrass warned, taking her elbow and steering her toward the door.

"Let's go down to that stupid store," Julia said, marching out the door, "and get this over with. I'll offer to pay them back or whatever, and we can get the hell out of here. It's not like it was a big deal."

"I'll be right back," I told Joel, following the unhappy little party out the door. I mostly wanted to make sure that Julia and Marcia didn't kill each other on mall property; we'd had enough homicides for one week.

We found a uniformed Vernonville Police Department patrol officer waiting at Rock Star Accessories with Carrie filling him in on the heist details. "Arrest her," she said, pointing a finger at Julia when we appeared.

"It might be best," Marcia said.

Julia whirled, her mouth open in a comic book "O" of astonishment. "What?"

"Maybe it's time you learned about action and consequence, sweetheart," Marcia said sadly.

I wasn't sure if the action-consequence link she had in mind was shoplifting and getting arrested, or ratting out your mom and getting cast adrift. A hard lesson either way.

"But you said—" Julia turned to me, pleading with her eyes.

"She has some information that might interest Detective Helland," I told the officer. "About the Jackson Porter case."

"They closed that one," the young officer informed me.

"I know. But Helland might still want to hear what she

has to say. I'll give him a call," I said to Julia. Underneath her obnoxious manner and air of entitlement, I sensed real distress about her mother's possible involvement in the Porter case; the least I could do was try to pave the way with a call to Detective Helland.

"Now, just a minute," Denny Snodgrass started.

Not interested in whatever lawyerly objection he felt compelled to offer, I walked slowly back toward the security office where I knew Joel would be anxious to hear what was going on. I made him wait while I dialed Helland's number. When the desk sergeant finally got him on the line, I filled him in on what Julia Cleaton had said. A long pause hummed over the line when I finished.

Finally, Helland said in a weary voice, "What part of 'case closed' doesn't resonate with you, Officer Ferris?"

"The part where you don't explain why Gatchel would have displayed the body in the window and the part where you haven't even figured out where he was shot," I said hotly, tired of being condescended to.

"What makes you think we haven't located the murder scene?"

"Have you?"

More silence. "No."

I bit back the "Hah!" that sprang to my lips. "It's easier to pin it on Gatchel, I'm sure, but—"

"This may surprise you, but I don't look for 'easy' in my investigations." Anger tinged his voice. "If you must know, we interviewed Marcia Cleaton and several other people with a grudge against Porter or the Olympus development. We found no evidence indicating any of them were involved in his death."

"Did you know Porter was at the Cleaton house on Sunday afternoon?"

"Did you get that from the daughter who even you admit is out to get her mom?"

"I'll take that as a 'no,'" I said with some satisfaction.

"I will talk to the Cleaton girl," Helland said. "Happy?"

He hung up before I could tell him how pleased I was that the Vernonville PD took citizen input seriously. Probably just as well.

"What was all that about?" Joel asked as soon as I laid down the phone.

I told him what Julia had said about the blood and about her mom meeting with Porter.

"I'll bet she did it," Joel said.

"Who? Julia or her mom?"

"The mom. Though if this were a made-for-TV movie it would turn out to be the girl because she's such an unlikely suspect. I'll bet Porter and the mom argued and she lost it."

"And ran to the bedroom or wherever, pulled out a gun, and shot him in her kitchen?" I raised my brows skeptically. "The blood was in the backyard."

"Maybe not quite like that," Joel said, thinking. "How's this: they were talking in the backyard because he was showing her how the resort would look over her fence."

"That's plausible," I admitted as Joel plowed on.

"But then he says nothing she can do will stop him from building the resort and she loses it. She comes at him with whatever's handy—grill fork, shovel, who knows?—and he pulls a gun on her!" He leaned back in his chair triumphantly.

"Why would he have a gun with him?"

"Because he's a lousy developer and everyone in the tri-county region wanted to kill him."

I wasn't sure I bought that, but I supposed it was possible that Porter had a gun. "So she wrestles the gun away from him, shoots him without anyone in the neighborhood hearing—"

"Silencer?" Joel's certainty was deflating.

"—drags him across the yard, and somehow dumps him into her trunk so she can bring him here?"

"The lawyer dude was in on it with her."

"Possible."

Joel embellished on his new idea. "He comes over Sunday night—the daughter's gone—he's thinking he's gonna get lucky, and finds her with a body in the backyard. The Porter dude's already deader than disco. He loves her . . . what can he do? He helps her move the body so the police don't glom onto her."

I tapped a finger against my lips. "Not totally impossible," I allowed. "But I still don't understand why they brought the body here."

"So there'd be more suspects," Joel said in a "duh" kind of voice.

I rather thought that the body being in Diamanté narrowed the suspect field since the murderer would have needed a key to get in the store, or been proficient with picking locks. Since Grandpa Atherton was the only person in the mall that I knew of who could get into locked doors without keys, it might behoove me to figure out who had keys. Finola, of course, and maybe her employees. Certainly the Monica she'd mentioned who'd been supposed to open on Monday.

"Hey, Harold," I asked the older guard as he came through the door, "how long has Diamanté rented that space?"

"A couple years?"

"What was there before?"

"A teen clothing store, I think—TeenAngster—and before that it was a formal-wear shop for years; you know, a place that rented tuxes and whatever."

Suspecting I knew the answer, I asked, "Does the mall change locks on the shops between tenants?"

He snorted. "Get real. That would cost money."

I wasn't surprised. I couldn't remember seeing a locksmith in the mall in the year that I'd been here except once when some pranksters dumped Super Glue into the locks on all the bathroom stall doors. Quigley's office, I figured, would have a list of all the former tenants for that space, maybe going all the way back to the eighties when the mall had first opened. Even without seeing the list, I knew it would be a daunting number. Multiply the number of tenants by the average number of employees for a store that size— five?—and then double the figure to account for employee turnover, and you might have an approximation of the number of people who'd once—still?—had keys. It was a hopeless task for an individual to pursue. It would take a police department with a lot of manpower to locate the former tenants and get lists—if the owners kept the data, which was unlikely—of all their former employees.

Woskowicz walked in just as I was set to resume my patrols. His bulk shrank the room.

"Ferris," he barked, pointing a finger at me. "Go home and get some sleep. I need you to work the midshift— Weasel's been called out of town for a family emergency."

Weasel had family? Hard to imagine. I didn't waste my breath asking why Woskowicz didn't just call in someone who was on a break day or otherwise not scheduled to work. Ever since I'd started working here, Woskowicz had gone out of his way to give me crappy assignments and tasks he hoped would make me quit. No way would I give him the satisfaction of complaining. I'd probably be stuck on midshift full-time if Weasel hadn't lobbied for that time slot.

"Right," I said equably, knowing my lack of reaction would

annoy Woskowicz. "I'm out of here." Dragging my gym bag from under the desk, I slung it over my shoulder. "Later, Joel."

I stopped by the Y, but the pool was clogged with noon-time swimmers and a mommy-baby class of some kind. Way too many swim diapers in the water for me. I got in a quick upper body weight workout instead, and then went home to try to sleep. Fubar met me with little prrp-prrps of pleasure when I came through the door at such an unusual time. He looked affronted, however, when I stripped and crawled into bed. Clearly, he'd thought we'd be engaging in a nice game of "chase the feather on the string" or going for a walk around the patio-home community, as I sometimes did in the evenings. We didn't go fast or far, but Fubar liked to cut ahead of me on the path, hide in a box hedge or a rhododendron, and pounce at my feet when I walked past. If he untied my shoelaces before I shooed him away, he won. Neighbors found this game less amusing than I did when he attempted to play it with them. I'd had to replace more than one pair of shoelaces snarled beyond redemption by his fast claws.

In my military days, I'd gotten used to grabbing forty winks whenever the opportunity presented itself, so I didn't have much trouble falling asleep. I awoke at nine thirty, made a quick meal of pasta with marinara sauce, packed a "lunch" for later, and headed back to Fernglen. Fubar was nowhere in sight; I assumed he was on the prowl. Lampposts cast pools of light in the acres of empty parking lot at the mall when I drove up. There was still activity around the movie theater entrance, but otherwise the place was still. The air was brisk with a hint of moisture as I hustled inside.

The security officer on duty, a burly black guy named Edgar Ambrose, greeted me with a laconic, "Yo, EJ."

"You by yourself?" I asked, looking around for the other officer who should still be here.

"You implying I need help?" he asked with a huge grin, showing a gold canine tooth.

"Not at all," I said.

"Dallabetta just left," Edgar said, pointing one of his meaty fingers at a camera screen. I watched as Dallabetta opened the door of her car in the jerky motion consistent with not enough frames per minute. The screen switched to another camera before she drove off. "And I'm outta here. Poker game tonight." He shifted his bulk from the chair and stood, running a hand over his grizzled head.

"Anything going on?" I asked.

"Nada."

That was our version of a turnover briefing.

"Later." Edgar lumbered out, and I spent some time watching the screens. Movie patrons left the theaters and some walked toward the stores, but the sliding iron gate, padlocked when the stores closed at nine o'clock, kept them isolated in the theater wing. Views from our working cameras cycled onto the twelve screens in front of me at five-second intervals. A lot of nothingness. When the final movie let out after midnight, I got on the Segway and glided down there, unlocking the padlock on the gate to make sure the theater and the door to the parking lot were properly secured. They were. Relocking the gate, I rode the Segway through the empty halls, thinking that the mall seemed a completely different place at night.

Sound echoed off the marble halls differently at night, without gaggles of shoppers to absorb it. And the low lighting Quigley's office insisted on to save energy cast a bluish glimmer on the slick floors and left shadow puddles where the dim fluorescents didn't penetrate. Purring into the Macy's wing, I saw lights on behind their grille and heard the *vroom* of vacuum cleaners; the contract cleaning crew must be hard at work. When I'd started working at Fernglen, I'd assumed that the mall employed a janitorial service to clean all the stores. But, no. Each anchor store had its own contract cleaners, and the smaller stores, like Diamanté or the Herpes Hut, did their own cleaning, with salesclerks vacuuming or dusting or mopping as required. The mall's janitors cleaned the food court and other common areas.

The vacuum sound faded behind me as I returned to the main corridor. The escalator was frozen in place, and the fountain lay silent. The inadequate lights gleamed on a wet patch and I slowed. Was the fountain leaking? Getting off the Segway, I shone my flashlight around the fountain, realizing the wetness wasn't a patch; it was a trail about ten inches wide that led from the fountain toward the housing that hid the escalator's innards. Agatha? I played the beam cautiously over the escalator but saw nothing. No way was I going to try to dislodge the housing and face down a pissed-off constrictor on my own. Making a note to suggest someone in maintenance check under the escalator tomorrow, I skirted it and zipped down the hall toward Nordstrom, going much faster than I did when I had to dodge shoppers. I completed my tour of the ground floor, took the elevator to the second floor, and repeated the sequence. Nothing was out of place. No one skulked through the halls carrying a body or even loitered in a corner, trying to sell drugs. Returning to the security office, I watched the screens again, fighting the urge to drift off as the digital clock in the corner of the camera screens ticked its way to two o'clock. A car pulling into the north parking lot, headed for the garage, perked me up. As I watched, an SUV followed it. Hello. I switched to the garage camera and watched as the two cars stopped side by side.

Hot damn. Maybe I should mosey out to the garage and see what the folks in those cars were up to at two in the morning. They might be carpoolers meeting up for the morning commute, but I didn't think so. This was a bit early even for the Type A's that dominated the D.C. workforce. The north parking garage connected to the mall near the Macy's, and I gunned my Segway down the corridors to the entrance, leaving it in the hallway as I quietly pushed through the door into the cold and drafty garage. The structure smelled of damp cement, and the wind gusted small snowflakes through the open bays. My keen deductive processes told me it had started to snow since I came on shift.

Standing still, just inside the garage, I listened. The murmur of voices and the clang of metal on metal reached me. I walked swiftly toward the voices, hand on the pepper spray canister on my belt. Pepper spray was the most lethal weapon the investment company thought its security officers needed because Fernglen wasn't rife with the gangs and druggies that plagued some malls. I'm sure there was an insurance liability issue affecting the investment company's choices, too. I'd heard the security officers at the Mall of America made their rounds in full gear with Kevlar vests and AR-15s. Not too different from patrolling the streets of Kabul. The prospect didn't appeal to me. Even when policing, I'd always preferred to rely on wit rather than weaponry. Still, I missed the security-blanket feeling of having a weapon on my hip as I penetrated further into the garage.

Passing one of the five-foot-diameter columns that kept the upper level of the garage from falling on the cars below, I saw a red sedan drawn up beside a dark green SUV so that the drivers could talk through their open windows. Exhaust drifted around them, the noxious odor trapped by the humidity. Noting the license plate numbers—both Virginia—I walked up to within fifteen feet of the cars before calling, "May I help you with something?"

I glimpsed a pale oval of face and a shock of dark hair in the sedan's side mirror before the windows buzzed up, the engines gunned, and the vehicles tore away, the SUV passing within two feet of me as it cornered onto the down ramp. Unfortunately, I couldn't get any details on the driver through the tinted window. Relatively certain I'd interrupted a drug deal, but with no proof to offer the police, I decided I'd call in the license plate numbers to the Vernonville PD when I got back to the office.

I had started back toward the door when a skritch of sound jerked my head around. I stopped and turned, scanning the empty garage. The only place to hide at this hour was behind the huge support columns. I studied each column carefully. There was something funky about the shadow of the column across from where the cars had been parked. I palmed the pepper spray.

"Who's there?"

Eleven

. . .

A figure clad in a black leather jacket and jeans stepped out from behind the column, hands held unthreateningly out to his sides. "Just me."

My eyes narrowed as I recognized the mall's newest cookie franchise operator. Of all the people I might have expected to see, he wasn't even on my list. "It's a little early for baking oatmeal scotchies, isn't it, Mr. Callahan?"

"Jay. It's never too early—or late—for cookies, in my opinion," he said, walking toward me, hands held palm out. He moved with the economical motion of an athlete. "Can I put my hands down now?"

I waved an impatient hand and slid the pepper spray back in its slot. "What the hell are you doing here?"

"Independent businessmen work long hours," he said. "In case you haven't noticed, the economy sucks."

"Uh-huh." I unlocked the door and passed through it as he held it open. The hall's warmth washed over me in a comforting wave. I hadn't realized how chilly I was until I came in. "And I didn't see your car."

"It's out there," he said, waving a hand toward the world at large beyond Fernglen's walls.

His answer fell squarely into the "duh" category and exasperated the hell out of me. I swung around, blocking his path. We faced each other with no more than a foot between us. "What were you doing in the garage? Did you know those men were going to be there?"

Jay's hazel eyes looked down into mine, and for a moment I thought he might give me a serious answer. Then, he said, "Why are you the only mall cop with a scooter?"

"It's a Segway, not a scooter," I said, then slapped myself mentally for responding to his comment.

"Let's have a cookie." He eased past me, his arm brushing mine, and I felt a jolt.

"I don't want a cookie," I said. "I want to know what was happening out there."

"I don't know." He kept walking. I got on the Segway and glided up beside him, keeping pace.

"But you have your suspicions."

"I have a suspicious nature," he said, with a small, lopsided smile.

Well, so did I, and I suddenly wondered if he'd been part of what was going down in the garage. It had looked like he was observing the men in the car, or even spying on them, but maybe he was a lookout for them—not a good one since I'd snuck up on them—or had been about to join them when I came up.

"I'm going to call the license plates in to the Vernonville PD," I warned him.

"Good idea."

We had reached the fountain by this time, our voices and

his footsteps echoing strangely in the empty corridors. We turned toward the food court and I asked, "Are you really going to make cookies?"

"Of course." He raised his brows as if surprised by my question. "If I don't, you might think I'm here for some nefarious reason. Can't have that."

"Are you a cop?" I shot at him. "An investigative journalist?"

I thought surprise flickered in his eyes, but he responded blandly. "I'm just an entrepreneur looking to make a buck off the American public's jones for sugar and fat and chocolate. It's better to work on my new recipes at night. Fewer industrial spies looking to steal my proprietary secrets." He looked around in an exaggerated way, as if expecting to spot a rival cookie mogul lurking behind the trash cans or under the counters of the other food stands.

I growled deep in my throat and spun the Segway around. As I glided off, he called after me, "Come back in half an hour for a cookie."

Back in the security office, I pulled up one of the food court cameras to see Jay Callahan lifting a huge stainless steel bowl. Then he disappeared into the back—the kitchen, I presumed—and didn't come out again. Scanning the outside cameras, I searched for his car but saw no vehicles besides my own. I kicked back in the chair, thinking. Maybe he lived within walking distance? If not, why had he gone to the trouble of hiding his vehicle? There was more to Jay Callahan than met the eye. Far more.

To resist the urge to stare at the food court camera the rest of the night, I descended to the first floor and got into the security office's vehicle, parked in its usual spot by the Sears entrance in the lower level garage. A white Buick, it had green lettering proclaiming FERNGLEN SECURITY stenciled on both sides. I cruised the mall's lots, checking for any other unusual activity, but saw nothing. The snow was falling harder when I returned the car to its slot, and snowflakes filtered through the yellow cones of light beamed by the headlights.

By the time I returned to Legendary Lola Cookies on the Segway as part of my routine patrol, over an hour and a half had passed since I'd left Jay Callahan. He was gone, but the smell of warm cookies lingered in the air. A paper plate bearing two cookies rested on the counter. As I drew closer, I saw that one had "MALL" written on it in blue icing and the other said "COP." Whatever else he'd been up to here tonight, he'd really made cookies. I was conscious of a faint feeling of regret that he hadn't waited for me, but I stamped it down and bit into the COP cookie. My watch told me it was four thirty, so I headed to the main entrance between the Nordstrom and Dillard's to let in the first wave of mall walkers. I arrived to find at least twenty people gathered on the concrete apron, stamping their feet to keep warm and exhaling great clouds of steam. I'd thought Grandpa Atherton might be among them, but I didn't see him.

"Where's Office Wedzel?" one woman asked as the crowd streamed past me into the hall.

"Family emergency," I said.

The mall felt livelier now with exercisers race-walking the halls, keeping within three feet of the walls to maximize their distance. The really gung-ho even went to the extreme of walking into alcoves and doorways. I motored up beside some of the walkers, chatting for a moment before showing them the photo of Robbie Porter. All I got were headshakes until I reached a slim, sixtyish woman wearing turquoise leggings with black stripes and a matching jacket. She had stylishly cut gray hair and looked sideways at me through fashionable rectangular bifocals. I pegged her as a corporate vice president or CFO or some such.

"I've seen him a couple times," she surprised me by saying. Her voice was pitched low, but her enunciation was crisp. "Is he a drug dealer?"

"Possibly," I said. "Why do you ask?"

"He always looks . . . furtive." She pumped her arms hard and passed a pair of amblers doing more gossiping than walking. I kept pace on the Segway. "And I've seen him with some sleazy looking types once or twice."

Excitement zipped through me. "Where?"

"In the east garage, on the second level where you come in to Dillard's. He sort of . . . hovers around there, like he's waiting for someone." She wrinkled her nose as if smelling something distasteful. "At first, I thought he was homeless, but there's just something about him . . ."

"When did you last see him?"

Her gaze drifted to the right as she thought. "Monday? On my way in here to walk. He was there, by the door. It's like it's his spot. He always wears a ski cap, a black one with a red pom-pom." She scrunched her fingers above her head.

Robbie Porter had been here at the mall on Monday morning! I didn't know what time the coroner had established for Jackson Porter's death, but odds were it was late Sunday night or early Monday.

"I reported him once, a couple months back," the woman said, "to the officer who's usually here."

"Officer Wedzel?"

She nodded. "That's the one. I didn't see the young man"—she nodded at the mug shot in my hand—"for a couple weeks after that, but he's been around, off and on, for over a month."

I wondered why Weasel hadn't noted the complaint in

the log. I knew damn well I hadn't read anything about a possible drug dealer lurking in the parking garage. Had Weasel approached Porter on his own? Called the cops? "Thank you very much," I said. "The police may want to talk to you. Is that okay?"

"Of course," the woman said, sliding a hand into the pocket of her jacket and handing me a card. It read, "Theresa Eshelman, Intellitot Day Care Center."

"You run a day care?" I asked, surprised.

"For thirty years now." She smiled. "We take kids from six weeks to twelve years old. The before- and after-school care market is huge in this area."

So much for my assessment of her as a corporate bigwig.

More walkers had appeared, and I marveled at the number of people who got up BCOD—before the crack of dawn—to exercise in a mall of all places. Pondering who to approach next, I wondered why they preferred the mall to a health club or the great outdoors. Because it was free and warm and safe, I decided, gliding up beside an older gentleman in a wheelchair. He sat hunched forward, yellow-gray hair straggling from beneath a navy blue knit cap. An afghan covered his lap, and strong hands propelled the chair down the slick hall.

"Sir," I said, "I was wondering if you've ever seen this man?" I held up the photo of Robbie Porter.

The man looked sideways. A pair of twinkling blue eyes met mine.

"Grandpa!" I lowered my voice. "What in the world are you doing? And where did you get that?" I indicated the wheelchair.

"I'm scoping out the situation," he said. "I wanted to observe the dynamics."

I rolled my eyes. "I thought you wanted to make time

with one of the walkers. How are you going to chat her up looking like that?" I gestured to indicate his frowzy appearance and, oh yeah, the wheelchair.

He waved a dismissive hand. "Don't you worry about my love life, EJ. I've got a handle on it."

Associating the words "love life" with my grandpa was just too strange.

"The wheelchair belongs to a friend. I promised to have it back by eight so she can get to her quilting class. What are you doing here at this hour?"

"The regular guy got called away and Woskowicz tagged me to do the midshift," I explained.

Grandpa frowned and I noticed he'd even disguised his brows by covering their snowy whiteness with a light brown dye and—was it possible?—adding longer hairs. Who'd ever heard of brow extensions? I asked him about them.

He nodded proudly. "Of course. You use false eyelashes and separate the lash hairs from the strand, work them in among your natural brow hairs, and glue them in place with the tiniest dot of eyelash glue. It doesn't take long at all once you get the hang of it."

I shook my head. I'd bought my last makeup item—a lipstick—before I left for Afghanistan the last time and never used it, yet I had a grandpa who could do brow extensions. I looked at my watch and realized it was time to get back to the office. "Here." I thrust my copy of Porter's mug shot at Grandpa. "Ask around."

In the office, I wrote a couple sentences in the online logbook about the garage encounter, noting down the license plate numbers, but leaving Jay Callahan out of it. I wasn't sure why I didn't mention him, but figured it served no purpose to have all the mall security officers looking at him sideways. I phoned the plate numbers into the Vernonville

PD, relaying my suspicions about drug activity, and the desk sergeant said they'd run them. No promise to get back to me. I hung up with a sigh, frustrated at not having the resources I was used to: no forensics people, no fingerprint database, no access to phone records or addresses (other than those available to the general public), no way to check backgrounds or warrants and priors. I really wanted to run Jay Callahan and see what he'd been up to before he bought out Legendary Lola Cookies.

I pushed back from the desk, massaging my aching knee. The door swung open and Captain Woskowicz sailed in, rubbing his hands together.

"Damn cold out there," he announced. "If I'd known the weather was going to be this crappy in Virginia, I'd've stayed in Newark."

I couldn't help wishing someone had kept him up-to-date on Virginia weather patterns. "Will Weasel be back tonight, or do you want me to work the midshift again?" I asked, logging off the computer.

His brows knit together. "Dunno. I haven't heard from him." Pulling out his cell phone, he dialed a number, listened, then flipped the phone closed in disgust. "Straight to voice mail again."

"Where was he going?"

"Hell if I know," Woskowicz said, looking at me like I'd asked him why Pluto wasn't a planet anymore.

"Well, what did he say when you talked to him?"

"He sent an email. Said there was a family emergency. That was about it." He shoved a hand in his slacks pocket and jingled the change. "Anything to report from last night?" His tone was tense, and I wondered what he was worried about.

I told him about the cars in the garage and my suspicions.

"You called the police?" he asked, blowing out a huge

breath. "Why the hell did you bother them with it? Two cars in the garage? Big freaking deal. You didn't even see an exchange of any kind."

"I just asked them to run the plates," I said. His irritation surprised me and made me question my decision. Had I misinterpreted what I'd seen? I remembered how the cars had peeled out when I challenged them. No, I decided, there was definitely something fishy going on. "Tonight?" I prompted Woskowicz.

"Nah. I'll do it myself, give you a break," he said, his tone switching from irritated to magnanimous.

"Magnanimous" and "Woskowicz" were mutually exclusive terms, and I stared at him for a moment, convinced he was up to something. "Great. I'll take off then and see you tomorrow morning."

"Yeah, whatever." He clomped back toward his office.

Joel came in, looking morose. I had gathered up my stuff, ready to leave, but the way his shoulders slumped made me hesitate.

"Something wrong?" I asked when he flung himself into his chair with a sigh.

"No," he said, but he kept his gaze lowered, fishing an apple and a large bottled water out of the backpack he usually hauled to work. He eyed the shiny yellow-green Granny Smith with loathing, then took a large bite, jaws working like a cow with its cud.

I sank back into my chair, watching him. His soft brown hair flopped over his brow, and his pudgy cheeks shone with the effort of munching the apple into oblivion. He swallowed and met my eyes sheepishly. "I'm on a diet."

"Ah."

"I need to lose a little weight." He patted his paunch, almost affectionately.

Men are so much more accepting of their bodies than women are, I thought, not for the first time. Where a woman would call herself "fat" and pummel her saddlebags or pinch her love handles viciously, a man says he needs to knock off a couple pounds and gives his excess flesh love pats. I sorted through several possible responses to Joel, including "Yes, you do," and "You'll have more energy and be healthier if you knock off twenty pounds," and finally settled on a neutral, "Why?"

"Well, there's this woman—"

Aha. Joel's face went all mushy as he thought about the woman. I suppressed a smile.

"I think she likes me, but her last boyfriend was really . . ." He trailed off uncertainly.

"Fit? Ripped? A hunk?"

"Yeah, all of that. He's a firefighter. And I'm—" He gestured to his soft body.

"Well, a diet's good, but what you really need is a workout plan." I leaned forward across the desk. "Cardio plus weight training will strip the weight off you in no time."

Joel looked at me hopefully. "Could you help me?"

I rocked back in my chair, surprised. "Me?"

"Yeah, you're always working out and you're buff. Could you show me what to do, help me with a training plan?"

"Kyra Valentine is the one who could help you," I said, never having seen myself as a fitness coach. "She was an Olympic track and field athlete, you know."

"She'd laugh at me," he said bluntly.

I knew Kyra wouldn't laugh at him, but she did tend to be a bit brusque sometimes, so I couldn't blame him for not wanting to ask for her help. I tapped my knee. "I wish I could help, Joel, but I really can't run with you."

"I hate running," he said, shooing that idea away with a

hand flap. "But you swim, right? And swimming's great exercise. Could I swim with you?"

If he swam with me, he'd see my leg. I stared at him, not wanting him to see my reluctance or guess the reason for it. Something in my expression must have given me away, though, because he sighed again and leaned over to turn on his computer. "It's okay," he said, his voice muffled. "I'll figure something out."

"No. I'll help you," I heard myself saying. "We can swim."

I headed out of the still quiet mall, trying to think of a way to keep my leg hidden from Joel at the pool. Maybe I could get a wetsuit. I scoffed at myself for even thinking like that and tried to focus on how grateful and relieved Joel had looked when I offered to help him train at the Y. Morning rush-hour traffic whooshed by on nearby I-95. An inch of snow covered my Miata, and I brushed it off with my hand, thankful it wasn't snowing any longer. My drive took me past a run-down area with single-family homes built in the fifties and sixties, and it triggered a memory. On impulse, I pulled into the neighborhood, remembering it from having dropped Weasel off one afternoon when his truck battery died. I didn't remember the house number, but I thought I would recognize it. South Pacific Street gave way to Bora Bora Place and I slowed. The houses looked amazingly alike: small, dingy, and unvalued, like the outgrown plastic soldiers or naked dolls at the bottom of a toy box. Tiny, winter-browned yards fronted houses clad with faded aluminum siding. Here and there, cheery curtains brightened a window or a coat of red enamel highlighted a mailbox, but the overall effect was dreary with a capital "D."

I almost cruised past Weasel's house but recognized the tree stump in the yard at the last moment. Pulling to the curb, I cut the engine and stared at the house. No curtains shielded the living room windows, but a sheet draped a window I figured was Weasel's bedroom. Nothing moved and no lights glowed in the house. What was I doing here? Just because Woskowicz couldn't get hold of Weasel didn't mean anything was wrong. Weasel was a big boy; maybe he was playing hooky. Still, since I was here, I might as well knock on the door. I swung my legs out of the car and zipped my jacket against the damp cold. A Siamese cat sitting in the neighbor's driveway eyed me as I walked toward Weasel's house.

"Pretty kitty," I said.

He turned and walked away, tail held straight in the air.

Passing Weasel's one-car garage, I stood on tiptoe to peer into the frost-rimed windows. Weasel's black truck sat in the garage, ragged Confederate flag sassing me through the back window, toolbox locked in the pickup bed, mud flaps with the girly silhouette hanging limply. Uneasiness prickled my skin. What was Weasel's truck doing here if he'd gone somewhere to visit his family? He probably flew, my logical side said. It didn't feel right, though. I continued toward the front door, more cautiously now. I had no real reason to think something was wrong, but I did. And I'd learned in my twelve years as an air force cop not to ignore my instincts. I glanced in the living room window as I passed it, but saw nothing except a saggy sofa and a big-screen TV.

Standing to the right of the door, I reached over and knocked loudly. The rickety house seemed to shudder with each blow. Nothing. I hammered with my fist, loud enough to startle the Siamese into hiding under the station wagon in his driveway. I tried the doorknob. Locked. I had three choices: (A) I could go home and mind my own business, hoping Weasel would show up at the office in a day or two, hungover from a three-day binge or depressed after his Aunt Laverne's funeral. (B) I could call the cops and ask for a health and welfare check on Billy Wedzel at 3462 Bora Bora Place. Or, (C) I could poke around a little more and see what I turned up. I voted (A) the most logical course of action and (B) the most efficient, but I went with (C).

I traipsed around to the back, the snow crunching softly under my boots. The one window on the side of the house was set high and frosted—a bathroom, I concluded, unable to look in it. The backyard was tiny, fenced, and held a rusty charcoal grill, a cracked concrete patio just big enough for the one webbed chair that sat there, and a newish red wagon tipped on its side. The latter surprised me and I wondered if Weasel had a kid, or maybe a grandkid. I was no better than Woskowicz, I decided. I knew almost nothing about Weasel's personal life or situation, even though I'd worked with him for a year.

The sagging mesh on the screen door shivered slightly in the freshening wind as I pulled it open to knock on the backdoor. Cupping my hands on either side of my face, I studied the kitchen. Fridge closest to the door, then stove, then sink. A card table in the middle of the linoleumed floor held a laptop computer, open, a coffee mug beside it. The sight of the computer made me gnaw my lower lip. Who left a valuable computer in plain sight when they were out of town? No one. As I pulled away from the window, a flash of color by the arched doorway on the far side of the kitchen grabbed my attention. Scrunching my nose against the glass, I tried not to fog it up with my breath. My eyes adjusted to the dimness and I saw that the splash of red I'd seen was a sock, and the sock was on a foot that lay tremendously still. The rest of the leg and body lay out of sight in the hallway.

I simultaneously tried the doorknob and dialed 911. Before the call could go through, a sharp voice behind me said, "Put your hands up and turn around slowly."

Twelve

...

I knew that voice.

Well, not that specific voice, but the type. Cop. Not wanting a bullet aerating my insides—I'd had enough of that to last a lifetime—I did as he asked. Spreading my arms wide at shoulder height, I turned around slowly.

"I was just calling you," I said with a slight nod at the cell phone in my hand.

"Yeah, right." The cop was tall, black, brawny, and skeptical. "We got a call from the lady next door to say there was a burglary in progress at this address. And I walk up to find you breaking and entering." His partner, a thirtyish white guy with male-pattern baldness, came around the corner.

"I wasn't breaking and entering," I said angrily. "I can see a foot through the window. The man in there is hurt or dead. I was going in to see if I could give aid."

The newcomer approached, and I stepped aside so he

could peer through the window. "She's right," he told his partner.

"Cuff her."

"But—"

The balding cop twirled a finger, and I obediently turned, putting my hands behind me. He snapped the cuffs around my wrists, the metal warm from being against his body, and the first cop lowered his gun and approached the door. He keyed his push-to-talk radio and called for an ambulance as his partner braced himself and kicked at the door near the lock. It splintered and gave way with a second kick. Observing their rough and ready entry, I thought morosely that my knee wouldn't take that kind of abuse anymore.

They plunged into the kitchen, and I positioned myself so I could see through the door. The sickly sweet smell drifting toward me told me all I needed to know even before the black cop called to his partner: "He's dead. Bullet through the head. Call Homicide."

I've always been more of an "ask forgiveness instead of permission" person, so I sidled through the door, careful not to touch anything, to see if the body was really Weasel. The smell was stronger in the kitchen, and I breathed shallowly through my mouth, inching my way toward the middle of the room while the cops cleared the rest of the house. Water dripped from the faucet at two second intervals, *plip . . . plip*, and cubes tumbled from the ice maker into the bin, startling me. I stared down at Weasel, positioned as if he were running from the kitchen, with one thigh perpendicular to his body and his arms outstretched. I couldn't say that I'd liked him, but I was sorry he was dead.

"Hey! You can't be in here!"

The black cop advanced on me, making shooing motions.

He stepped carefully over Weasel's body and nudged me toward the exit.

"Officer—?"

"Bruden," he supplied. "Now get your ass out that door before I kick it out."

"Officer Bruden," I said, moving slowly toward the door, his bulk crowding me along. "I think this death could be connected to the murder at Fernglen Galleria earlier this week. You might want to call Detective Helland—it's his case."

"Thank you for thinking of me," Helland's voice said from the doorway. He didn't sound grateful.

Eyes widening, I turned to catch the full brunt of his icy glare. No hint of smile lightened the lean face, the strong jaw, the high brow with a shock of white-gold hair falling across it. "Let me tell you—" I started.

"I've been called out for exactly two homicides this year, Miss Ferris," he said, moving into the kitchen, which suddenly felt crowded, "and you've been front and center both times. Should that make me suspicious?"

"No, I—"

"Because it does. I have to ask if your presence is more than coincidence." He eyed me ruminatively while digging a pair of latex gloves out of his pocket and slipping them on. "I'll talk to you when I'm done here." He nodded at Officer Bruden, who nudged me toward the door again.

"Can you at least uncuff me?"

Bruden looked at Helland, who nodded. Bruden unlocked the cuffs, and I made a show of massaging my wrists, which neither man appreciated because they'd gone back to examining the body. I exited before Helland changed his mind about the cuffs.

The barren backyard was an unappealing place to wait, but I made myself comfortable on the webbed chair on the patio after brushing snow off it. Even so, dampness seeped through my uniform pants and I rose to pace the yard. Blythe Livingston arrived, as did a clutch of uniformed officers, crime scene techs, and someone from the coroner's office. Neighbors peered from behind their blinds, and the woman next door, probably the one who'd called the cops on me, hovered near the fence that divided her yard from Weasel's, cradling the Siamese in her arms. As I watched, she raised a cell phone and snapped a picture of me. Incensed, I started toward her, but she scurried inside, the screen door banging behind her.

Detective Helland emerged after forty-five minutes, gave some direction to the waiting patrol officers, and sauntered toward me.

"Now can I—"

He shook his head. "Come." Taking me by the elbow, he led me around the house to the street side and down the driveway to a dark red Chrysler LeBaron. For one chilling moment, I thought he was going to recuff me, stuff me in the backseat, and haul me off to the station under arrest. Instead, he opened the front passenger door and said, "I need coffee. I know I can't handle your story without more caffeine in my system."

Keeping my mouth shut for once, I sat quietly as he drove smoothly to the nearest Starbucks. The gentle vibration of the car and the warmth blasting from the heater almost put me to sleep. I was more tired than I had realized. Not too crowded in the late morning, the Starbucks welcomed us with coffee-scented air and a cheery babble of conversation. When we ordered, Helland looked at me. "You're the suspect—you pay."

I was happy to pay, figuring he couldn't be planning to toss me in jail if he was making me buy him coffee, could he? Wouldn't that be seen as a bribe or a conflict of interest or something? And he'd paid at the food court two days ago.

Taking our steaming cups, we found a table for two behind a display shelf laden with CDs and mugs. Helland took the lid off his cup and blew across the hot liquid. I took two long gulps of my hot chocolate, needing the infusion of sugar and fat.

"Okay," Helland said, sipping his brew. "Here's where you convince me not to toss you in jail and throw away the key. What the hell were you doing in William Wedzel's house, standing over his dead body?"

"I wasn't even in the house when the officers arrived," I protested. "Captain Woskowicz hadn't been able to get in touch with him, so I stopped by on impulse. It was on my way home."

"Do you do a lot of things on impulse?" he asked, sounding genuinely curious. He seemed like the type who planned everything from A to Z, lived by to-do lists, and considered "spontaneity" a dirty word. I recognized that in him because I was much the same way.

"Not usually, no," I admitted. "Unless you count joining the air force."

"We'll come back to that," he said, "but for now I want to hear about Wedzel."

I told him Weasel hadn't worked his shift last night, that he'd emailed Woskowicz with some tale about a family emergency. "Only now I don't think it was Weasel who sent the email," I said. "When Woskowicz said he couldn't get hold of Weasel and didn't know if he was working tonight, I just decided to stop by. It didn't seem Weasel-ish. He spends more time on his cell phone than I spend sleeping.

His house was on my way home. When I saw his truck in his garage, I got worried for real and went around to check the back. I saw his foot through the window and had just called 911 when Officer Bruden jacked me up."

"I'll check on that," he said.

I rolled my eyes. "Good."

"Even if you did call 911, you could still have killed him. You might have been coming back to see if the body'd been discovered yet." He kept his ice blue eyes on me as he took another sip of coffee.

"I couldn't have killed him," I said. "I was at work when it happened." I crossed my fingers, hoping that was true.

"How do you know that?" he asked sharply, his eyes narrowing. "We don't have a time of death."

"He's been dead awhile; I could tell from the smell." At the memory, I swallowed hard to avoid gagging. "And his arm was limp when the officer checked for a pulse, so rigor had already gone off. That takes—what?—twenty-four to thirty hours, right?"

"Give or take," Helland acknowledged.

The couple at the table next to us gave me an uneasy look and moved to a table at the far side of the coffee bar, muttering about "sickos."

I ignored them. "Weasel worked his shift as usual on Tuesday night, so he left—alive—at about seven in the morning. Woskowicz got the email about Weasel's 'family emergency' before noon yesterday, because he came in and told me I was working the midshift. So, he had to have been killed some time Wednesday morning, when I was at work, in full view of dozens of people."

"Hmph," Helland responded, apparently unimpressed by my reasoning.

"Since I'm no longer a suspect, does that mean you'll reimburse me for the coffee?"

My question surprised a laugh out of him. He looked almost human with a smile warming his handsome features. I felt a flicker of attraction.

He sobered quickly. "So what's your theory? I know you've got one," he added in a resigned voice.

"Weasel saw something Sunday night," I said promptly. I'd had a lot of time to think about it while I was waiting in the backyard. "He saw Porter's killer or something that would identify the killer."

"You mean Gatchel?"

I gave him a look. He was being deliberately obtuse. "No. It wasn't Gatchel."

Helland let that pass, looking at me from under half-lowered lids. "So, if Wedzel saw something, why didn't he speak up during the investigation?"

I'd thought about that, too, and had an answer ready. "Either he didn't realize the significance of what he'd seen, or, more likely, he decided to capitalize on his knowledge."

"Blackmail?" Helland's brows drew together. "Blackmailing a murderer is a dicey game."

"Obviously."

The implication hovered between us, unnamed but very much present. I buried my nose in my cup and inhaled the chocolate smell before draining the last sweet drop.

"Shit," Helland muttered under his breath, clearly pissed off that his closed murder case had just been reopened. He glared at me as if it were my fault. "You've got whipped cream on your nose."

After Detective Helland dropped me back at my car with

an order to sign my statement at the station later, I called
Captain Woskowicz to let him know about Weasel.

"Damn," he said after a moment's silence. "What am I
going to do about the midshift?"

Mr. Sensitivity. "Did Weasel have any family?" I asked,
thinking about the wagon in the backyard.

"How the hell should I know?" Woskowicz said. "It's the
police's job to notify them."

"I know that," I said, controlling my temper with an
effort, "but I thought we might want to send a card or
flowers."

"Weasel wasn't a flowers kind of guy," he said.

He had me there, although I rather thought the flowers
were meant for bereaved family members rather than the
deceased. I let it go, planning to look up Weasel's data when
I got back to the mall. I'd buy a card, at least, and pass it
around for everyone to sign.

"Now I've got to hire another officer," Woskowicz grumbled, hanging up without saying good-bye.

I drove home slowly, battling fatigue. My body clock was
all messed up. I wanted to power through the day, rather
than taking a nap, though, so I could sleep normally tonight
and get back on schedule. Fubar was nowhere to be seen
when I entered the house, but a small rodent leg of some
kind by the cat door told me he'd been by. Picking the leg
up with a paper towel, I disposed of it outside, then came
back in for a long shower and a change of clothes. As I pulled
an orange sweatshirt over my head, I wished I had access
to Weasel's computer and phone records. I knew the police
would check them and wondered if they held any clues to
his murder. If, as I suspected, he'd been blackmailing Porter's killer, how had he contacted him or her? Could he have
been stupid enough to arrange for a payoff at his house, or

had the killer tracked him down? Nothing about Weasel's death was staged; the killer left him where he'd fallen, not bothering to "display" him as he had Porter. That led me to believe we weren't dealing with a serial killer with some sick mental pathology; we were dealing with someone who was really pissed off at Porter and who needed to kill Weasel to tie up loose ends. Someone ruthless. Whoever it was hadn't killed in a fit of passion—he or she had planned it, working out the logistics of getting Porter's body to the mall and into the Diamanté window.

As I was trying to figure out what Weasel had seen Sunday night—surely not the murderer lugging Porter's body through the mall or he would have called it in—the phone rang. Squeezing water out of my hair with a towel, I picked it up. "Hello?"

At first all I heard was nasal breathing. Then, "Is this Officer Ferris?" The voice was male, youngish, hesitant.

"Yes. Who's this?"

"I hear you've been looking for me."

Robbie Porter! "Ro—"

"Don't say my name! I need to talk to you. I know who murdered my dad."

I caught my breath. "You need to go to the police."

"I can't. I've got a sheet. They won't believe me. Besides, they're looking to shut down my entrepreneurial activities." A weak laugh ghosted over the phone.

Translation: he thought they'd arrest him for pushing drugs. "I don't care about your business dealings." Ooh, bad choice of words. "Just tell me what you know about your father's murder."

"Tonight. Ten o'clock. You know where. Come alone. If I smell a cop, I won't show."

"Wait! I—"

But he had hung up. I stared at the phone until it emitted an irritated beep to tell me it was off the hook. I replaced it on the cradle.

Clearly, Grandpa and I had struck a nerve when we showed his photo around this morning. Someone we talked to had passed the word to Robbie Porter. I thought briefly about calling the police. Helland would certainly want to know that Porter's son had been in touch. But if I called him, he'd take over the meet and maybe scare Robbie away. I didn't want to call Helland, I admitted to myself, because then I'd lose my chance of finding the killer and presenting the solution to Helland, gift wrapped. Grandpa! I could use his help if I was going to meet up with Robbie Porter tonight. And why did the kid think I knew where to meet him? Somewhere at the mall, probably, but where? I'd figure that out later. For now, I needed to get hold of Grandpa Atherton.

A feathery sensation on my ankle sent goose pimples up my leg. I jumped and looked down to see Fubar sitting at my feet, twitching his tail. "You scared me, you dumb feline," I said.

He looked pleased.

I couldn't get hold of Grandpa, so I left a message and went back to Fernglen, wearing straight-legged jeans, a red henley shirt, and low-heeled boots. I was too hyped from finding Weasel's body and getting Robbie's call to sit around at home. I went straight to Merlin's Cave, hoping to talk to Kyra. Luckily for me, if not for Kyra's bottom line, no customers waited for her attention. She looked like a gypsy princess today in a red skirt embroidered with gold, an off-the-shoulder peasant blouse, and her hair kinked loosely around her shoulders. A dozen thin bangles circled each wrist. Spotting me, she hurried over and threw her arms around me.

"I just heard," she said. "Are you okay?" She drew back and studied my face.

"Mostly," I said. "It's not like Weasel and I were bosom buddies."

"Still," she said.

"Still."

Viewing a dead person, especially a person you know who died violently, takes it out of you. We went behind the counter, and I sat on a swiveling desk chair while she perched on the stool in front of the cash register. "I'm making you some tea," she announced.

Oh no. Kyra was a health nut, and her tea invariably tasted like the inside of an old tennis shoe smells. She picked up a sachet loaded with twigs and leafy bits, and probably eye of newt or something similar, and popped it into a delicate china cup patterned with yellow roses. She poured bottled water into the automatic tea kettle and plugged it in, looking at me expectantly. I talked quickly, hoping to escape before the water boiled.

I told her about how I came to find Weasel. "How did you hear about his death?" I asked.

"Quigley emailed everyone. Just a short note about 'a member of our mall family has passed on.'"

Water bubbled in the kettle, and she poured it into the cups. Steam rose in an odiferous cloud that reminded me of walking near a lakeshore after there'd been a fish die-off. Kyra took a long, satisfied sip of her tea and raised her brows at me. "I'm letting it steep," I said, launching into an account of my phone conversation with Robbie Porter.

"What did the police say?" she asked. When I stayed silent, she leaned toward me. "You did call them, right?"

I gave a tiny shake of my head.

"EJ! What are you going to do? Meet up with this drug dealer?" Her strong brows drew together.

"He said he wouldn't show if there were police around. But I won't go alone," I said, forcing myself to sip the tea. It was bitter, but not as nasty as I'd expected and I found the warmth soothing. I took another cautious swallow. "Isn't tonight your hot date with Mr. Lola's Cookies?" I asked to distract her.

"It's not really a date-date. Just a 'welcome to the mall' drink." She winked. "Now, who—"

A customer walked in, interrupting Kyra's question. She rose with a tinkle of bangles to ask if he needed help, and I was happy with the interruption since I knew she wouldn't think Grandpa Atherton was an adequate backup for me. The young man with Kyra was going on and on about Area Fifty-One and a book he'd self-published about his journey to the Krill galaxy aboard an alien spaceship, so I waggled my fingers at her and left, headed for Diamanté.

Thirteen

...

Entering the well-lit boutique, I looked around for Finola, but a woman I didn't know came forward from the dressing room area. Muted voices told me customers were trying on clothes behind the slatted doors. "May I help you find something?" she asked with a professional smile. Younger than Finola by six or eight years, she was about my height but carried an extra twenty pounds, mostly through her bosom and waist. Great legs showed below the above-the-knee hem of a burnt orange skirt topped with a striped, cowl-necked sweater. A tousled bob highlighted with several shades of dark blond framed a face wider at the jawline than the brow. Heavy makeup almost concealed the scars left by long-ago acne along her lower cheeks.

"I was looking for Finola," I said.

"Oh, she left early for an appointment. I don't expect her back today," the woman said, her gaze going past me to a pair of women who came in behind me. They beelined for a sales rack, and hangers clacked as they rustled through the dresses.

"Are you Monica?" I asked before she could latch onto the newcomers.

"Yes." A shadow of suspicion darkened her eyes.

"I'm EJ Ferris, a security officer here at the mall, and I think Finola told me you were supposed to open the morning that Jackson Porter's body turned up in the store window."

"The police already talked to me," she said, her face closing down.

"Great," I said, ignoring the slight shift in her posture that told me she was ready to charge past me and make a sale to the women now holding sequined camisoles against their torsos. "Then you can tell me what you told them. Why weren't you here at ten o'clock that morning? Did you lock up the night before? Did you notice anyone weird hanging around, or anything out of place?" I bombarded her with questions, hoping she'd answer at least one.

"Finola locked up Sunday night," she said. "I didn't work Sunday at all." She seemed to think that cleared her of all blame. Maybe it did.

"And Monday morning?" I smiled, carefully keeping any hint of censure out of my voice.

"I was sick. Stomach flu, if you must know."

"Did you know Jackson Porter?"

Her gaze flicked away from me. "I've only worked here a little more than a week. I don't know too many of the customers."

Which didn't answer my question. Before I could call her on it, she said, "You'll have to excuse me," and shouldered past me to ask the shoppers if she could start a dressing room for them.

I browsed the racks for a few minutes, watching Monica and getting a feel for the store. Monica ignored me, flitting capably from the dressing rooms to fetch another size for a customer, then ringing up a sale with a chirpy "Have a good day." She was clearly planning to avoid me, so I forced the issue by scooping up a pair of earrings crusted with blue and green Swarovski crystals that my mom would love and marching to the cash register. "I'll take these."

She took the earrings from me, swathed them in layers of yellow tissue paper, and slid them into a glossy bag. She mellowed enough to give me a small smile after glimpsing the price tag. When I handed over my credit card, she said, "You know, there *was* a strange pair in here, oh, last Thursday or Friday. They didn't look like the Diamanté type, if you know what I mean."

"What did they look like?"

She wrinkled her longish nose. "Late teens or early twenties, maybe, wearing that camouflaged gear some of the kids like these days. Not at all the Diamanté style. More like army surplus or even Salvation Army. The girl had about seventeen piercings in her ear"—Monica fingered her left ear—"and the boy wore a 'Save the Shenandoah Salamander' tee shirt. I mean, what the heck is a Shenandoah salamander?"

"An endangered amphibian?" I guessed, taking the small bag from her. Her description sounded remarkably like the pair who had visited the Herpes Hut, and I wondered, excitement pricking along my spine, if there could possibly be a connection between the reptile "liberation" and Porter's death. Thanking Monica, I left the store, letting my brain cycle through possible links. Could the young man be Robbie Porter? I wished I still had his mug shot on me so I could show it to Monica. Or, if the two were "Save All the Critters to Keep the Environment Diverse" eco-warriors, maybe they had a grudge against Porter because of his development activities. That felt more like it to me. Developers routinely bulldozed animal habitats and drained wetlands, according to popular report. I'd bet one or more of Porter's projects threatened some creepy crawly or slimy slitherer. Not politically correct terms, I know, but I prefer my animal buddies to have no fewer than two and no more than four legs. And fur or feathers as an exterior covering beat scales or wet skin every time.

I wondered how I could get a list of all of Porter's developments and find out which of them, if any, had sparked demonstrations or protests from animal rights groups. If my brother Clint was around, he could run the information down in no time. Digging up data that corporations or heads of state wanted to keep buried was his bread and butter. I'd send him an email when I got home; with luck, he'd be stateside.

Three thirty and time to meet Joel at the pool came all too quickly. Donning my one-piece suit, I showered, tied my towel around my waist, and padded barefoot to the lap pool, my gut twisting. Relieved to see that Joel wasn't out yet, I slipped into the water, shuddering at the sudden cold, and trod water to warm up. Only one other person was in the water, swimming laps in the far lane. A bored teenage lifeguard sat in the tower, swinging the whistle that hung from a lanyard around her neck. Joel emerged from the men's room on the opposite side of the pool a few moments later, wearing lemon-colored trunks and a tee shirt. He carried a rolled-up towel and wore flip-flops.

"Hi," he said awkwardly, looking like he thought the whole idea was a mistake. He shuffled out of his flip-flops and laid his towel on top of them, gazing at the water with much the look of a kid eyeing a heaping plate of brussels sprouts.

"Let's get started," I said, motioning him into the water. He started to lower himself into the water, but his hand slipped on the wet tile, sending him into the pool with a splash. His yellow tee shirt ballooned around him, and he swatted at it, trying to flatten the air out of it. Watching him burp air from under the shirt, I realized with a jolt that he was wearing it as camouflage for his body, much as I had contemplated wearing a wetsuit to hide my leg. I felt suddenly more comfortable with him and stripped off the goggles that sat atop my head. "You'll need these," I said.

"I'll get a pair tomorrow," he promised, adjusting the band.

We set off at a slow crawl; Joel barely managed a length and a half before stopping to gasp for air. "Swimming's hard," he huffed.

"That's why it's good for us," I agreed, urging him to complete the lap. "It'll be easier tomorrow."

"Tomorrow! I was thinking maybe once a week—" He swallowed a mouthful of water and coughed.

"Tomorrow," I said firmly.

We swam for only twenty minutes. Joel's arms were trembling as he hauled himself out of the pool. I eased myself out of the water by pressing my arms straight against the deck and half turning in the air to land on my butt. I had completely forgotten about my knee until Joel's gaze strayed that way.

"Looks like it hurts," he said. There was no hint of revulsion in his voice, merely interest and concern.

"Not so much anymore," I said, drawing my towel over and snugging it securely around my hips. And that was that. Joel headed toward the men's locker room with a wave and a weary, "Thanks, EJ."

I took two steps toward the women's locker room and then turned around, calling after Joel, "What's her name?"

A smile split his face and he stood straighter. "Sunny."

By the time the clock rolled around to nine p.m., I still hadn't heard from Grandpa, which worried me slightly. Chances were he was tailing someone or undercover somewhere and had his phone turned off, but it wasn't like him to be out of touch for so long. I didn't have time to do it now, but I decided I'd swing by his place on my way home from the mall. I had hoped to hook up with Grandpa before meeting Robbie Porter, to get him to rig me a wire or something so there'd be a record of my conversation with the young drug dealer, but I wasn't worried about winging it alone. Nothing in Robbie's background pointed to violence. He seemed to be a low-level druggie who sold a bit on the side to support his habit. I'd decided he was most likely to be in the garage near where Theresa Eshelman had seen him. If I didn't find him there, I'd wander around until I spotted him. It'd be easier to find him by using the security cameras, but I didn't want to alert Woskowicz to what I was doing by going into the security office.

A two-car accident and a detour made me late, and it was dead on ten o'clock when I pulled into the Fernglen parking lot. Before I had parked, a car cruised toward me, its brights blinding me. It pulled up alongside my Miata, and I recognized the security office's green and white car. Of all the bad luck. Captain Woskowicz rolled down his window as I got out. Poking his head forward, he opened his door but stayed in the car with the engine running. "The mall's closed," he said gruffly. "Oh, it's you, Ferris. What the hell are you doing here?"

I swung my door shut and said as casually as I could, "I think I left my gym bag upstairs."

"And you need it at ten o'clock at night?"

"I . . . uh, need it for my workout first thing in the morning. My iPod's in there."

"I don't know why you bother working out with that bum knee of yours anyway," he grumbled, pulling his head back into the car. "Hey, and while you're up there, get my coffee cup, would you? I left it by the coffeepot."

"No problem," I said, slowly unclenching my fists.

Damn. Now I would be late meeting Robbie because I was going to have to go all the way up to the security office and back. I felt Woskowicz watching me as I walked to the entrance, using my key to let myself in. I walked as fast as I could, half jogging although it made my knee hurt, through the deserted halls to the security office, unlocked it, and did a scan for Woskowicz's stainless steel mug. It was where he said it would be. I scooped it up and glanced at the camera screens. The view I needed wasn't showing. Rather than take the time to pull up that camera, I relocked the door and retraced my steps, conscious of my watch ticking past ten after ten.

I hurried out the door and over to where Woskowicz waited in the car. "Here." I thrust the warm cup at him.

"No gym bag?" He eyed my empty hands.

"I must've left it at the gym," I said with a helpless shrug. "Stupid of me."

"You got that right." He guzzled his coffee and wiped the back of his hand across his lips. "Why don't you come in at six tomorrow instead of seven? I'm beat."

"Sure thing," I agreed, anxious to be rid of him.

He took another sip of coffee, elbow casually propped on the door, seemingly in no hurry to resume his patrol.

"Well, I'd better be getting home if I'm coming in early," I said. I started the engine and pulled away slowly, watching in the rearview mirror until Woskowicz finally put the car in gear, wove around a light post, and headed toward the theater parking area where a few cars testified to a movie still showing. Playing it safe, I drove across the lot until I was sure he was out of sight, and then I flipped a U-turn and sped back, turning into the garage this time so Woskowicz wouldn't spot my car if he circled the mall again. Hopefully, he wouldn't bother to cruise through the garage.

Locking my car, I started up the ramp to the next level where I expected to find Robbie Porter. My knee ached from jogging to the security office, and I leaned over to massage it as I walked. I came to the top of the ramp and turned the corner, scanning for Robbie Porter. No cars blocked my view of the dark garage. A thin wind whistled through, and I dug my hands into my pocket. I was ready for spring. Suddenly, running footsteps from my left startled me. I hurried forward and caught a glimpse of a dark figure running toward the northwest corner where the elevators and stairs were. Foreboding gripped me. Pushing myself, I sprinted to where the figure had started from. There, I found a huddled figure slumped against the wall.

"Robbie!" I shouted. No movement. I dropped to my knees beside Robbie Porter, taking in a waxy white face framed by a gray hoodie. Unseeing eyes stared at me, and a thin line of drool crawled from his slack mouth. Robbie's sweatshirt sleeve was pushed up, and rubber tubing encircled his left arm just below the bicep. A needle, plunger pushed all the way down on the syringe, was buried in the vein. I put my fingers to his throat and thought I felt a faint pulse. "Hang on, Robbie," I commanded, frantically pulling my cell phone from my pocket and dialing 911. When I'd given the information to the operator, I shrugged out of my jacket and tucked it around Robbie's thin form.

The ding of the arriving elevator pulled my head up, and I realized the running person couldn't use the stairs because they were locked. He or she had had to wait for the elevator. I leaped up and took off toward the elevator, convinced whoever waited there knew something about what had happened to Robbie. Maybe he was a fellow druggie and they'd shot up together. Or maybe his—or her—role was more sinister. I heard the doors shush closed before I was in view of the elevator, and I fumbled for my keys as I ran so I could unlock the stair door. I took the stairs two at a time, using the banister to take the weight off my wrecked knee. Skin peeled off the palm of my hand as I slid it along the metal railing. On the second step from the bottom, my knee collapsed and I fell forward, banging into the door and bruising my shoulder. Damn. I fumbled for the release bar and leaned against it, spilling out into the lower level in time to see the runner dash out the garage entrance. I tried to stand, but my knee gave way again and I crumpled to the ground. An engine started and tires squealed as whoever it was escaped.

Damn my knee! Damn it, damn it, damn it. I sat for a minute with my leg stretched out straight on the cold cement, tears of pain and frustration leaking from my eyes, and throttled my knee with both hands. The thought of Robbie alone upstairs made me move. I pushed up, keeping all my weight on my left leg, and hopped to the elevator, which gaped open just two yards away, its light welcoming in the darkness. I lightly tapped the button for the upper level, using my elbow in case were any fingerprints—small hope— and sagged back against the wall. I had screwed this up royally. If Robbie Porter died, it would be partly my fault for not going to the police with information about the meeting.

The door dinged open on the upper level and I hopped out. It took a moment for my eyes to adjust to the dimmer light after the elevator's relative brightness, and when they did, I saw a man bent over Robbie Porter's still figure.

"Hey!" I shouted. "Get away from him."

The man looked up, fumbled at his ankle, and straightened, saying, "Well, if it isn't déjà vu all over again." Even though the words were light, Jay Callahan's expression was sober with his lips drawn into a grim line. "He's dead."

"What are you doing here?" I asked, moving closer. I was pretty sure he'd reholstered his gun when he recognized me. The question was: why did he have it out in the first place?

"What's wrong with your leg?" he countered.

"I fell down the stairs chasing whoever was here with Porter," I said, drawing even with him. He wore jeans again, and the black leather jacket, and smelled faintly of some spicy aftershave.

"You saw someone?" Jay's eyes narrowed.

"Not well enough."

"What were you going to do if you caught him?"

"Take him down," I said coolly, my eyes daring him to dispute it. "Hey, weren't you supposed to go out with Kyra tonight? Why are you lurking in the garage again? And don't tell me you're inventing cookie recipes or I'll smack you." I glared at him.

My ferocity got a faint smile from him. Before he could answer—assuming he was going to answer, which wasn't a safe bet—sirens sounded, getting closer by the second. "I called 911," I told him.

"Me, too." He held up a cell phone. "It's too late for this guy, though." He gazed down at the man sprawled against the wall.

"Robbie Porter."

Jay snapped his head around to stare at me. "Any relation to the murder vic?"

"His son."

We didn't have time for more as a police car and an ambulance barreled up the ramp and around the corner, lighting up the garage with strobes of red, white, and blue. Jay and I both raised our hands to shoulder height as the EMTs leaped out of the ambulance and ran toward Porter, while the cops stalked suspiciously toward Jay and me. One officer called for backup and a homicide investigator while the other one led Jay some distance away from me to keep us separated. It was going to be a long night.

The responding homicide detective wasn't Detective-Sergeant Anders Helland, so I got away sooner than I expected. I told the new detective—Detective Lyons—about Robbie Porter being Jackson Porter's son, so I knew I'd get a call from Detective Helland as soon as the two detectives compared notes. The detective accepted my story about coming back to the office to look for my gym bag and stumbling upon Robbie Porter—I'd give the whole story to Helland when I talked to him. I told Detective Lyons I'd chased someone who'd been near the body, and he looked at me as if I were nuts.

"Are you kidding me? You don't wanna be chasing after drug dealers, ma'am. Some of 'em would just as soon shoot you as talk to you. Sooner," he added reflectively.

"What do you think happened here?" I asked.

"Too early to tell." He shrugged. "Maybe he owed his supplier. Maybe he and another punk were shooting up and got hold of some bad stuff. Maybe he was depressed about his father's death and the guy who ran was an innocent bystander who stumbled over the body and couldn't be bothered to play good Samaritan."

"Suicide?" I wasn't buying that. Who committed suicide in a mall parking garage? And I hadn't noticed a plethora of innocent bystanders wandering the parking garage after ten o'clock at night. Speaking of which . . . I looked around for Jay Callahan, but he and the original patrol officers had disappeared. Maybe they'd taken him down to the station to grill him. I felt distinctly pleased by the thought and hoped the cops got more straight answers from him than I had.

It wasn't until I was on my way home at almost midnight that I realized Captain Woskowicz had never turned up, despite the coming and going of cops and evidence teams and the ambulance and, eventually, reporters in news vans. No way could he have missed all that activity if he was keeping an eye on the camera screens or patrolling the parking areas as he had been when I ran into him. Which led me to believe he was either sleeping like the dead in his office . . . or not at Fernglen at all.

Fourteen

. . .

A rude pounding on the front door jolted me awake at just after five o'clock Friday morning, which was just as well since I needed to be at work at six. Fubar sprang off the bed where he'd been curled at my feet in a rare moment of human-feline bonding—he didn't indulge me often with cuddling, perhaps thinking it would spoil me—and trotted toward the front hall. Expecting it to be Grandpa Atherton—after all, the last time I was rudely awakened that's who it was—I snugged my green silk robe around me, muttering, "Hold your horses," as the knocking sounded again. I found myself limping as I walked to the entrance way, and I hoped I hadn't really damaged my knee last night.

Only the faintest hint of dawn showed to the east as I pulled open the door, and said, "Grandpa, where—"

But it wasn't Grandpa Atherton on the stoop. A tall, blond, pissed-off homicide detective glared at me. He'd ditched his suit jacket and was tieless with his shirt open at the throat. My sleep-fogged mind found his slight dishevel-ment, the haze of stubble along his jaw, surprisingly attrac-tive. The cold nipped at my bare feet, and I remembered that I had bed head, morning breath, and was wearing only the slinky robe I'd bought as a gift for myself when I grad-uated from Basic Military Training School. After two months of marching, uniforms, and deprivation, I thought I deserved a bit of luxury.

"Why the hell didn't you tell me you had a meeting set up with Robbie Porter?" Detective Helland asked. His tone made Fubar hiss.

He had a right to be mad, so I bit back the response that jumped to my tongue. "Come in, make yourself some coffee, and I'll be with you as soon as I've dressed," I said, pulling the door wider.

For the first time, Helland appeared to notice my state of undress. His eyes traveled from my bare feet to the place where the robe gapped open to show a bit of cleavage to my tousled chestnut hair. Something like interest flickered in his eyes. As he stepped into the hallway, Fubar pounced on his black wing tip, working furiously to untie the laces.

"What the—?" He looked down and said, "That is the ugliest cat I have ever seen."

"Fubar, stop," I said, reaching down to pull the cat away. I noted that despite his disgruntlement, Helland hadn't kicked Fubar.

"Fubar?" Helland's brows rose. "As in—"

"Fouled up beyond all recognition," I said, replacing the more colorful "f" word some people used to start the popu-lar military acronym. "Because he is. And I am." Holding a squirming Fubar who wanted to return to assaulting Hel-land's laces, I retreated to my bedroom, leaving Helland to do whatever the hell he wanted.

I emerged twelve minutes later dressed in my uniform, with clean teeth, brushed hair, and the confidence that comes with all that. I found Helland in my kitchen, examining my spice rack. He held my Operation Achilles mug in his large hands, the one given to me by a British friend that I never let anyone else use, and half a pot of coffee sat behind him on the counter. Fubar streaked past me and out the cat door.

"You alphabetize your spices?" Helland asked.

"I don't imagine you're here to critique my organizational habits," I said, maneuvering past him to get to the coffee. For some reason, I really, really wished my retiling job were done; I didn't like Helland seeing my kitchen half-dressed, as it were.

That reminded him he was mad at me. "I cannot believe you arranged a meet with Porter and didn't tell me. You're interfering with a murder investigation. I ought to arrest you."

I couldn't resist the urge to needle him just a bit. "I thought that case was closed. Gatchel did it, right?"

He ground his teeth. "You know damn well Wedzel's murder raised some questions. Your irresponsible hot-dogging—"

"You're right. I'm sorry. I should have called you after Robbie contacted me. I screwed up."

He stopped in mid-rant. "Well," he said after a moment, "that takes all the fun out of chewing you out. But I still reserve the right to arrest you for *fouling* up my investiga-tion."

His emphasis on "fouling" made me smile. "How did you know I'd talked to Robbie?"

"Please. You didn't expect me to believe that you just happened to trip over him in the middle of the night, did you?"

"No." I sipped my coffee. "I was going to call you this

morning when I got to work and fill you in. In fact, I've got to get going—I'm due in at six."

"Uh-uh." He shook his head. "Not until you've told me everything you know. And I damn well mean everything." Setting his mug—my favorite mug—on the counter, he crossed his arms over his chest.

I sighed and brushed my bangs out of my eyes. It was time for a trim. "He called me yesterday, after I'd been showing his photo around like you asked me to." I told him everything I knew, which wasn't much.

"This guy you chased—did you get a description?"

"No more than I gave Detective Lyons last night. Medium height—somewhere around five-ten or eleven, I'd guess, medium build, black clothes, fast runner. I never saw his face, so I can't even say if he was black or white."

"You're sure it was a man?"

"Could have been a woman." I shrugged. "I know it's not much to go on. Do you have autopsy results yet?"

He shook his head. "Maybe later today. But it looks like a drug overdose. Not exactly a shocking end for an addict."

"How do you think this connects to Jackson Porter's death? Or Wedzel's?"

"We don't know that it does," he said. "Gatchel could still be good for Porter's death. Wedzel's murder could be completely unconnected—he surprised a burglar, maybe—and the kid's death could be the simple overdose it looks like."

I stared at him in disbelief. "You don't believe that! What are the chances that these three deaths occurring within the same week are coincidence?"

"Slim," he admitted, "but it's my job to find the link—not yours. So go back to reuniting lost kiddos with their parents and tracking down mega snakes and leave the murder investigation to me. I *will* arrest you for obstruction of justice if you get in my way again."

The steely look in his eyes convinced me he was serious. "Oh, that reminds me," I said. I told him about talking to Monica at Diamanté and my theory about the twosome who had probably freed Kiefer's reptiles and might have had a grudge against Jackson Porter for destroying habitats with his building projects.

"Thin," he said. "Only a moron would think that killing one developer would stop building projects in their tracks."

"If all murderers were Mensa material, the jails wouldn't be overcrowded," I pointed out, miffed that he had dismissed my theory so easily. My gaze fell on the microwave clock. Five fifty-four. "I'm late. Out." I herded Helland unceremoniously ahead of me through the garage door. I could see his gaze noting the screwdrivers arranged in descending size order on the Peg-Board, and the rake, snow shovel, and broom hung neatly on the far wall. "Don't say anything," I warned. I'd taken grief from my family my entire life about my passion for order. My brother Clint insisted that's why I'd joined the military, because no other organization on the planet would appreciate my "anal-retentive obsessiveness" (Clint's words) so much.

Helland laughed, a surprisingly pleasant sound, and ducked under the garage door as it rose. I waited until he drove off and then took off at a speed no cop would condone.

Even though I was running late, I stopped by Grandpa Atherton's place. I hadn't heard from him in twenty-four hours and I was getting worried. Not "file a missing person report" worried, but concerned enough to stop by. The community, with its lookalike cottages and knee-high iron fences useless for penning up even a teacup poodle, was quiet. Knocking on Grandpa's glossy blue door, I waited for a response. None came. No sound drifted from inside, and I didn't see any movement. Either Grandpa was up and out awfully early, or he hadn't spent the night here. I chewed the inside of my lip, wondering what to do. Nothing, I finally decided. Grandpa was an adult. My mom might think he needed a keeper, but that was because he got up to antics that made her nervous, not because he was infirm or losing it mentally. Maybe he'd spent the night with one of his lady friends. I returned to my car, resolving that I'd take action if I hadn't heard from Grandpa by the time my shift was up.

I walked through the doors of the security office at twenty after six, debating whether or not I should ask Woskowicz why he hadn't shown up in the garage last night. The smell of stale coffee permeated the room as I slung my jacket over the back of my chair.

"You're late," Woskowicz barked, emerging from his office. Bloodshot eyes blinked from between pouchy lids. He swiped the back of his hand under a red and irritated nose, then sniffed. His white uniform shirt was crumpled, with a smear of something at the cuff. "And why the *hell* do I have to learn from the morning news show that a death occurred at my mall last night?"

"You were on duty," I observed neutrally.

"Screw that! You were at the scene—you're all over the damn news reports. I should fire your useless ass."

It was turning out to be a banner morning: I'd been threatened with arrest and firing, both before seven o'clock. The day could only go up from here.

"I was surprised you didn't come down to talk with the police," I said. Actually, I was more surprised that he hadn't come down to score some face time with the reporters.

"Oh, you were, were you?" He advanced toward me, an ugly look twisting his face. I held my ground. He stopped a yard and a half away and swiped at his nose again. "I have a cold," he said, "not that I owe you an explanation. Took some NyQuil and it knocked me out."

Hm. He looked more like he'd been knocking back tequila shots. Or snorting cocaine. The thought popped into my head as he dabbed a tissue under his nose. Could Woskowicz have a drug problem? That might explain some of his erratic moodiness and current symptoms. But just being a bastard could account for his personality, too. Was it even remotely possible that Woskowicz knew Robbie Porter, maybe bought drugs from him? I closed my eyes to try to picture last night's runner in my head. No, no way it was Woskowicz. He was too damned big. The person I'd chased had been shorter and less bulky. I opened my eyes to see him staring at me suspiciously.

"That's too bad," I said. "You'd better go home and rest. Maybe have some chicken soup."

"Well, if you aren't Little Florence Nightingale," he said. "Maybe now that you've finally turned up I can get out of here."

I didn't remind him that my shift didn't officially start until seven o'clock, that I had done him a favor by agreeing to show up early. He waited a moment, to see if I'd respond, then stiff-armed the door and tromped away.

Grandpa Atherton's words about finding another job came back to me. Maybe he was right. Why was I putting up with Woskowicz? I liked my coworkers and the whole Fernglen family, and I liked feeling like I was doing something akin to police work, rather than working as an insurance claims adjuster or a teacher or pet groomer, but I had to admit that this career had its downsides, too, not least of which was the way real cops—Detective Anders Helland came to mind—sneered at us mall cops.

I reviewed the log, such as it was, and saw that Woskowicz had typed up a paragraph about Robbie Porter's death,
making it look like he was actually on the scene, helping
the investigators. He must have gotten details from a newscast. What a worm. I noticed that one of Macy's loss preven-
tion officers had asked for our help with a shoplifter late
yesterday afternoon, and the Christian graffiti artists had
tagged a school bus, of all things, with the entire text of John
3:16. A parenthetical remark from Joel said the bus was at
the mall to deliver a middle school band to play. Fernglen
had a small stage, more of a dais, near the fountain, where
Santa took requests at Christmas and the Easter Bunny
posed for photos in the spring. The rest of the year, Quigley's
office scheduled in a variety of performers to entertain mall
patrons.

Joel came in before eight and plunked a bag of baby carrots on his desk. I bit into one, appreciating the crunch.
Helping myself to another carrot, I filled Joel in on the
night's events and watched his eyes get rounder.

"And Woskowicz never even showed?"

"He said he had a cold and his meds knocked him out,"
I said neutrally.

Joel blew a raspberry. "It's good to be king," he said. "If
one of us fell asleep on duty, he'd fire our butts faster than
a speeding locomotive."

"As well he should," I said. "Look, my knee aches, so
I'm going to do dispatch today and keep an eye on the cameras. You take a turn at the patrols." Low man on the totem
pole usually got stuck with the boredom of dispatch duty,
so Joel's face brightened.

"Wilco," he said, standing and tucking his uniform shirt
more securely into his slacks. "Who else is working today?"

I checked the schedule. "Tracy and Harold come in at

nine thirty. It's just you and me until then." Our staggered schedule ensured an overlap of officers on duty during the peak hours when the mall was open.

"I'd better get to it, then," Joel said, self-importantly.

"Yeah, keep an eye out for the python."

Joel bustled out, and I scanned the screens for fifteen minutes, not seeing anything of interest except a news van parked outside the garage. An idea hit me and I took advantage of my solitude to slip back to Captain Woskowicz's office. The desk was bare of papers, but I took that as a sign of work avoidance rather than efficiency. His computer was off. Glancing over my shoulder to ensure I was still alone, I zeroed in on my target: Woskowicz's metal trash can. Brimming with used tissues, it looked like a certain source of plague or worse. Unwilling to fish through it with my bare hands, I found a ruler in Woskowicz's desk drawer and used it to sift through the can. Sure enough, halfway down, I came upon two empty NyQuil bottles. Not proof that Woskowicz had told the truth, but enough to allay my worst suspicions.

Returning to the front, I turned on the small television mounted high on the wall that kept us abreast of news. A perky reporter was relaying the details of Robbie Porter's death, ending with, "Unless you have a fancy to die buying, you might want to avoid Fernglen Galleria where this is the second death in a week. Rumor has it that a giant python is also at large in the mall. I'm—"

I muted the television with an internal groan, hoping Curtis Quigley hadn't been watching.

No such luck. Quigley burst through the door on the thought, radiating outrage. Today's paisley bow tie quivered with the force of his emotion. He pointed a stiff finger at the television. "Did you see that? Did you hear what she said?"

"No one will pay any attention to that," I said soothingly. "They—"

"Nothing of this sort has ever happened to me before," he said, pacing. "Two deaths in one week! A homicide and a drug overdose! Three deaths if you count Officer Wembley—"

"Wedzel."

"—who at least had the common decency not to die at Fernglen. I will not countenance all this dying in my mall. Only once before has someone died on one of my properties and that was a man who suffered a heart attack while his wife tried on St. John suits."

And who could blame him? The price tags on the designer knitwear would give anyone a coronary.

"You need to fix this, EJ," he said. "The chairman of the board of Figley and Boon Investments"—the conglomerate that owned Fernglen—"has been on the phone with me already this morning, wanting to know what I'm doing about all this. Please contact the investigators in charge of the case and tell them I want an update. And tell Captain Woskowicz—" He broke off and looked around. "Where is Captain Woskowicz?"

"He worked the night shift," I said, "and went home sick this morning."

"Well, tell him that I want to see a plan to prevent further incidents of this kind. On my desk first thing Monday morning." And with an emphatic nod of his sharp chin, he returned across the hall to his office.

I jotted a note for Woskowicz—"Submit plan to prevent mall murders"—then crumpled it to write something less facetious. As I turned back to the security log on the computer screen, intent on compiling some statistics for our weekly report, weariness caught up with me. Using the sink in our small unisex restroom, I poured out the sludge Woskowicz had left in the bottom of the coffee carafe and brewed another pot. Maybe caffeine would kick-start me. Steaming mug in hand, I kept an eye on the cameras for a while and then briefed Tracy and Harold when they showed up for their shift. The mall opened soon after that, and I stayed busy answering calls about Agatha spottings, a lost toddler, a soda spill in the Dillard's corridor, and a fire in the wastebasket in the movie theater men's room.

I filled in the time between calls by researching "animal+rights+activists+violence" via Google, and Jackson Porter's development projects. The first search generated a results list that would take a full-time staff of twenty people a week to sort through. Near as I could tell, roughly every fifth citizen in the United States was willing to burn a puppy mill to the ground (after removing the dogs, of course), shoot scientists who used lab animals for experiments, or booby-trap construction sites to discourage development. Such acts were officially called "animal enterprise terrorism," a new one for me. On a whim, I printed out photos of people identified as belonging to some of the more radical groups, thinking I'd run them by Kiefer and Monica on the one-in-a-billion chance they might recognize one of them.

The Jackson Porter list was more manageable, although still lengthy. He had a lot going on, especially considering the current state of the economy. I clicked through some of the articles, stopping when a familiar face startled me. Under the headline "Protestor Arrested for Assaulting Developer" was a three-year-old photograph of a very angry-looking Dyson Harding, Kyra's college friend, beaning Jackson Porter over the head with a placard. I skimmed the article and then stared at the black-and-white photo for a long moment, trying to figure out if it was just coincidence that Dyson Harding had led a protest against one of Porter's projects three years back and was now at it again, or if he had a vendetta against the man.

Only one way to find out. I called Kyra and asked if she could set up a meeting with her old buddy. "Today would be good," I told her.

She called back minutes later. "He'll meet you at noon," she said. "At the museum on campus. He's only got an hour between classes, so don't be late. Want me to come with you?"

"Thanks," I said, "but I think I can handle it on my own. What's he going to do if I piss him off? Chuck a pot shard at me?"

She laughed, but said, "Be careful. Dy's got a temper."

Fifteen

. . .

Two hours later, with Joel back in the office as dispatcher, I took my lunch hour and drove to the Vernonville Colonial College campus on the western edge of Vernonville. A pond complete with ducks and fountain for aeration fronted the combined student center and administration building, a newish edifice built to look old with red brick salvaged from the destruction of a nineteenth-century warehouse. I knew this because of the handy college brochure I picked up just inside the sliding glass doors that gave way to a maze of halls and offices. I stopped a passing student and asked for directions to the archaeology museum.

"I'm a math major," he said, staring at me as if I'd asked for a lemonade recipe.

"Right," I said, as if his non sequitur made sense.

A girl's voice piped up from behind me and I turned. "It's out the door to your right, down that walkway, and behind the building that looks like a pyramid."

"Great, thanks," I said, smiling at her. She smiled in return and continued on, weighed down by a backpack that looked like it held enough supplies to climb K2.

I followed her directions, wishing I'd worn a heavier jacket, and found myself in front of a small, square building with smoked glass windows and metal letters over the door spelling out "Richard D. Ruxton Museum of Archaeology." I figured old Dick Ruxton was a big-time donor. A muddy green SUV was the only vehicle in the small lot that fronted the museum. Pushing through the glass door, I found myself in a dimly lit space with a linoleum floor. Glass display cases lined the walls, and what looked like an Indian encampment of some kind, complete with teepee and canoe, sprouted from a display in the center of the room. Dr. Dyson Harding, half-eaten sandwich in hand, gestured to me from the far side of the room. He had on the same jacket he'd worn at the mall, and bread crumbs dotted his soul patch. He looked professorial and soft, not like a radical primed to take violent action to protest overdevelopment.

"I thought you might like the chance to see our museum while we talked," he said, swallowing. "Kyra said you're interested in archaeology."

Only when it provided a motive for murder. "I haven't been into it very long," I hedged. "I got interested when I was in Afghanistan. Some of the sites there are fascinating." Not that I'd been to any of them. We were strictly confined to base when not on patrol.

His eyes lit up. "What a fabulous opportunity. My area of specialty is early paleo-Indian settlements in Virginia, but I wouldn't turn down the opportunity to visit the BMAC." He chuckled.

At my blank look, he said, "The Oxus Civilization?"

I nodded in an "oh, yeah" kind of way, as if that had clarified anything.

"Right. So, Kyra said you were interested in helping with my petition drive?" His brown eyes, magnified by the glasses, studied me.

Damn Kyra. "I was hoping to find out more about it. What exactly are you protesting?"

His face darkened. "The destruction of hugely important archaeological sites by profit-driven developers."

"Specifically . . . ?"

"On that site by the mall, where Jackson Porter Developments wants to put up a golf resort—as if there weren't enough water-hogging golf courses in the county already— there's evidence of a pre-Clovis settlement. I've found unfluted bifacial tools on that site!"

Sounded like something used in prehistoric spa treatments.

"It needs to be protected, excavated, mined for the richness of historical, anthropological, and archaeological data it undoubtedly contains, not destroyed to cater to the recreational whims of the tiny segment of society that can afford to pay two hundred bucks to chase a dimpled ball around." He caught my upper arm and dragged me to a display case. "Look!"

I looked. What appeared to be chunks or bits of stone sat under the smudged glass, attended by labels with incomprehensible phrases like "flake blanks," "flint-working," and "refined biface preforms." My eyes glazed over. "Fascinating," I murmured. "And are these similar to the artifacts you were trying to protect when Porter's company broke ground for that Hyacinth Hills shopping center?"

Harding stiffened beside me. His voice when he spoke no

longer sounded like that of an enthusiastic professor going on about his favorite subject. It held an undertone of menace. "What are you really here for, Ms. Ferris? I get the feeling you're not quite the amateur archaeologist Kyra made you out to be."

"She exaggerates."

He blinked his eyes slowly, studying my face in unspeaking silence.

"I read that you were arrested for assaulting Jackson Porter three years back," I admitted. "And I was curious how it came about that you were protesting another of his developments. Surely there are other developers despoiling the landscape?"

"Are you mocking my work?"

"No, I'm not," I said truthfully. "It seems like important work, and I can see you take it seriously. I'd just like to know where you were last Sunday night."

Harding's lips thinned to a straight line. "You mean when some public benefactor killed Porter?"

I nodded, casually taking a step back from Harding, who was leaning uncomfortably close.

"You may be wearing a uniform, Ms. Ferris, but it's not one that gives you the right to question my movements." A fleck of spittle appeared at the corner of his mouth, but he didn't seem to notice. "You spend your days protecting the Mecca of crass consumerism, making sure spoiled shoppers have a pleasant experience lapping up the products that greedy corporations make them think they need. Do you know what life was like in this area fifteen thousand years ago? What people had to do to survive?" He was almost shouting.

"No," I said.

"No. You don't." An eerie half smile spread across his doughy face. "Are you married, Ms. Ferris? Do you have kids?"

The abrupt change of topic caught me off guard. "That's none of your business."

His gaze shifted to my left hand. "No, you don't. Pets?"

Something in my reaction pleased him because his smile grew. "When someone threatens what's important to me, I strike back."

I faced him stonily, unflinching, thinking that his soft exterior covered an iron will, and wondered what his coworkers thought of him. My mind flitted to the biology professor in Alabama who had opened fire at a department meeting, killing three of her colleagues. "Are you threatening me?" I asked, squaring my shoulders.

"Not at all," he said. "Just making my position clear." He blinked mildly.

"Well, thank you for your time, Harding," I said, deliberately omitting his title. I started for the door, angling toward it so I could keep an eye on him.

"Any time, Ms. Ferris," he called after me with fake bonhomie. "Any time. Tell Kyra I'll be by early next week to pick up the signatures she's collected."

If it were up to me, I'd bar him from the mall, but I just said, "I'll let her know." The door was only two steps in front of me and I burst through it into the weak February sunshine, feeling like I'd emerged into fresh air after weeks spent below ground in some dark, noxious cave. Dyson Harding was a nutter, a psycho, and it wouldn't surprise me at all to learn that he'd graduated from framing professors he disliked to murdering developers who stood in the way of his academic priorities.

I was in a burger drive-through, getting lunch before returning to the mall, when my phone rang. I recognized the number. "Grandpa!" I answered. "Where have you been?"

"Sorry, Emma-Joy," he said, sounding chipper. "I just got your messages. Can you come pick me up at the hospital? Confounded doctor says I can't drive for a couple of days."

Cold clutched at me. "The hospital? What—?"

"Nothing serious. I'll tell you when you get here." He gave me directions to a hospital about halfway between here and D.C.

I phoned Joel to let him know I'd be late getting back to work, grateful that Woskowicz wasn't around to grouse about it. "Anything going on?" I asked.

"Nada. We'll hold the fort until you get back. I hope your grampa's okay."

"Me, too." I hung up and headed for I-95, munching my burger as I drove. Visions of heart attacks, strokes, and hip-breaking falls whizzed through my head. Pulling into the hospital lot twenty-five minutes later, I took a deep breath. I walked as quickly as I could, my knee complaining the whole way, up the path to the hospital lobby. A hugely pregnant woman, whooshing air in and out as her husband counted, waddled by me, blocking my view. When she passed, I saw an old woman sitting at an information desk, a confused-looking couple studying a hospital directory, and Grandpa Atherton, standing near a window, his hands swathed in gauze with his fingers peeking out. His carriage was as erect as always, although his white hair was mussed and he wore what looked like a painter's white overall.

"Grandpa!" I rushed to him and hugged him. He smelled like charred rubber. "What on earth—"

"Let's talk in the car, Emma-Joy," he said. "I've had enough of this place. It's full of sick people."

Laughing, I took his arm and we proceeded to my Miata. "When are you going to get a real car?" he asked, stooping to get into the passenger seat. "Something with four doors?"

I slammed his door, climbed into the driver's side, and wended my way back to the interstate. "Now," I said, once we were cruising along at seventy-five, "spill it."

Grandpa awkwardly adjusted the heater to a warmer setting and said, "An old colleague got in touch yesterday—he needed my help with a little op he was running in Georgetown—and I've been strictly incommunicado. By the time we finished debriefing and they dropped me at the hospital, my phone battery had died—"

"What's wrong with your hands?"

"Just a first-degree burn," he reassured me. "No worse than a sunburn. Those incendiary devices are tricky."

"What—?"

"If I told you, I'd have to kill you," he said, interrupting my question.

I'd heard that quip a thousand times before, both from Grandpa and my friends in the military intelligence community, and I just rolled my eyes. "Doesn't the CIA have anyone under eighty they can use in their ops?" I asked.

"The CIA doesn't run ops on U.S. soil, Emma-Joy," he reminded me.

"Then who—?" I cut myself off. "Yeah, yeah, I know . . . you'd have to kill me."

He chuckled, but his voice was serious when he asked, "What's this I hear about another body at the mall? It was on the television at the hospital. A drug overdose?"

I told him about Robbie Porter's contacting me and last night's adventures. "You need to back away from this one, Emma-Joy," Grandpa said, surprising me. "That's three bodies in a week, assuming young Porter was the victim of foul play."

"You're advising me to be cautious, Mr. Incendiary Man? Is this a 'do as I say, not as I do' situation?"

"I'm a professional. I trained—"

A flash of anger whooshed through me. "So am I! Present tense. You retired twenty-some-odd years ago."

A wounded silence filled the car.

I sighed. "Look, Grandpa, I'm sorry. The situation is getting to me. I got my butt chewed by Detective Helland this morning, and Curtis Quigley pitched a hissy before I had my first cup of coffee. Then I met with a nut-job activist who might have killed Porter and who practically threatened to turn Fubar into kitty litter. I've had about four hours sleep in the last thirty-six and I'm cranky. I'm sorry. Please?"

"You're my favorite granddaughter," Grandpa said, reaching over to pat my knee with his mitted hand. "How'm I going to stay mad at you? Do you still need help catching those car artists?"

"And how," I said, relieved.

"Good, because I've got just the device to trip them up."

"How are you going to work your gadgets with your hands like that?"

"This is just for show," Grandpa said, waving his hands in the air. "Comes right off. I'll have those cameras in place this evening some time, and we'll have a line on those vandals in two days, tops."

"What did the doctor say?" I asked suspiciously as I pulled onto his street.

"He's a fussbudget," Grandpa said. "Doesn't know what he's talking about. Probably wrapped my hands up like this so he could charge my insurance company an extra thousand dollars for the gauze. I'll be just fine, Emma-Joy—don't you worry."

With that, he hopped spryly out of the car and proceeded to his front door. A second later he turned around and called to me, a sheepish look on his face, "Do you have your key? I left mine—well, I can't say where—when I sanitized before the op."

With a sigh, I got out and unlocked his front door. "You're sure you're okay?" I asked, hugging him again. He felt thin and bony beneath the coverall.

"Dandy." He winked and closed the door.

Back at the mall, I found Joel scanning the camera screens while playing a game of computer solitaire. "Busy day, huh?" I asked.

"Dead," he said. "How's your grampa?"

"Feisty," I said with a smile. "You want to go back out on the mean streets of Fernglen?"

"Sure thing," Joel said, abandoning his card game and standing. "Hey, you got a call from Elena Porter. She wants to talk to you."

I couldn't imagine why. First, I'd found her husband's body, then her son's. She must think I was some sort of jinx. "Did she say what she wanted?"

"Uh-uh. Says she's not up to leaving the house but that you can stop by any time this afternoon." Joel handed me a message slip with an address scrawled on it. "We can skip our swim this afternoon if you get tied up with Mrs. Porter." He tried to make it sound self-sacrificing, but I could tell he was trying to wiggle out of our training session.

Stifling a smile, I dashed the faint hope on his face. "No way. See you at the Y at four."

As much as I didn't want to face Elena Porter's grief,

I couldn't bring myself to ignore her request. So, when my shift ended, I found myself headed toward the Porter estate, an overlarge home on an acre of lawn, part of a gated community of similar houses owned by Vernonville's nouveau riche. The old money had homes on the east side of town, along the river. Even though the houses had different architectural styles—faux Georgian, faux Tuscan, faux Mediterranean—they looked depressingly similar in their newness and fauxness. A black MDX, a silver Mercedes, and a blue Volvo station wagon were parked in the semicircular drive fronting the Porter home. I left my Miata at the curb and walked up the drive.

Catherine Lang, the woman who had been with Elena Porter at Diamanté, opened the door when I rang the bell. Her dark hair was pulled back from her face and twisted into a knot low on her neck, and she wore a brown cashmere sweater with a deep V-neck over matching wool slacks. "EJ Ferris," I reminded her. "Mrs. Porter asked me to stop by." A melancholy piano tune played from deeper inside the house.

"Oh, yes," she said, opening the door wider. "Elena's distraught, as you can imagine. I'm trying to help out where I can, but, well, there's not much one can really do at a time like this, is there?"

She didn't wait for an answer, but led the way down a plushly carpeted hall to a large room with two cranberry leather sofas facing each other over a massive marble cocktail table. Other than that conversation grouping and a gleaming black grand piano, the room was empty, although I noted depressions in the carpet where other furniture pieces had stood. Faded squares on the pale green walls spoke of paintings that had been removed, and I speculated briefly that the Porters might have been selling off their stuff. Was Jackson Porter's development company on the rocks? Or was Elena Porter just undertaking a redecorating project?

A flood of sad and angry music issued from the piano and wrapped itself around me. I half closed my eyes to listen as Catherine said, "Elena, that mall cop is here." She cast me an apologetic look.

"EJ Ferris," I reminded her.

The music stopped in mid-measure as Elena Porter stood up behind the piano, her blond hair flatter than before, looking unwashed, and her plump cheeks sagging under their own weight. I was surprised to see she was the talented pianist, not having associated the socialite with musical virtuosity, or, I realized shamefacedly, any real depth of emotion. "You play beautifully," I said.

"Thank you," she said, coming around the piano to join us. "There was a time, when I was at Juilliard, but then I met Jackson—" She shook her head.

"I'm so sorry about your son," I said belatedly.

"Thank you." She stood as if stuffed with sawdust, arms hanging at her sides, so weighed down with grief she couldn't move. Or maybe she had taken something, Valium or the like, to take the edge off.

"Let's sit," Catherine Lang suggested, guiding her friend to one of the sofas.

I perched on the edge of the sofa across from them, feeling awkward and out of place. What was I doing here, invading this woman's grief? It was clear she was much more affected by her son's death than she had been by her husband's murder. "You asked me to come by—?"

With a glance at Elena, Catherine Lang spoke again. "Elena heard you found Robbie before—that is, was he alive when you found him? Did he say anything?"

Was this a case where a white lie would be comforting,

something along the lines of "He said to tell his mother he loved her and he's sorry?" Both women's gazes were glued to my face. "No," I said gently. "He was unconscious. He died almost immediately. I don't think he was in any pain," I offered, knowing it was hopelessly inadequate. My mind went back to the image of Robbie sprawled against the garage wall, his flesh as pale as the cement, his dark hair hanging limp across his forehead, his eyes open but unseeing. Describing his last moments in detail would not comfort his mother.

"How did you come to find him?" Catherine asked. She reached for one of her friend's hands and held it as Elena's gaze drifted to the window and its view of the tan sweep of lawn declining to the curb.

"He called me."

At that, Elena looked at me. "He did? Why?"

"He said he knew something about his father's murder."

"What could he—" Elena began, only to be trampled by Catherine Lang's "I won't believe Jackson was into drugs!"

Elena and I stared at her. Her cheeks reddened. "I'm sorry. But if Robbie knew something, wouldn't that mean—"

She left the thought unfinished. I wondered if she were right. Could Porter have been a drug dealer or manufacturer? Were his development projects fronts for distribution? Or maybe he was a hardcore user and his habit was sucking all the money out of his bank accounts. That might explain the missing furniture. I reined in my thoughts. I was speculating way ahead of the evidence, always a risky thing to do.

"Jackson was a bastard," Elena said. A little color showed in her cheeks. "A bastard. But I never knew him to take drugs." She looked bewildered. "And my Robbie. Last year, when he came out of rehab, I hoped—" She began to sob, turning aside to bury her face in the sofa.

"I'll let myself out," I said, acutely uncomfortable.

Catherine Lang nodded as she patted Elena's back and murmured to her. Walking quickly to the door, I opened it and took a deep breath of the cold air that blew in. The brief visit made me want to connect with my family, and I dialed my mom's cell phone number as I slid behind the wheel. Not getting an answer, I left an affectionate message and hung up. Dad's number also went to voice mail. Huh. They must be traveling. The only thing that detached my father from his cell phone was an on-camera performance or airline restrictions. Becoming aware of a figure watching me from the front window, I put the car in gear, filled with a new resolve. This murderer had had things his or her own way long enough. I was going back to the scene of the crime to get some answers.

Sixteen

. . .

At midnight, the parking lot behind the mall was an expanse of black nothingness, lit only by the occasional lamppost. Joel's minivan, the vehicle his parents had passed along to him and which his financial situation obliged him to accept despite the van's rock-bottom rating on the "cool" scale, glided to a stop outside the delivery door closest to Diamanté. Very few of the stores had doors opening directly to the outside; most opened to narrow halls that mall patrons never saw. They were used mainly for deliveries.

"Okay, Joel, you're the body," I said, hopping out of the van. I swept my gaze along the mall's roofline, making sure we were between the fields of vision of the two nearest cameras.

I thumbed the push-to-talk radio clipped to my shirt. "Can you see us, Edgar?"

"Negatory," came the reply in the big man's laconic voice.

Woskowicz had stuck him with the midshift until he hired a replacement for Weasel.

"Why do I have to be the body?" Joel asked, nonetheless moving to the back of the van and arranging himself in a supine position in the cargo area.

"Because," Kyra explained in an exasperated voice, "if we two weak womenfolk can carry your hefty corpse into Diamanté, then it proves anyone could have offed Porter. We've already been over this." She looked sleek and dangerous in a black turtleneck over polypropylene running leggings that showed the formidable muscles in her thighs.

I'd asked Kyra for her help as soon as I got home from the Porter's house, and run the idea past Joel at the pool. They'd agreed to help me reenact the crime, hoping we might learn something useful. Since we had no idea where the murderer shot Jackson Porter, we were just doing the body-disposal bit. We'd clued Edgar in so he wouldn't call the cops on us if he spotted us behaving suspiciously.

Kyra eyed Joel where he lolled artistically, eyes closed, on the van's floor. "Do you suppose he was already naked when they took him in, or did they nakedify him after they got him in the store?" We pondered Joel whose cheeks flushed pink, making him look like the world's healthiest dead man.

"I don't know," I finally said. "We'll keep him clothed for now." I winked at Kyra.

"You are not taking off my clothes, even in the interest of catching a murderer," Joel said, alarmed, rising to a half-sitting position.

"Lie down, corpse," Kyra said, shoving at his chest. "I've got his legs." Hooking her arms under Joel's knees, she dragged him to the edge of the van.

I moved in near his shoulders, awkwardly maneuvering until I could get my hands into his armpits. "Okay. Don't drop him."

"Yeah, don't drop him," Joel pleaded from the corner of his mouth.

We took ten steps toward the mall, Joel's butt sinking closer to the asphalt with every step, a crescent of pale flesh showing where his sweatpants pulled down. Finally, Kyra said, "I've gotta put him down for a moment. He weighs more than a blue whale. You ever think about mixing in a salad?" she asked him.

Joel played dead, but I noticed he sucked in his stomach. I bit back a smile.

"You know," I said, "if the murderer had this planned out, maybe he brought along a dolly or something."

"Or found one inside?" Kyra suggested.

"Stay here." Leaving my friends, I used my key to unlock the delivery door. The hall that snaked behind Diamanté and a dozen other stores branched off to my left. Ahead and to my right were the restrooms and the janitorial supply closet. And right outside the men's room sat the huge, gray trash bin Fernando and the other janitors hauled around all day. Bingo! Grabbing it by its thick, rubber lip, I hauled it outside.

"That's more like it," Kyra said.

"Yuck," Joel said.

"You're dead. You don't get a vote on mode of transport," I told him. "Ready?" With a lot of effort and some serious grunting, Kyra and I hefted Joel so he lodged butt-down in the trash can, his arms and shins draping down the sides.

"No way could one person have done this," Kyra said, panting.

The muscles in my arms and chest burned. "Maybe a

strong man," I said. "And he'd probably have had to drag him, which would've scraped up his feet if he'd already been naked."

With Kyra pushing and me pulling, we got the trash can into the hallway and let the door bang shut behind us. It was easier going on the smooth linoleum, and we arrived behind Diamanté a minute later.

"Time?" I asked.

Joel looked at the stopwatch on his wrist. "Ten minutes and twenty-three seconds since we pulled up," he said.

"Okay. Since we don't have a key to Diamanté, we just have to guesstimate from here on out. Say thirty seconds to get the door open, a minute to push the trash can to the display window. How long to undress the body?"

Kyra shrugged. "Three or four minutes if there were two of them? Longer if it was a solo routine."

"Sounds about right. So, twenty-five minutes, tops, from start to finish?"

They nodded.

"And the only cameras they had to worry about were the exterior ones since there aren't any in these back halls," Joel said.

"How would the murderer know that?" Kyra asked.

"With a little recce," I said. "Wander back here like you're going to the bathroom, then drift down the hall. It's not like the cameras are hidden or anything. The mall wants people to know they're there to discourage shoplifting and vandalism."

We retraced our steps to the outer door. As we started back toward the van, I asked, "So what did Weasel see, if anything, that got him killed?"

"It's not likely he was patrolling down the delivery hall," Joel said.

"The car." I knew it. "He was driving around and he saw the car, van, whatever. He probably didn't think much about it until the next day when he heard about the murder."

"Or," Kyra suggested, "he stopped and challenged whoever it was."

"Not Weasel," Joel and I said together. "He was too lazy," Joel explained.

"And I can't believe even Weasel could come across a murderer disposing of a body and not call it in," I said.

"So, he saw the car and noted the plate number," Joel said, climbing into the driver's seat of his van. "And then what? Phoned up the murderer the next day instead of giving the info to the police?"

"Or maybe he saw whoever it was walking back to the car *after* propping up Porter in the window," Kyra said.

"Or maybe someone paid Weasel to murder Porter and then rubbed him out to make things nice and tidy," Joel said, swiveling his head around to look at Kyra in the backseat.

"Eyes on the road. You've been watching way too many Robert De Niro movies," Kyra said disapprovingly.

We rode in thoughtful silence as Joel drove back to my place. Without more data to work with, it was impossible to figure out exactly how the murderer had moved Porter's body or how Weasel had gotten a line on the murderer, if he had. It was completely possible that his murder had nothing to do with the Porter case; it wouldn't surprise me at all to learn Weasel numbered ex-cons and other undesirables among his personal acquaintances. I sighed. About the only thing this exercise had accomplished was proving it was possible to get a body into Diamanté without being spotted, and it was likely Porter was still clothed when he arrived at the mall. Big whoop. That and a fiver would buy a cup of coffee.

Saturdays are Fernglen's busiest days, and we had a full complement of officers, including a still-sniffling Captain Woskowicz, on duty by opening time. Grandpa Atherton called to tell me he had his cameras in place and would keep me posted. I volunteered to do dispatch duty for the morning, to which Woskowicz just grunted before disappearing into his office and closing the door. Keeping an eye on the cameras, I went back through the log for the week, organizing the data to put it into a PowerPoint presentation for the weekly Monday-morning briefing to Quigley and his staff. With two deaths at the mall, this week's briefing would be considerably longer than usual. Putting the data into succinct bullets, I did a slide on Jackson Porter's death and one on Robbie Porter's, ending with the same status on both: OPEN. I put together a slide about the Herpes Hut liberation, finding a photo of a Komodo dragon to jazz it up a bit. I ended that one with an optimistic status: ninety-eight percent of animals recovered. I didn't point out that the one snake still at large was a fifteen-foot python.

Titling the next slide "Vehicle Vandalism," I clicked back through the log entries to list the dates and approximate times of the graffiti attacks, adding the type of car in another column. Leaving a space for today (because I was sure the taggers would get in their one-a-day quota before the day was over), I listed the data for Friday, then Thursday, and all the way back to Monday and Kenneth Downs's BMW. When I reviewed last Sunday's entries, I couldn't find one related to vehicle vandalism. I checked again, reading through each entry carefully. Nothing.

I pushed back in my chair and tapped a pencil against the desk. Huh. Several explanations immediately popped into my mind. It had happened on Weasel's shift and he hadn't bothered to log it. Possible. The taggers had taken the day off, maybe to attend a tagger's convention or because they ran out of spray paint. Unlikely. The person whose car got vandalized hadn't reported it. Even more unlikely. Car owners needed a report for their insurance. Unless . . . I sat up straight, excitement prickling along my arms. Unless they had a good reason for not reporting it, like they didn't want it known they were at the mall. Was it even remotely possible that the taggers had spray painted the murderer's vehicle? I forced myself to take a deep breath and think it through. Maybe the owner had reported the vandalism to the Vernonville PD, rather than to us.

Jabbing at the phone buttons, I waited for what seemed an eternity for the officer who answered the phone to get back to me: no reports of vandalism from Fernglen Galleria last Sunday. I hung up. Taking another deep breath, I called Grandpa and told him what I suspected. "It's more important than ever to get a lead on the taggers," I said. "With any luck, they'll remember what car they vandalized last Sunday."

"That's good thinking, Emma-Joy," Grandpa said. "I'm on it. Out here."

I debated calling Detective Helland. He'd probably sneer at my theory, the way he had when I suggested the pair who liberated Kiefer's reptiles might have a connection with Jackson Porter. Reluctantly, I decided I had to call him anyway. He had the resources—if he chose to use them—to check with body shops to see if any of the suspects had had a car repainted this week. I couldn't do that.

A long silence greeted my new theory after I laid it out for Helland. Finally, he said, "Do you have any idea how many paint and body shops there are within a fifty-mile radius of here?"

"Dozens."

"Hundreds. No way can I spare the manpower to call them all to see if, by chance, they've painted one of a dozen cars owned by one of the people connected with this case." His tone was more weary than scornful. "But it's not bad thinking on your part, and if you catch up with the taggers, let me know. I could certainly move forward with more specific information, like make and model."

I hung up, slightly miffed by his condescending "not bad thinking on your part." It was damn good thinking, and as soon as Grandpa got a bead on the taggers, I'd prove it to Detective Helland. I finished up the briefing presentation by eleven o'clock, emailed it to Captain Woskowicz, and summoned Joel to the office so I could take a quick lunch break and get back on patrol. Sitting in the office was driving me stir-crazy. If I looked for another job, it would have to be something where I could be out and about, not a jail sentence in a cubicle.

In the food court, I bought a salad from the deli place and settled at my favorite table, away from the crowd, partially hidden by the spreading branches of a ficus. I hadn't taken more than two bites of my chicken Caesar—sans dressing—when Jay Callahan plopped into the chair opposite me, smiling broadly. His dark red hair curled around his ears, and his hazel eyes surveyed my meal with pity. "You need a cookie to go with that." He produced a chocolate chip cookie and waved it under my nose.

"I haven't worked out in two days." The sessions with Joel didn't count since coaching him didn't burn nearly as many calories as my usual lap swimming. "No cookies."

With a shrug, he took a bite of the cookie. I forked up another unexciting mouthful of romaine.

"Heard any more about our body?" he asked.

"Robbie Porter's body."

"I heard the autopsy said it was a drug overdose—heroin. No sign of foul play."

I looked up from my rabbit fodder. "Really? Where'd you hear that?" And why hadn't Helland bothered to fill me in when we talked? I could just hear him say it was an official investigation and he didn't share with civilians.

"Sources." He grinned.

"Since when does a cookie mogul have 'sources'?" I asked.

"'Mogul'—I like the sound of that." He pushed back in his chair so it balanced on two feet and smiled, teasing me with his nonresponsiveness.

I laid my fork down with a snap, breaking one of the plastic tines. "Look—who or what are you? I don't believe you're really a cookie franchisee. There's not a single other merchant at this mall who spends as much time lurking in the garage after hours as you do. I'm surprised we didn't run into you last night."

Interest flickered in his eyes. "Why? What were you up to last night?"

I didn't see any harm in telling him about our reenactment. "I half expected you to turn up," I said when I'd finished. "After all, you've been Johnny-on-the-spot at every after-hours event this week."

"Other fish to fry," he said briefly.

I scanned his face. "C'mon, tell me who you're with. You feel like a fed. DEA? FBI?"

Clanging the chair's legs back down, he leaned toward me and whispered, "Can you keep a secret?"

Warily, I nodded, conscious of the chocolate chip sweetness of his breath at such close range. His eyes had flecks of gold in the hazel irises. A deadly serious look settled on his face. "I'm an industrial spy for Keebler, reporting on mall cookie recipes for the elves. I'm really an elf myself, but I grew taller than the norm, so they send me out on these missions because I blend in better with the populace at large. Get it, at *large*? And, I think you're really cute, for a non-elf." The irrepressible smile broke out again.

Caught between amusement at his outrageousness and annoyance at my gullibility—I'd thought he was going to tell me the truth—I caught his right ear between my thumb and forefinger and pinched it.

"Ow."

"Where're the pointy ears, elf boy?"

He gave me a wounded look. "Sure, make fun of me like all the elf boys and girls do. They don't even let me join in elf games. I've had to file more than one ear-discrimination suit."

I couldn't help myself: I laughed. He grinned, clearly pleased at having amused me.

"Well, elf boy, I've got to get back to work."

"Have they found that python yet?" Jay asked, gallantly gathering up my tray and trash.

"No," I said. I'd reported the wet trail I'd found on the night shift to the maintenance crew, and they'd looked under and around the escalator. Nothing. "I'm afraid maybe whoever turned the other reptiles loose kept Agatha. I don't know what she's worth, but probably a lot."

Jay's question reminded me that I hadn't checked in with Kiefer lately, so I headed to the Herpes Hut. The store was doing a booming business—maybe some of the publicity about loose snakes had paid off—and Kiefer looked harried.

"No, I haven't heard anything about Agatha," he said when I asked. "There was a guy in here yesterday, convinced he'd seen her in the Sears appliance center, but it was just some of that ducting for clothes dryers. The crinkly silver stuff. Who thinks a python is silver?" He shook his head.

Leaving Kiefer to his customers, I Segwayed to Diamanté, intending to ask Finola if she had an address or phone number for Velma Maldonado, Jackson Porter's alleged mistress. I hadn't thought to seek her out earlier, but it struck me that she might know something about Porter's comings and goings, and maybe his business dealings, that would shed light on his murder. I didn't know if Helland had bothered to get in touch with Ms. Maldonado, but I figured it couldn't hurt to talk to her.

Diamanté also had a surfeit of customers, and I had to wait ten minutes, browsing the racks, before Finola could break free. When I told her what I was after, she scrunched up her face doubtfully. "I don't know . . ."

"I just want to talk to her," I said. "I won't tell her you gave me her data."

"Oh, what the hell," she said, pulling out a business card and scribbling something on the back of it. "It's not like she's ever going to darken my door again without a sugar daddy to foot the bill. Jackson didn't used to like them quite so young or quite so dim," she said with a hint of venom in her voice.

"Did you and he have a thing?" I asked.

She looked up, instinctive denial on her face. Then, a rueful smile tugged at the corners of her mouth. "Is it so obvious? It was years ago. But we were still friends, still . . . fond of each other."

What my brother would call "friends with benefits," I suspected. Finola handed me the card. She'd written "Destiny's Dance Studio" on it. "She's a dance teacher," Finola explained. "I don't have her number, but I'm sure you can catch up with her at the studio. Monica says she practically lives there."

I was confused. "Monica?" I looked around the store but didn't see her.

"Yes. She's Velma's mother. Didn't you know?" Finola raised her penciled brows.

My flabbergasted expression must have answered her. "A month or so after Jackson took up with Velma, late last year, he asked if I would hire Monica. He said she'd lost her last job when the store she was working for folded. For old times' sake, he said." She snorted. "At the time, I had all the help I needed, but when Joanie got pregnant and quit a couple weeks ago, I told him I'd give her a chance. She's really good with the customers," she added.

"Thanks," I said dazedly and walked out of the store, staring at the card in my hand. Jackson Porter's girlfriend's mother worked for Diamanté. The implications flooded over me as I paused by the Segway. Monica had a key to the store. She was supposed to open the shop the morning he died, but conveniently didn't show up, ensuring someone else discovered the body. She denied knowing Jackson, even though she'd surely met him if he was in a relationship with her daughter and recommending her—Monica—for jobs. I stopped and thought. She hadn't actually denied knowing him, I realized, thinking back on our conversation; she'd implied it by saying she'd only worked at the store a short time. Did Helland know about this connection? Somehow, I doubted it.

Seventeen

. . .

I worked the rest of my shift on autopilot, anxious for the moment I could ditch my uniform and head over to Destiny's Dance Studio to talk to Velma Maldonado. I considered calling ahead but decided not to give her a chance to say she didn't want to talk to me. In between discouraging teenagers from skateboarding in the mall and telling a middle-aged woman she couldn't have her ferret on a leash because pets weren't allowed at Fernglen, I spun theories about why Monica or her daughter might have wanted Jackson Porter dead.

Maybe Monica hated Porter for carrying on with her daughter. Maybe Velma hated him because he was cheating on her or dumping her. Maybe . . . the possibilities were almost endless, and I forced myself to stop thinking about them since I was just guessing in the absence of data. At three thirty that afternoon, though, I pulled up in front of Destiny's Dance Studio, determined to get some facts. The studio sat in a high-end strip mall on the north end of Vernonville. Like the other stores in the center—a tea shop, an Amish furniture store, a Realtor's office, and a Christian bookstore—it had a green awning, and the studio's name swung on a wooden sign hung over the sidewalk. Cars jammed the parking lot, and girls ranging in age from three to midteens scurried from the lot to the studio, freezing in thin dance gear of leotards, tights, and, on a few of the girls, short flippy skirts.

I followed a giggling trio into the studio, which had a counter on the left and dance costumes pinned to a cork-board along the right-hand wall, mixed in with photos of award-winning dance ensembles hoisting trophies. Dead ahead was a studio with a large glass window through which I could see girls of about ten pliéing under the watchful eye of a thin woman in her fifties. I didn't figure her for Velma Maldonado. Parents, mostly mothers, milled around, craning their necks to watch their little ballerinas in the studio, chatting with each other, and texting on cell phones.

"May I help you?" asked a harried-looking woman from behind the counter. She was stout with improbably black hair and the whisper of a matching mustache.

"I'm thinking about starting my daughter in dance," I lied, "and a friend recommended your studio. She said Velma is just fabulous with kids. I was wondering if I could observe a class?"

"Oh, sure." The woman nodded, turning to accept the check a client held out to her. "She's in Studio D right now with the hip-hop class. To your right." She pointed with her chin toward the hall that branched off on either side of the lobby.

I took the right-hand branch, passing one studio with adult tappers making a racket and another where teenage girls in leotards practiced split leaps. The last studio on the right had a smaller window than the others, just a porthole set into the door above a large red "D." I peered in, nodding my head in tempo with the Black Eyed Peas song leaking around the door. Six tweens, including two boys, undulated their bodies in sync with the beat. A slim young woman stood with her back to me, showing one girl how to start a movement in her left hand and let it ripple up her arm, through her shoulders, and down her other arm. The teacher wore a classic pink leotard with black tights and had her black hair pulled back into a messy ponytail. When she turned, I saw delicate features with a slightly broad nose, sloe eyes, and a lush mouth. Velma was half Filipina, I decided, and probably no more than twenty-five years old.

The hip-hop tune reminded me of how much I'd liked dancing, back before my knee got shot up. I let myself feel melancholy for a moment, as I watched the kids gyrate and spin and fling their bodies around exuberantly. Ten minutes later Velma cut off the music with a remote and clapped her hands. "That's it for today. On Tuesday we'll start learning our routine for the recital."

"Yay," the kids chorused, rushing for the door and the waiting mothers who had gathered in the hall behind me. I stepped aside to avoid being flattened, then slipped through the door as the last dancer exited. Velma was removing a CD from the stereo and didn't see me enter.

"Miss Maldonado?"

She spun around with fluid grace. "Yes?" Her skin was almond colored, smooth, and unlined.

"I understand you were friends with Jackson Porter," I said after introducing myself.

"Yes?" Her tone was warier.

"Can you tell me about him?" I left my question open-ended, not knowing exactly what to ask.

"Why should I? I already talked to the police. Are you a reporter?"

Interest flickered in her eyes, and I saw her making mental calculations about how much her story might be worth if a tabloid was interested.

I explained who I was, and after a moment she said, "There's nothing much to tell. We dated for a while and he died."

"Was he worried about anything recently? Did he mention anyone being mad at him?"

"Besides the usuals?" Pulling a pot of lip gloss from a tote bag, she stuck her pinky in it and smoothed the goo over her lips. The scent of licorice drifted to me.

"The usuals?" Her nonchalance took me aback. Who talked so easily about their lover being hated by a posse of people?

Cynicism gleamed in her brown eyes. "He got hate mail from enviro-nazis every week, especially when one of his developments made the news, along with pictures and videos of the poor, helpless creatures he was exterminating." Her tone made it clear she wasn't shedding too many tears about the demise of some obscure rodent or amphibian. "And, of course, there was always Elena." She rolled her eyes.

"His wife knew about you?"

"Oh, please. She'd have had to be blind, deaf, and dumb not to know. I was just one in a long line. I had no illusions that I was the end of the line, either. Jackson had the attention span of a mayfly—here today, gone tomorrow. It was fun while it lasted, and I'm sorry he's dead, but I'm off to the Big Apple next month—I got a part dancing in an off-off-Broadway play—and our . . . liaison was coming to an end, anyway." She drew out the word "liaison" as if she liked the feel of it on her tongue.

"How did you two meet?"

"I went out with Robbie a couple of times when we were in high school." Tears sprang to her eyes, but she dashed them away. "I can't believe he's dead. He was a nice boy, really liked me, but he always seemed kind of lost, you know? Anyway, I ran into Jackson at a charity thing last fall and, well, one thing led to another."

"What did Robbie think about that?" I asked.

"What do you mean?" She looked genuinely puzzled.

"That you'd moved on from dating him to dating his father. That would rile a lot of guys." To say the least. It might drive some men to murder. Was that what Robbie Porter had wanted to tell me—that he'd killed his father? Maybe his conscience got to him and the overdose was suicide, not an accident and not murder.

"Robbie and I were never that serious," Velma said dismissively. Pulling a pink cardigan from her dance bag, she shrugged her slim arms into the sleeves. "And Jackson, well . . ." She trailed off, as if unsure how to characterize her relationship with Jackson Porter, or unwilling to. "Look, I've got to go." She slung the dance bag over her shoulder.

I followed her out of the small studio. After threading our way through knots of bumblebee-costumed preschoolers, we reached the lobby. "Porter got your mom the job at Diamanté, didn't he?" I asked.

"Yeah? So?" She waved to the woman behind the counter and pushed open the door, letting in chilly air.

"So what did she think of your relationship?"

Velma turned to face me on the sidewalk fronting the parking lot, the wind tugging strands from her loose ponytail and blowing them across her face. "Where do you get off being all judgmental about what Jackson and I had together? 'What did Robbie think? What did your mom think?' Who cares? It was between me and Jackson. Period. We enjoyed each other's company. We had great sex. Get over it." She gave me a condescending once over. "Maybe you just need to get laid."

She beeped open a dark blue Honda CR-V parked in front of us, flung her bag onto the passenger seat, and climbed in. Without a word of farewell, she backed out and drove away.

I stood as if rooted to the sidewalk, shocked by her words. Was I judgmental? I sorted through my thoughts about Velma and Jackson, colored by Finola's description of him as a "sugar daddy." Yes, I had to admit their relationship seemed more like a business transaction than a love affair to me, but it wasn't my business. I had no right to judge Velma. Or Jackson Porter, for that matter. I drifted toward my car, annoyed with myself for letting my personal feelings influence the interview. I'd never learn anything more from Velma. Remembering her last words made me bang my hand against the steering wheel. Was it really so obvious I hadn't had sex in the modern era?

"Yes," Kyra said unequivocally when I asked her that question as we ate dinner at a Thai bistro before her roller derby bout. I'd swum with Joel and dressed in my favorite midnight blue sweater. "You might as well be wearing a chastity belt over your clothes."

I choked on a pepper that seared my mouth, and swallowed half a glass of water. "You're exaggerating," I said when I could talk again.

Kyra just grinned in a know-it-all way. "Tell me you've gotten laid since moving to Vernonville."

I shoveled a forkful of noodles into my mouth to account for my silence. Truth was, I hadn't had sex since the night before my unit shipped out to Afghanistan, almost three years ago. My boyfriend at the time, Ross, had spent that last night with me, and we'd parted tearfully in the morning. Then had come the long, celibate eleven months in Afghanistan—Ross had sent me a "Dear Jane" email two months into my tour—followed by months in the hospital and more months in rehab for my knee, then more time getting settled in Vernonville. Since then, it just hadn't come up, so to speak.

"I haven't been in the mood," I told Kyra. "With my knee—"

She blasted a laugh that had the tiny Thai waitress shooting us a worried look. She lowered her voice. "Since when do knees play a part in S-E-X? You just need to get your mojo back, girlfriend. Find an attractive man and let nature take its course. Stop thinking so much. I guarantee you that not one man in a hundred gives a damn what your knee looks like. You're the only one with hang-ups about it." She sat back in her chair. "There. I said it. I've been thinking it for months, and now I've said it. Are you mad at me?"

I tugged at the neckline of my sweater, which had a habit of slipping off my shoulder. "No," I said finally. "I'm not mad. You're probably right." Knowing she was right didn't mean I could move past it immediately, though. I'd grown up in the Hollywood culture that defined women by their physical beauty, where birthmarks were lasered off, cheekbones surgically enhanced, and cellulite thighs suctioned. Even though I'd escaped into the military, which valued a body for how many push-ups it could do or how fast it could run a mile, not how it looked, I couldn't completely ditch the cultural indoctrination of my younger years. And besides, now my knee would get failing marks from both my worlds: it looked like crap and crapped out when I needed it.

Apparently satisfied that she'd said enough, Kyra resumed eating. Her long kinky hair fell forward into her noodles, and she flipped it back impatiently. "So do you think Velma could have killed Porter?"

"Maybe, but I don't see why she would. Her mom looks like a better bet to me—maybe she had the hots for Porter herself, or she was mad at him for taking up with Velma."

"Sounds to me like Velma is well able to look after herself," Kyra said, chasing a mussel around her plate with her fork.

"Yeah, and so is your buddy, Dyson Harding," I said. "He struck me as someone with a real capacity for violence. And he's seriously perturbed about that development going in and burying his precious fluted whatevers."

"Flutes?" Kyra knit her brow. "He found instruments?"

"Something to do with arrowheads, I think," I said. "Or tools. I didn't stick around for the lecture. The point is, he's rabid on the subject."

"What about that girl who said she found blood in her backyard and that her mom killed Porter?"

"Marcia Cleaton," I said slowly, realizing I'd let Julia Cleaton's mother drift off my radar after telling Detective Helland about her. "I'll see if I can get Helland to tell me what she said when he interviewed her." Fat chance. When I'd learned about Cleaton, the police still thought Gatchel killed Jackson Porter. I wondered if Helland had followed up after we'd found Weasel's body.

My cell phone rang and I glanced at it. "It's Grandpa," I said with an apologetic look at Kyra as I answered it.

"Emma-Joy, I've got 'em." Grandpa Atherton's excited voice greeted me. "We're going south on I-95 and just passed the first Fredericksburg exit."

" 'Them?' You're chasing the taggers?"

"That's affirmative."

"You were just supposed to get a license plate number!"

"My hidden camera caught them as they spray painted a van, but their license plate is covered with mud and I couldn't get the number. So I decided to follow them."

"But you're not supposed to be driving."

"Oh, I'm not," he said. "My friend is."

What friend? Before I could ask who was with him, he said, "Oh, they're getting off."

He read me the exit number, promised to keep me updated, and told me to get my fanny on the road.

"On my way. Don't—" He hung up before I could tell him not to try to confront the taggers on his own.

Twenty-five minutes later, I pulled my Miata up behind the dark blue van Grandpa Atherton told me he'd borrowed for "the op," and took stock of my surroundings. We were parked on a quiet residential street in Fredericksburg, lined with 1980s-vintage two-story houses with two-car garages and well-kept yards graced by mature trees. That was about all I could make out in the dark. Getting out of my car, I closed the door quietly and advanced on the van. When I reached the driver's window, I rapped lightly on the tinted glass. The window buzzed down, and I found myself looking into the amused face of Theresa Eshelman, the mall-walking day care center owner. The silver strands in her short gray hair stood out, and she wore a red cashmere sweater.

"Wha—" I started.

Grandpa Atherton leaned forward from the passenger seat. "You know Theresa, don't you, Emma-Joy? Theresa, this is my granddaughter, Emma-Joy Ferris."

"EJ," I said, shaking hands awkwardly through the window.

"We met that morning I was asking about Robbie Porter," Grandpa said. "She offered to help me with my wheelchair. This is our first date."

"You really know how to show a gal a good time, Grandpa," I said drily.

Theresa laughed. "Your grandfather is the most interesting man I've met in years," she said.

"'Interesting' is one word for him," I agreed. "Where are the taggers?"

Grandpa pointed out his window to a house on the north side of the street. I noticed he'd ditched his gauze mitts but had bandages strapped around his palms. The house was pale—white or tan—and the garage door was up a bit more than a foot, maybe to let a cat in and out. "Stay here," I told Grandpa and Theresa, "and call the police if I'm not back in fifteen minutes."

Without waiting for an answer, I crossed the street. The house was quiet. Light leaked in thin stripes through blinds and slipped past the edge of drawn curtains on the ground floor, but didn't provide enough illumination to make out much. Shadows moved behind the drapes of what I took to be a living room or family room. I hesitated on the driveway. Knock? Or check out the garage? The convenient gap between the garage door and driveway called to me. It struck me that maybe not being a police officer bound by rules and regulations and the need for probable cause and warrants could be a good thing. With a flash of regret for my sweater, I dropped to the ground and scootched under the door on my back, turning my head sideways to avoid scraping my face on the rubber gasket edging the door. I stood and brushed off my clothes as best I could before pulling a mini flashlight from my pocket. I kept it in the glove box of the Miata for emergencies.

Turning a slow three hundred sixty degrees, I ran the beam over the bare walls and gray-painted floor of a standard-issue suburban garage. A red lawnmower hunkered in one corner, a bicycle hung from an overhead rack, and an old Frigidaire hummed near the door I presumed led to the kitchen. Most of the space, however, was taken up by a white van with ELMER'S ELECTRICAL SUPPLY stenciled on the side. I peered through the passenger window, spying a pair of paint-stained work gloves in the foot well and sunglasses clipped to the visor. A partition separated the seats from the back of the van, and I couldn't see anything incriminating. I tried the windowless back door. Locked. However, the sharp smell of spray paint seeped from the van, and I stifled a cough.

Something nudged my shin hard, and I stumbled against the van, eliciting a dull clang. My heartbeat tripled, and I swung the flashlight toward the floor, ready to use it as a weapon if I had to. The beam picked up the tricolor coat, heavy muzzle, and long ears of a basset hound, who regarded me hopefully from a pair of brown eyes. His tail whisked back and forth across the garage floor. He nosed my shin again, then sat.

"Nice dog," I whispered. "Nice, quiet dog."

He apparently took that as an invitation, because he stood on his hind legs, put his forepaws on my thighs, and snuffled vigorously at my slacks, no doubt smelling Fubar. Reaching out a tentative hand, I patted his bony head, mentally cursing myself for not having taken the time to scope out the place before I rolled under the door. I was lucky I hadn't been attacked by a Rottweiler or pit bull, or ratted out by a Yorkie or Chihuahua.

"Woooo." My new buddy pointed his nose up and howled.

I didn't know if that was hound for "Let's play fetch," "You smell like a stupid-ass cat," or "Come quick! There's an intruder in the garage." I clapped my hands around his muzzle to shut him up. "Ssh."

He looked up at me dolefully from his droopy eyes and wagged his tail, apparently not offended by my attempts to silence him. I dug in my jacket pockets, thinking I might have a leftover energy bar or something I could bribe him with while I slipped under the door. All I found was a lint-crusted cough drop that had worked its way out of the wrapper. I offered it to the hound on the flat of my hand, and after a moment of snuffling, he licked it up. With a final pat on his head, I hurried toward the gap under the door.

I was almost there when the door to the house squeaked open and a bar of light pierced the garage. I flicked off the flashlight and dropped to my haunches behind the van as a young man's voice called, "Dolly? Are you back?"

The basset hound—who I guess was a her, not a him—trotted over, tags clinking, to investigate the new game I was playing as I huddled against the rear of the van. She thrust her nose toward my face and gave me a comprehensive lick. I made shooing gestures. "Go see your daddy," I whispered.

"Woohr. Whuf!" she said.

"Dolly?" Footsteps clopped down the two stairs into the garage. "Did you do your chores?"

I gave Dolly a shove, barely budging her. Who knew bassets weighed so much? After a long moment, she ambled away, responding to the man slapping his hands against his thighs. With a sigh of relief, I heard him greet the dog. "Good girl," he said. Footsteps climbed the two steps again, accompanied by the clicking of the dog's toenails, and I tensed myself to duck under the garage door as soon as the man closed the house door. Before I could move, a motor hummed and the door rattled toward the floor, trapping me in the garage.

Eighteen

• • •

Well, shit. This was not good. Blackness enveloped me now that the closed door kept all ambient light out. I clicked the flashlight back on, wondering if there was a door to the side yard I might have missed. Nope. My choices were raise the garage door and alert everyone inside with its rumbling, sneak into the house and hope there wasn't someone standing in the kitchen to call the police, or spend the night in the garage and hope I could sneak out when they raised the door in the morning. Or, maybe . . . I pulled out my cell phone and dialed Grandpa's number.

"I'm trapped in the garage," I said when he answered. "I need a distraction, something that will get them to open the garage door or leave the house for a few minutes."

"We're on it," Grandpa said. He hung up before I could ask what he had in mind.

Time seemed to crawl in the cold, dark garage, but it wasn't more than ten minutes by my watch before the door jerked and grumbled upward. Hidden by the van's bulk, I rolled under the door before it was a quarter of the way up. I stood pressed up against the garage's brick exterior, listening with a smile to the playacting going on inside.

"I don't know how your cat could have gotten in here," the young man's voice said. "Dolly was in here, and she doesn't much like cats."

"But I'm sure I saw my naughty little Clementine slip under the door," Theresa said in a dithery voice not at all like her usual manner. "She's such a naughty kitty."

"Which house did you say you're in again?" the man asked. "I don't think I've seen you around the neighborhood."

His voice seemed closer, and I imagined the three of them bending to look under the van and peering into the garage's dark corners, trying to find the imaginary cat.

Theresa stepped out of the garage and paused on the driveway. "That one over there," she said, pointing vaguely. "We're visiting family, isn't that right, honey-bunch?"

"Absolutely," Grandpa said, joining her. "And it wasn't my idea to bring the dang cat—you can believe that," he said, apparently to the man who was still out of my line of sight. "Traveling with a carsick feline yowling the whole way is nothing but torture. If I'd had my way, we'd have left her at that rest stop in South Carolina."

"Now, Ralph, you know you don't mean that," Theresa said, batting at his arm playfully.

"Well, she doesn't seem to be here," the man said, emerging from the garage. He was on the short side, maybe five-nine, and light brown hair hung to his shoulders. He looked even younger than he sounded, no more than twenty.

Deciding it was time for me to play a role, I stepped out

of the house's shadow, saying, "Gran, Gramps, we found your kitty. She's safe at home."

Theresa turned toward me without missing a beat and said, "Thank goodness. I guess we disturbed this young man all for nothing." She winked at me.

"No prob," the man said, hitching up the cargo pants threatening to slip off his skinny butt. His tee shirt proclaimed "Jesus is Lord" over the image of a rising sun. "I'm just glad your cat turned up."

"Hey, haven't I seen you at the mall?" I said, studying the man's narrow face with its slightly pug nose and thin lips. "At the Fernglen Galleria?"

"Uh, maybe. I shop there sometimes," the man said uneasily, glancing over his shoulder at the van.

"I think you do more than shop," I said, still pleasant. "In fact, our cameras captured you spray painting a car just this evening."

"No way! We know where all the cam—" He cut himself off, his gaze going from me to Theresa to Grandpa. "Hey, what is this? Mary Beth!"

Before I could explain who I was, the front door opened and a plump girl about his age, dressed in identical chinos and tee shirt, stepped onto the stoop. The porch light glowed on a frizzy halo of blond hair. She held a dripping cherry Popsicle in one hand. "What's up, Murph?" Her voice was sweet and young, and she was wide-eyed as she took us all in. Dolly pushed her way out from behind the girl and trundled over to greet me.

I patted the dog absently as I introduced myself, deliberately not mentioning Grandpa or Theresa, in case the taggers took it into their heads to report us for trespassing or something. When I said I worked in mall security, Mary

Beth and Murph exchanged nervous glances. "I know you've been tagging cars in our lot," I said. "We've got your latest artistic effort on film," I added with a look at Grandpa who gave a confirming nod.

"It's our calling," Mary Beth said, apparently unperturbed at having been found out. She drifted toward us, licking the Popsicle as she walked. I noticed she was barefoot. Brrr. "We evangelize through our art."

"Using other people's vehicles as your canvas," I pointed out. "That's known in certain circles as criminal vandalism." The similarity in sound between "vandalism" and "evangelism" struck me.

"Jesus didn't believe in the concept of personal property," Murph put in. "He was all about share and share alike. Remember the feeding of the five thousand with the young boy's fish and loaves?"

I was a bit hazy on Bible specifics, but I didn't remember Jesus saying anything about being in favor of vandalism. I didn't pursue the point, merely saying, "I have something serious to ask you."

"Are you going to arrest us?" Mary Beth asked, slipping an arm through Murph's. I noticed the slim gold band on her ring finger and thought that this young, spacey couple didn't seem to go with the solid suburban home. "Because we're ready to go to prison for our evangelism, just like Paul did."

"No. Actually, I'm willing to forget the whole thing under two conditions."

"Yeah?" Murph asked suspiciously. He seemed a bit more pragmatic than Mary Beth.

"First, that you stop tagging cars at Fernglen. It really pissed off my boss when you got his Karmann Ghia earlier this week."

"That was Matthew 7, wasn't it Murph?" Mary Beth

asked. "'Do unto others' is one of my favorite texts," she explained.

"And?" Murph prompted.

"And you tell me about the car you tagged last Sunday. You only do one a day, so—"

"We do eight a day," Murph said proudly, "at different malls."

Damn! Why had I never thought to check with other malls to see if they were having the same graffiti problem we were?

"We want to spread the word as widely as possible," Mary Beth said. A line of cherry juice trickled toward her chin, and she swiped at it with her tongue. "We go from outside Richmond to Quantico."

"Why do you want to know?" Murph asked. "Heel, Dolly!"

Dolly gave up sniffing at Grandpa's shoes and ambled toward Murph.

"She's diabetic," Mary Beth explained, "and needs insulin shots every day. That's why we're dog-sitting while Murph's parents are on a cruise. They didn't trust the kennel to—"

"Why?" Murph asked again.

I explained about the murder and my theory about the murderer's car.

"So we could help catch a murderer by telling you about the car?" Murph asked.

I nodded. "Maybe."

"That was the red Lexus, wasn't it?" Mary Beth said, wrinkling her forehead. The last bit of Popsicle broke off the stick and made a cherry splat on the driveway. Dolly snarfed it up with a move a striking cobra would envy.

"Nah, the Lexus was at the Short Pump Town Center. Fernglen was the black SUV."

"Second Corinthians," Mary Beth nodded. "But it was dark blue."

"Black."

"Blue. Or maybe dark green." She faced me. "It was hard to tell because we blessed that car so late and it was blacker than the devil's heart in that parking lot."

"What time was it?"

"About eleven," Mary Beth said just as Murph declared, "Just before midnight."

They glared at each other and I interrupted. "Do you remember what model?"

They looked at each other doubtfully. "CR-V?" Mary Beth offered, tapping the Popsicle stick against her lip.

"I thought it was something more upmarket than that," Murph said, brow wrinkled in concentration. "An MDX or Cayenne."

Mary Beth shook her head, making her frizzy hair tremble like dandelion fluff. "No, it was a CR-V, or maybe a Highlander. And it was definitely not black."

Murph faced me squarely. "Black."

"Not," Mary Beth muttered from behind him.

"Where did you write the verse?"

"At the Fernglen Galleria," Murph said, giving me a "duh" look.

"I mean, on what part of the car?"

"The hood," they said together. "In orange and yellow with lime green accents," Mary Beth added, swishing her hand through the air as if wielding a can of spray paint.

"Okay," I said, convinced that they'd told me all they could. Besides, I was getting darn cold and I noticed Theresa shivering. "Thanks for your help."

"So we're good?" Murph asked. "No police?"

"Not this time," I said. "But if any more cars in my lot get 'blessed,' all bets are off."

"Deal." He stuck out his hand and I shook it.

With a final pat on Dolly's head, I trailed Grandpa and Theresa back to the van. "Thanks for tracking them down," I said.

"I'm afraid you're not much better off than you were before," Theresa said.

"Well, I wish they could've been more specific, but at least we know the murderer drives a dark-colored SUV. That rules out a lot of vehicles. You were fantastic back there, by the way."

"Community theater," she said. "You should see my Norma Desmond." She struck a dramatic pose with the back of one hand against her forehead.

"*Sunset Boulevard* is one of my favorite movies," Grandpa said. "But the musical—"

I left them to it. I wanted to be long gone before Grandpa broke into his rendition of "C'est Moi."

I swung by the auditorium on my way home to try to catch the end of Kyra's bout, but she was already gone. By the time I got to my house, it was after eight and I was beat. Fubar met me at the door and twined between my ankles. "Nice to see you, too," I said, picking him up. Cradling him in my arms, appreciating the weight of his solid body and the feel of his fur tickling my chin, I headed for the kitchen. I found a single Sam Adams at the back of the fridge and made a mental note to go grocery shopping tomorrow. I put Fubar down to open the beer, and he scampered off as I pried the top from the bottle. He probably figured that thirty-seven seconds of cuddling had fulfilled his quota for the week.

After scrambling an egg with some chives and feta

cheese, I wandered into the living room and sank onto the love seat, putting my plate on the ottoman. I ate distractedly, my mind turning over everything I'd learned this week. Finished with my dinner, such as it was, I pulled my lap desk onto my thighs and started writing down my thoughts, connecting some with circles and arrows. When I was done, I had a list of suspects for each killing and possible motives:

Jackson Porter

Wife
(alibi)

Gatchel
(business deal gone wrong)

Robbie
(inheritance)

Velma Maldonado
(dumped by JP?)

Monica Goudge
(hated Velma's association with JP?)

Dyson Harding
(protect archeological dig)

Marcia Cleaton
(preserve view/property value)

Finola?
(woman scorned?)

Miscellaneous antidevelopment people

Weasel

Porter's killer

(blackmail killer?)

Random burglar

Someone from personal life

Robbie Porter

Dad's killer
(Robbie knew something incriminating)

Drug customer/dealer

Suicide
(guilt for killing dad?)

Accidental overdose?

I wished I had access to the alibi information Detective Helland had no doubt collected. Surely he'd managed to rule out some of the suspects? I also wished I could get hold of vehicle registration records and find out what kinds of cars the suspects owned. I knew Velma drove a black CR-V, and I'd seen a dark MDX parked at the Porter house, but I didn't know who it belonged to. A hazy memory of a green SUV of some kind parked in front of the college museum made me wonder if it belonged to Dyson Harding. Tomorrow, I'd call Helland and tell him what I'd learned from Mary Beth and Murph. Maybe then he'd share some of his information with me.

"This is an open police investigation, thanks to you," Detective Helland said when I called from work Monday morning. "And—"

"Thanks to *me*? How is it my fault you haven't sewn this up yet?"

Ignoring my interjection, he continued, "—and we don't share police files with the general public."

"Even when a member of said public provides you with valuable information about the vehicle that the murderer used to dispose of the body?" I made no attempt to soften my bitter tone.

"*Might* have used to dispose of the body. And narrowing it down to 'dark blue, green, or black midsize SUVs' doesn't exactly point a finger at somebody." Someone in the background yelled, "Helland! Livingston!"

"Gotta go," he said. "Thanks for doing your civic duty." The smile in his voice made me bang the phone down harder than I'd intended, causing Joel to look up.

"No luck?" His expression was sympathetic.

"Arrogant, snide, unbearable—"

"Put that to music and you'll have a Top 40 hit," Joel suggested.

Growling, I stalked from the office and mounted my Segway. My knee had improved, but it still ached more than usual and I was grateful for the Segway's smooth ride as I patrolled the Fernglen halls. I gave directions to several people, helped a woman find her car, and was just coming in from the parking lot when I spotted a familiar figure. I zoomed forward, wanting to catch up with Julia Cleaton before she arrived at the bright yellow Volkswagen she was headed toward. "Julia!"

The girl looked over her shoulder, spied me, and broke into a run. She dropped two shopping bags to fumble for her key and had just gotten the door open when I pulled up behind the compact car, effectively blocking her in.

"What was—" I started.

Her gaze dropped to the bags at her feet and the penny dropped. "Ah. You thought someone reported you for shoplifting."

She crossed her arms over her chest, the skimpy white tee shirt under a black sundress with quarter-sized pink polka dots not remotely adequate for the February chill. "You can look in the bags if you want to. I paid for everything." She dug in a pink messenger purse and brought out a handful of crumpled receipts. "There!"

"No one accused you of shoplifting," I said.

"Then why did you chase me?" Her young face showed confusion.

I didn't point out to her that it only became a chase when she started running. "I was wondering if you and your mom talked about what was worrying you."

"The blood?"

I nodded. A sunny smile lit her face. "Yeah, and everything's copacetic. She didn't kill him."

"Then the blood was . . . ?"

"She told me a coyote killed the neighbor's cat in our yard. She didn't want me to see it and get all upset, so she helped Rosa—our neighbor—bury it that morning and hosed away the blood when she got home from church, not knowing I'd already seen it.

"That's great," I said.

"She was really pissed off that I said what I did, though, and that the detective asked her about it."

"Maybe she wasn't so much pissed off as hurt," I suggested, mentally crossing Marcia Cleaton off my suspect list.

Julia looked thoughtful. "Maybe I can make dinner tonight," she said after a minute. "I know how to do tuna casserole. And I can clean my room before she gets home from work, and not complain about practicing my French horn."

"Sounds good." I suppressed a smile. There was hope for Julia yet.

Nineteen

. . .

I took my lunch break at noon and sought out Kyra, anxious to talk to her about tracking down the graffiti duo. Not wanting to be bothered by people who take my uniform as an invitation to interrupt my meal with questions about where they get refunds for defective Rollerblades or how to apply for a job at the mall, I picked up loaded baked potatoes in the food court and toted them to Merlin's Cave. We ate in Kyra's small office with her sitting by the door so she could see if a customer came in.

"Well, finding the killer's a piece of cake now," Kyra said when I told her about tracking the taggers to their home and learning about the SUV. She leaned back in her chair, balancing the potato on her knee. Today's outfit of royal blue, star-printed tunic over matching leggings with boots made me think of a mod Merlin.

"It is?" I mashed butter evenly through my spud.

"Sure. You just find an opportunity to scratch some paint

off the hoods of the suspects' cars and see if there's an orange Bible verse underneath."

"With lime-colored accents," I reminded her. I cocked a brow. "And the fact that vandalizing cars is illegal shouldn't bother me? Or that someone might catch me at it and run me down or shoot me?"

"You'd be careful, of course," Kyra said. "Be stealthy. Didn't they teach you that sort of thing in the military?"

"We didn't go in much for vandalism," I said. "Come on. I need a real plan. I suppose I could call all the body shops and ask about someone getting their SUV repainted." Just thinking about all those calls made my dialing finger hurt.

"That would take for-damn-ever," Kyra said. "And besides, this dude's too smart to get the work done around here someplace. He hasn't gotten away with killing three people by being stupid or careless."

"If you want to scrape paint off cars' hoods, you can start with your buddy Dyson's SUV."

Kyra wrinkled her nose. "Uhm—"

"Doesn't sound like such a good idea now, does it?" I didn't know what Dyson Harding would do if he caught someone defacing his ride, but I suspected it would involve maiming and a possible jail sentence.

Leaning toward a small mirror propped on her filing cabinet, Kyra picked a bit of broccoli out of her teeth and didn't reply.

"So, I guess I'll start dialing my way through the Yellow Pages when I get home tonight," I said, crumpling up the cardboard boat my potato came in.

The chimes near the shop's entry tinkled, and Kyra peered toward the front of the store. "Speak of the devil," she murmured, rising to greet her customer. "Stay here."

Curious, I peeked around the corner and saw Dyson

Harding, soul patch neatly combed and glasses in place, hovering near the door. "Kyra!" he said, coming forward to greet my friend with a hug.

She pulled back after only a second and said, "What brings you to the mall today?"

"How are you coming with the petition?"

"I got a few signatures," she said, walking to the counter and pulling the clipboard out from beneath it.

Harding studied it. "I was hoping for more," he said, dropping it onto the counter with a disgruntled bang.

"Sor-ree!" Kyra said. She had her back to me so I couldn't read her face, but her tone of voice was plain enough. "I've got a store to run, Dy; I can't be trotting up and down the halls asking folks for their John Hancocks."

He put up a placating hand. "I know, Kyra. I'm sorry. It's just that this is so important, not just to me, but for the country."

I hummed a bar of "America the Beautiful" under my breath.

"How important is it, Dy?"

Something in Kyra's voice stung him because he reared back and said, "What's that supposed to mean?"

"It means I know you. You can be pretty determined."

His eyes glittered behind narrowed lids. "You've been talking to that friend of yours, the one who pretended she was interested in archaeology but who wouldn't know a pot shard from a Harris matrix. She's not on our side."

"And whoever isn't for us is against us?" Kyra asked.

"Precisely."

"Like Jackson Porter."

She was pushing him too hard. I decided it was time to make my presence known. Stepping out of the office, I said,

"I've got to run, Kyra, or I'll be late picking up my Harris matrix at the dry cleaner."

Harding literally jumped at the sound of my voice but recovered quickly. His gaze slid from Kyra to me. "You think this is funny?"

I ignored his question, picking up the clipboard and scanning the text. Before he could say anything else, I added my name to it.

"What are you doing?"

I responded to his hostility with a smile. "Signing your petition against the Olympus development. There." I tucked the pen under the metal clip.

"But—" He stared at the petition as if I'd put a hex on it. "But you—"

"I'm no more in favor of the development than you are, Harding," I said. "And a petition's an easy, legal way to register my opinion. Not like, say, murder."

"You are really something," he said, disgusted. "I thought you, at least"—he looked at Kyra—"understood how important this is. I guess I was wrong." He swept up the clipboard and stalked out of the store, brushing against the chimes so hard it sounded like a hurricane was gusting through. Hurricane Dyson.

"Was it something I said?" I looked at Kyra with mock confusion.

She didn't smile. "You might remember he's a friend of mine. You don't have to make fun of him."

Her reaction took me aback. "You're the one who warned me about him. And you were the one goading him a minute ago."

She turned away, pretending to straighten a rack of horoscope booklets on the counter. "Yeah, well, his methods might be questionable, sometimes, but he wouldn't kill any-one. He might be a little . . . volatile, but he's trying to do the right thing here."

"That depends on how he goes about it," I said. "Three people are dead. Your pal Harding might well be involved: he's a zealot and zealots think the usual rules don't apply to them. He's also smart enough to have pulled off the murders. And he drives an SUV."

"So we might as well toss his butt in jail and throw away the key," Kyra said. She wouldn't meet my eyes.

"Fine by me," I said, her attitude finally making me angry.

"So much for due process and evidence and innocent until proven guilty," Kyra said. "Now I know why you can't get a job as a real cop—it's your attitude, not your knee, holding you back."

I sucked in a breath as her words jabbed at me. Part of me recognized that Kyra was defending Harding because she used to date him—what did it say about her judgment if he turned out to be a murderer?—but most of me was too hurt to accept an excuse for her wounding words. Without another word I turned on my heel and left, careful not to set the chimes clanging. I was halfway back to the security office on my Segway before I let myself think about what had happened in Merlin's Cave. What *had* happened? One moment, Kyra and I were tossing around ideas about how to track down the murderer's car and the next we were spit-ting hurtful things at each other. Dyson Harding happened, I decided. And where did Kyra get off accusing *me* of ignor-ing due process when *she's* the one who wanted to go around keying people's cars to see if they'd painted over some Christian graffiti? Righteous indignation carried me back to the office, but I decided not to go in. Instead, I parked the Segway, thumbed my radio to let Joel know where I was, and entered the management offices, needing a little back patting and approbation.

When I told Curtis Quigley that I'd tracked down the taggers (with the help of outside "contractors"—Grandpa and Theresa Eshelman), he came around his desk, beaming, to shake my hand. "Excellent work, Officer Ferris. Will the police need me to testify? I'm perfectly willing to do so, you know, to ensure the miscreants get what's coming to them. When I think what they did to my Karmann Ghia—" The tips of his ears flushed pink.

"Well, I don't think they'll be facing prosecution—"

"What?"

Reluctantly, I told him about the deal I'd struck with Murph and Mary Beth.

"You just let them go?" His face was an almost comical mask of dismay.

"I don't have arrest authority," I pointed out. "And they wouldn't have told me about the murderer's car if I hadn't promised not to point the police at them."

Tugging his cuffs down, he retreated behind the desk. "You had no right," he said. "They are criminals. They need to pay for what they did. I asked you to stop the vehicle vandalism, not investigate a murder. That's the police's job."

I straightened my back. I had expected kudos from Quigley, not abuse. "I did stop it," I pointed out. "They won't be tagging cars at Fernglen."

He harrumphed and sat, still obviously dissatisfied with the solution I'd negotiated. "Tell Captain Woskowicz I need—"

The door to his office pushed open and his new assistant, a young woman named Pooja, scurried in, her brown eyes wide with excitement. "Mr. Quigley?"

"What is it?" he asked testily.

"Outside." She looked over her shoulder. "It's . . . it's Ethan Jarrett."

"The movie star?" Quigley couldn't have looked more confused if she'd announced that Jabba the Hutt was slithering through the halls.

Pooja nodded breathlessly. "Yes. And he's asking for EJ."

"Officer Ferris?" Quigley asked incredulously.

They both looked at me, Pooja with curiosity and Quigley with suspicion, and I heaved a sigh. "I'll get rid of him."

"Get rid of him! No, no," Quigley said, practically leaping over his desk in his hurry to fawn at the movie star's feet. "If he wants to see you—I don't know why—but take all the time you need. If only we had time to get reporters over here. Having Ethan Jarrett in the mall would boost customer traffic significantly."

Quigley led the way out of his office, hurrying with his hand out toward the tall, handsome man standing relaxed by Pooja's desk, eyes hidden behind aviator sunglasses. He wore pressed jeans, a crisp white shirt open at the neck, and a navy blazer.

"Mr. Jarrett," Quigley said. "Such an honor! I'm Curtis Quigley, director of mall operations. How can we help you today?"

"Call me Ethan." The actor removed his sunglasses and smiled the smile, the endearing one where his lips quirked up on one side, that had made two generations of female moviegoers swoon. I knew he was in his midfifties, but good genes or discreet plastic surgery made him look no older than forty. With evenly tanned skin, a square chin, thick brown hair cut short, and piercing blue eyes, he deserved the title of "World's Sexiest Man" that some magazine had bestowed on him not once, but twice.

"Ethan, then." Quigley almost quivered with pleasure. "We can arrange a private shopping experience for you if—"

"I wouldn't put you to the bother," Ethan said. "I was hoping I could steal EJ for a bit, if you can do without her for an hour or so?"

He turned the smile on me, and I couldn't help but respond with a smile of my own. "Hi, Ethan. You're looking well." I let him gather me into a huge bear hug while Pooja and Quigley looked on in astonishment. His solidity felt comforting, and I hugged him back tightly.

"Can I take you to lunch?" He looked down at me fondly.

"I already ate," I said. "And I'm on duty."

Quigley interrupted. "No, no—take her to lunch. Absolutely! We can spare Officer Ferris—EJ—for a while. You just go." He made shooing motions at me, clearly befuddled by my lack of enthusiasm about dining with one of Hollywood's top moneymakers. "I'll clear it with Captain Woskowicz."

"Thanks, Curtis," Ethan said, holding the door for me.

Resigned, I passed through the door, and he followed after signing an autograph for Pooja.

"It's a nice enough mall," Ethan said, matching his pace to my slower one as we walked. "Bigger than I realized."

I laughed. Ethan probably hadn't been in a mall since *Dead to Rights* turned him into an action star in his late twenties. His clothes were custom-made, and he had a shopper on his staff, Sally, who went slumming at Tiffany's or Harry Winston's to pick out gifts for Ethan to present on the right occasions: birthdays, Christmas, anniversaries. I knew; I'd received more than one elegant jewelry box myself and always made sure to thank Sally.

"Where shall we eat? Citronelle?"

In downtown D.C., a good hour and more from here each

way, plus at least two hours in the restaurant. "I can't, Ethan. I've really got to work. Let's just grab a coffee—okay?—and we can get together tonight."

He accepted the rebuff with good grace. "Whatever you want, EJ."

We—okay, Ethan—attracted stares and not a few gasps on our way to the Bean Bonanza. For once, no one was tacky enough to interrupt us, and we settled on a bench near the kiosk once we got our coffees. A philodendron in the planter behind us tickled my cheek, and I automatically scanned the shrubbery for any sign of Agatha. I told Ethan what I was doing and he laughed. "A python? Really? I'll have to work that into a script." Everything in his life was fodder for a script or developing a character or some other aspect of his career, but I was used to that.

We chatted about his latest movie until he asked, "What about you? Solve that murder you told me about?"

I sighed. "Not yet. In fact, now there's two more bodies to worry about." I spent fifteen minutes bringing him up-to-date.

"If I were writing the script, I'd play it so everyone thought it was the wife, or maybe the son—does he have to die?"

"'Fraid so." Too many years in Hollywood surrounded by dead bodies created by makeup and special effects could really warp your sense of reality.

"Hm. Well, then I'd make it look like the wife until the final scene where it turns out to be the mistress and her new lover. Or maybe the gorgeous mall cop he seduced and—"

"Ethan!"

He grinned at me, and I heard at least one passing shopper gasp. I couldn't blame her; the full-wattage Ethan Jarrett grin had the knock-out power of a Muhammad Ali punch.

I started to rise, but he put a hand on my knee and held me in place. "How's it doing?"

I didn't like talking about my injury, not even with Ethan or my mom or Kyra. "Fine."

My tone of voice should've ended the discussion, but Ethan said, "You need a job where you're not on your feet all the time. I could hook you up at my production company— I'd make you a vice president, in fact, with an eye toward turning over the reins to you—"

"No!" It came out too harshly, and Ethan looked wounded. "It's not like we haven't talked about this before. I appreciate the offer—I really do—but I love police work."

His perfectly groomed brows rose. "But you're not doing police work, are you? You're a glorified security guard, hired to provide a façade—"

"Thanks for the support," I said, turning my head away so he wouldn't see my tears.

He tried to turn my face toward him. "You know I'd be happy to pay—"

"Is everything okay, EJ?"

Jay Callahan's voice came from beside us, and I looked up to see him staring disapprovingly at Ethan's hand on my knee. I brushed it off, my face flushing. I blinked rapidly to get rid of the lingering tears.

"Everything's fine, Jay," I said.

"Because if this guy is bothering you . . ."

Either Jay didn't recognize Ethan or he didn't care about making a good impression; either way, it made me smile. I stood and Ethan followed suit, eyeing Jay narrowly. "Ethan," I said, "this is Jay Callahan. He owns the Legendary Lola's franchise in the food court. Jay, meet my dad."

"Your dad!" Jay's eyes widened, and he looked from me to Ethan before his lips curled into a slight smile. "I can see the resemblance," he said, extending his hand to Ethan. "It's a pleasure to meet you. Your daughter's a pistol."

Nothing bugged Ethan more than me or Clint calling him "Dad" in public and making it abundantly clear he couldn't possibly be the forty he looked. He contented himself with a sideways look at me and gripped Jay's hand. "Tell me something I don't know."

Both men laughed and I rolled my eyes. "I've got to get back to work." I stretched up to peck Ethan on the cheek. "Dinner tonight?"

"I'll send the limo to pick you up. Your mom's anxious to see you. She'd've come with me today except she's got a slight cold."

A gaggle of middle-aged women who'd been hovering by the Bean Bonanza sliding sidelong looks at Ethan got up their courage and came over, exclaiming over his brilliant acting and begging for autographs. I felt no compunction about deserting him since he lived for the fans' adulation. I slipped away only to find Jay at my side a moment later. "I'll walk with you," he said, falling into step beside me.

"Lucky me." My tone verged on the sarcastic, but I was surprisingly pleased to have him accompany me.

"So, the humble mall security officer is really a Hollywood princess in disguise," he teased, his shoulder brushing mine.

"Not hardly," I said discouragingly. "I renounced my crown when I joined the military."

"Why aren't your names the same?"

"They are. He's Ethan Jarrett Ferris, but uses Ethan Jarrett as his stage name. I was named after him—EJ."

"I wouldn't think you'd fit in with the Hollywood crowd," he said, studying my profile, "although you're certainly beautiful enough to make it in the movies."

"Oh, please," I brushed aside his compliment. "And I fit in far too well for far too long. I did the whole scene, including bad grades, too many parties, lots of booze. I woke up with a hangover the day after my high school graduation and took a good, long look in the mirror. It was ugly. I went down to the recruiter's office that afternoon and signed up."

"I'll bet that went over well with your folks." Jay's hazel eyes held interest and a hint of a smile.

I smiled back. "Like a turd in the pool . . . like maggots in the flour . . . like a dent in the Bugatti." I'd run out of comparisons. "You'd've thought I announced I was joining the Taliban instead of the United States Air Force."

Jay laughed. "Oh, come on. It couldn't have been that bad."

I just arched one brow. "How did your folks take it when you told them you wanted to be a cop?"

If I'd hoped to trip him up, I'd failed. He merely smiled and lifted a hand in farewell as we reached the turnoff for the security office. "Have fun at dinner tonight. Tell your dad I really liked his last movie, the one where he was a starship captain."

I shook my head and pushed through the door of the security office, thinking about how to discourage questions about Ethan. No one here knew about our relationship, and I wanted to keep it that way. I semiregretted telling Jay, but something told me I could trust him to keep a secret. Maybe it was the way he stayed mum about who and what he really was.

When I went off shift at three, I debated running by Merlin's Cave to see if Kyra wanted to make up. We rarely disagreed and I didn't like feeling cut off from her; still, she started it, I told myself, deciding just to head home. She should apologize first. Something crinkled in my jacket when I put it on, and I reached in and pulled out the photos of eco-terrorists I'd printed off the Internet. I'd forgotten to show them to Kiefer or Monica to see if they recognized any of them as the man and woman who had been traipsing through their stores in camo gear. The Herpes Hut was only a little out of my way, so I decided to drop in there before heading to the parking lot.

Kiefer was alone in the store, using a long-handled scrubbing pad to clean algae off the terrariums' walls. A faint stink of wetness and reptile poop made me wrinkle my nose. When I told him what I wanted, he willingly put down the pad and stripped off his rubber gloves. "Sure, let me look at them." He leaned over the counter where I'd spread the eight photos, the beads on the ends of his dreads clicking against the glass.

"That's the dude," he said, stabbing a finger down on the second-to-last page. "I don't see the chick, but this is definitely the guy."

I studied the photo he indicated. It was three years old and featured a young man with light, crew-cut hair, thin lips, and an angry expression. He was front and center in a crowd of demonstrators raising their fists and apparently shouting at someone outside the frame. The caption identified him as Henrik Dawson, leader of the animal rights group Freedom for All Animals. Kiefer and I looked at each other. "Maybe he decided LOAF made a better acronym than FFAA and changed the name?" Kiefer said.

I nodded. "'Lovers of Animal Freedom' sounds a lot like 'Freedom for All Animals.' I'll get this photo over to the police and let them know that you've ID'd our buddy Henrik. Maybe they can roust him and he'll tell them where Agatha is."

"I hope so." Kiefer turned sad eyes toward the empty

enclosure. "I know it sounds foolish because it's not like snakes are affectionate or companionable, but I miss her."

"It doesn't sound silly to me," I said, gripping his shoulder. "We'll get her back."

Twenty

. . .

Heartened by my success with Kiefer, I hurried over to Diamanté to see if Monica could ID Henrik Dawson as well. She was outside the store, talking on a cell phone, which snapped shut when she caught sight of me. Her angry frown and hostile glare told me she'd talked to Velma.

"You keep away from my daughter," she said by way of greeting. A soft blue blouse cast an unflattering light on her complexion, making her look sallow. Another short skirt showed off legs encased in brown tights and knee-high boots.

"I only asked her a couple of questions about Porter," I said. "I thought she might remember something that would point us toward his murderer."

"I know what you're really doing," Monica said.

That put her ahead of me.

"You're looking for a scapegoat. You think that just because Velma slept with Jackson that she killed him. Well, she didn't. She loved him and he loved her. He was going to divorce Elena and marry my daughter." She blinked rapidly, depositing mascara flakes under her eyes.

I had no answer to her astonishing declaration. Velma Maldonado hadn't struck me as being a woman madly in love—quite the opposite in fact. Had Velma exaggerated the nature of her and Porter's feelings for each other to appease her mother's sense of propriety? Or had Monica invented this fairy tale of star-crossed love because she was embarrassed by Velma's being Porter's mistress?

"Could she have borrowed your key to the store? Maybe without you knowing . . ." I let my words trail off suggestively, knowing that sometimes you get more information from an interviewee who is off balance, either frightened or mad. My words fanned Monica's anger to new heights.

"Are you implying—? You think that I—that Velma—?" She thrust her chin forward pugnaciously. "Yes, I have a key, but Velma never borrowed it. And it's not like I'm the only person with a key. There must be dozens floating around. And they're cheapo anyway. If you jiggle them good, some of them will unlock stores they're not supposed to. I know because Mr. Song at Himalayan Imports"—she nodded to the shop across the corridor—"let me in one morning when I forgot my key. The security in this place wouldn't stop a disabled six-year-old from breaking in."

Monica continued to blast the mall's security shortcomings while I reflected that she was largely correct. With the exception of the jewelry stores, which had advanced alarm systems tied into private response companies, most of the stores in the mall worried far more about shoplifters during the day than burglars breaking in after hours. As an eager-beaver newcomer, I'd gone to Woskowicz and Quigley after I'd worked here a couple months with a plan for beefing up security, and gone down in flames. No money, Quigley said. No need, Woskowicz said.

Pursuing the topic with Monica would clearly get me nowhere, so I stopped the flood of words by holding out the photos I'd shown Kiefer. "Actually, I've got some photos I want you to look at. Have you ever seen any of these people before?"

Monica gave me a suspicious look but reached for the sheaf of copies. Her eyes widened and her gaze flicked to me when she got to the photo of Henrik Dawson. "This guy. Why, he's the one who was in the store, the one I told you about."

"Thank you very much," I said with satisfaction.

"Did he kill Jackson?"

"I don't know," I said, "but I'm on my way to the police station now to give this information to the detective in charge of the case." Not that I expected him to be grateful.

"I suppose you expect me to thank you for this?" Detective Helland said half an hour later, waving the photo of Henrik Dawson I'd given him. We stood by a vending machine in the Vernonville Police Department while it spewed out pale brown mystery liquid. I'd arrived at the brick building in the town's center—two blocks of shops and restaurants in Colonial-era buildings fronted by brick sidewalks—ten minutes earlier and spent the time examining the pleasant, caramel-painted walls of the waiting area while the desk sergeant sent for Helland. A divorced husband and wife were doing a kid hand-off in one corner of the waiting room, and I thought how sad it was that some marriages ended with such hostility that the former lovers could only meet safely in a police station. The toddler wailed and reached for his father as the mother hoisted the kid in her arms and headed for the door, a slightly older child clinging to her hand. Helland came to fetch me, and I turned away from the sad scene.

"Of course I don't expect you to be grateful," I responded to what was probably a rhetorical question. "I've known you for a week now and my expectations are low."

Helland glared at me for a moment, and then a brilliant smile lighted his face. "I've got to say you're persistent." He took a cautious sip of his coffee and made a face. Turning, he headed down a linoleumed hallway and I followed, even though he hadn't asked me to. Instead of the official photos of cops and former police chiefs I expected, the walls were hung with landscape photographs showing scenes from around the region. I stopped in front of a particularly evocative photo of the Blue Ridge Mountains with a smear of mist hazing their outline. Tiny gold letters in the corner proclaimed "A. Helland."

"You took this?" I asked, astonished. It was good, so good I wouldn't have minded hanging it in my living room.

Helland glanced over his shoulder but continued down the hall. "It's a hobby." With an impatient gesture, he motioned me into his office. I was still thinking about the photograph and how it revealed a creative—even sensitive?—side of him I'd never have expected.

I looked around with unabashed curiosity. More landscape photos—black-and-white studies of trees—decorated the wall behind his desk. A fish bowl with a lone Siamese fighting fish sat on a credenza near a computer printer. File folders, case binders, a computer, and other office paraphernalia took up most of the available space on the desk and bookshelves. The absence of personal items made it hard to get a read on his family situation. Not that it was anything to do with me, I told myself hastily. He could be married with six kids and it wouldn't make a difference to me.

Gesturing me to a red-padded, straight-backed chair, Helland settled into the swivel chair behind his desk and leaned back, arms crossed over his chest. "Tell me what you think you've got here."

I pointed to the photo of Henrik Dawson in the middle of his desk. "I'm damn sure we have the guy who stole the reptiles from the Herpetology Hut. And he might be Porter's killer."

"How do you figure?" He raised a skeptical brow.

"I did a little online research and there's more than one environmental group pissed off at Porter's development activities. I know it's a long shot, but isn't it possible this Dawson guy thought he could stop Porter's building projects by killing him?"

"Possible, but not likely," Helland said dampingly. When I started to protest, he held up a hand. "Still, it's worth talking to him. We'll pick him up."

I smiled internally, but kept it off my face. "Ask about Agatha when you find him."

"Agatha?"

"The stolen python. What else have you got? Any leads on Wedzel's murder? Or Robbie's death?"

Helland thumped a hand on a file folder. "The ME has ruled Robbie Porter's death an accidental overdose. Only his fingerprints on the syringe and the rubber tubing. No defensive wounds or signs of a struggle. Enough heroin in his system to take out a rhinoceros."

I pondered that. Could Robbie have committed suicide? It seemed strange that he'd choose the mall garage as his location and set up a meeting with me, but maybe he was being considerate in an odd way by ensuring his mom or a friend didn't find his body? "And Weasel? I mean Billy Wedzel? Anything on his death?"

"It wasn't suicide," Helland said, as if it hadn't been blatantly obvious at the scene that Weasel hadn't shot himself in the back of the head. "We're checking into some of his associates. Did you know that he ran a very profitable eBay business?"

"Weasel? Really?" I couldn't picture Weasel haunting garage sales and thrift shops for castoffs to resell online. Then the penny dropped—the virtual auction house was a popular place to fence stolen merchandise. "Do you think he was auctioning off stolen stuff?" That might explain where the missing Macy's merchandise ended up. I wondered idly how Weasel had gotten a key, but then realized it wouldn't have been that hard if he was friendly with a former employee.

Helland shrugged. "We're checking into some of his customers."

"So you think he was killed by a—what? Fellow thief? Dissatisfied customer?" It didn't ring true for me. The timing—so close on the heels of Porter's death—was too coincidental.

"I don't think anything yet," he said. "I don't theorize in advance of the evidence."

Sure he didn't. Was he trying to convince me he was a robot? "At least tell me you've been able to eliminate some of the suspects in Jackson Porter's death."

"We've been able to eliminate some of the suspects." His gaze mocked me.

The man was exasperating beyond belief. "Specifically . . . ?"

Helland stood, towering over me, even from behind the desk. A lock of blond hair fell over his forehead. "Thank you for coming in with your information, Officer Ferris. The Vernonville Police Department is always grateful when citizens take an—appropriate—interest in reducing crime in our community." From the way his mouth tightened at the corners, I knew he was fighting a smile.

I rose and smiled sweetly even though I wanted to belt the man. "Always happy to help out, Detective Helland. It's clear you need all the help you can get."

I started toward home but just before turning into my neighborhood, gave the Miata some gas and sped toward Wilderness Avenue, a misnamed street that comprised a large part of Vernonville's business district. It had a cluster of banks and office buildings, including a two-story structure with "Jackson Porter Development" in large red letters across an incongruous log-cabin façade. I'd passed the building hundreds of times but never been in. Now, I wanted to see where Jackson Porter had worked and meet some of his employees. I'd been proceeding under the assumption that there was something personal about his murder, because of the humiliating way his body was left, and I hadn't thought much about his professional connections. But really, other than family members, who's most likely to want to kill you? The people who put up with your donkeylike laugh for forty hours a week, the coworkers you irritate with your choice of radio channels, or the subordinates whose ideas you steal.

I opened the car door and hesitated. I had no business being here. I wasn't a "real" cop, as Captain Woskowicz and Detective Helland frequently pointed out. I wasn't related to Porter. Still, finding the man's body naked in a display window had affected me. So had Weasel's and Robbie's deaths, even though I hadn't liked the one and hadn't known the other. It galled me to think that a murderer was having the last laugh, getting away with . . . well, murder. I got out of the car and strode across the parking lot, trying to think up a plausible reason for being here. I decided I'd tell whoever asked that I wanted to know if there was some place I could make a donation in Porter's name, in lieu of flowers. Weak, but possible. I'd actually make a donation, too.

The inside of Jackson Porter Development could just as well have been a dentist's office or an accounting firm. Nondescript furniture and wall hangings in a small waiting area anchored halls leading off to the right and left. A vaguely familiar scent, sharp and unpleasant, permeated the room. A receptionist's desk sat directly across from the doors, but no one sat at it as I entered. A sappy orchestration of "Muskrat Love"—one of the stupidest songs ever recorded—filtered through hidden speakers. Other than that, the office was quiet. Too quiet. Maybe the firm *had* gone out of business when Porter died? But no, the front door was unlocked.

"Hello?" I called.

"Oh!"

The sound came from behind the desk, but still I saw no one. I started across the tan carpet toward the receptionist's desk just as a head popped up. It was a woman with frizzy, carrot-colored hair, a wide mouth, and brows penciled on in thin arcs that gave her a permanent look of surprise. "Just a minute," she said, her voice as reedy as a piccolo. "I'm— that is—I wasn't expecting anyone."

The head disappeared for a moment, and then she stood, placing a bottle of daffodil yellow nail polish on the desk. *That's* what the smell was—acetone.

"I was doing my toenails," the woman said. She put one bare foot, with tissue woven between the toes, on the desk so I could admire the yellow-painted nails.

"Nice," I said, completely at a loss.

"It's my spring color," she confided, tightening the top

on the polish bottle. "I know it's technically still winter, but I'm ready for sunshine and tulips. Aren't you?" She smiled, displaying a mouthful of braces despite the fact that she had to be close to thirty.

"Uh, yes."

She held out a slim hand. "I'm Kitty Heisterkemp. Can I help you?"

I shook her hand. "Emma-Joy Ferris. I'm here about Jackson Porter—"

Kitty's eyes widened in her thin face. "Didn't you hear? He *died*." She said it with such astonishment I'd've thought Porter's death was the first in the history of humankind if I didn't know better.

"Yes, I—"

"That's why there's no one here," she said with an expansive gesture. "The boss gave everyone the week off. She said we need to regroup, give the lawyers and accountants time to do their thing. Whatever that is." She wrinkled her nose. "But not me. I'm here to answer the phones and keep up with the mail. It's pretty lonely." She pointed to a romance novel splayed on the desk, a bodice ripper if the cover was anything to go by.

"Have you worked here long?" I asked, trying to feel my way toward a question or two about Porter.

"Almost nine years," she said proudly. "Since I graduated from Vernonville High." She waggled the fourth finger of her right hand to show off a class ring set with a red stone. "It's been great. I've gotten raises almost every year. I've learned so much you wouldn't believe it. And I like everybody here. We're just really close, you know? Like a family. Except . . ." She trailed off, then resumed with a bright smile. "And Jackson is—was—a super boss. He didn't get all uptight if you came in a few minutes late, you know?

And he was always friendly. Not in an inappropriate way," she hastened to add, "except . . ." She shook her head, swishing her carroty hair around her ears. "I've never had a better boss."

She'd probably never had another boss, period, if she started working here right after high school.

"Who's the boss now that Porter's dead?" I asked, deciding to go with the flow of Kitty's artless prattle.

"Catherine," she said. She pulled at her lower lip. "Well, she's not really the boss boss, not the owner, but she's the office manager and she's the one who gave us the week off. I guess the owner would be Elena, right? Jackson's wife." She nodded as if pleased to have figured that out.

"Catherine?"

"Catherine Lang. She started working here after her husband died—about three years ago. Wasn't that just awful what happened to him?"

"What happened to him?" I was still taking in the news that Catherine Lang worked for Jackson Porter. I don't know why I was surprised—there was no reason it should have come up in my conversations with either Elena or Catherine—but I was. Maybe because Catherine Lang hadn't struck me as the worker-bee type.

"You know. It was in all the papers because he was rich or famous or something, although I never heard of him. It's not like he was ever *People*'s sexiest man, you know." She giggled, sounding more like a teenager than a woman almost my age. "That's my favorite magazine—*People*."

Shocker.

The phone rang and Kitty reached for it. "Jackson Porter Development," she said, sounding surprisingly mature and professional.

"I'll come back next week when the office is open," I

mouthed at her, slipping away as she reached for a message pad.

I climbed back into the Miata, not sure if I was glad or sorry that the office was essentially closed. On the one hand, I hadn't gotten to meet any of Jackson's coworkers and get their take on him. On the other, Kitty was a fount of information and she probably wouldn't have chatted so freely on an ordinary day. On balance, I thought things had worked out to my advantage.

Back at my house, having fed Fubar, changed out of my uniform, and snacked on carrots and hummus, I plunked myself down in front of the computer to do some research. I'd found Henrik Dawson via Google—maybe I could dig up more about the other suspects. It wasn't like having law enforcement databases at my fingertips, but there's a surprising amount online about almost everybody, most of which the Average Joe doesn't even realize is out there for any old snoop to locate.

I studied the list of suspects I'd drawn up and left on the kitchen table, adding Henrik Dawson's name. I decided to eliminate Gatchel on the grounds that I thought Weasel's murder was connected to Porter's death and Gatchel was six feet under when someone shot Weasel. I also eliminated Robbie since he no longer posed a threat to anyone. Since I had talked to her this afternoon, I started with Monica Goudge, typing in her name and "Vernonville" as key words. A healthy list of hits popped up. Over the course of the next forty-five minutes, I learned that she was part of the altar guild at St. Mary's Church (her name was in the parish's online bulletins), that she quilted (from an announcement about an exhibit by local quilters two years back), and that she'd been involved in a nasty car wreck almost five years earlier (from the *Vernonville Times*). I found her address and phone number easily and MapQuested the house, discovering it was only two miles from me in a middle-class suburb where the houses went for more than Monica could afford on Diamanté wages. She must have another source of income—inheritance, alimony, big settlement from the car crash, whatever. I leaned back in my chair, thinking. Nothing came to me.

Typing in Velma's name, I skimmed through a bazillion dance recital programs that listed her. Several dance studios featured group photos of dancers that included Velma in a variety of sequined or floaty costumes, wearing tap shoes or ballet slippers and a self-conscious smile. In the earliest photos, she was maybe ten or twelve. In the more recent ones, she looked sleek and sophisticated, Broadway bound. A three-year-old engagement announcement popped up, and I saw that she'd been planning to marry a Bryce Underfield. Wondering if the marriage had ever taken place, I read the announcement and learned that the bride-to-be was the daughter of Victor and Monica Maldonado. Keying in Victor's name, I got a photo of a good-looking Filipino man with skin the color of teak and short black hair. The article said he'd been convicted of practicing medicine without actually being a doctor—yowza!—and was having his resident alien status revoked and being deported to his native Philippines. The article quoted friends and coworkers who said they had no idea his medical degree from a Manila university was forged and offered testimonials from patients who swore he'd cured them of various illnesses. I could see why Monica had resumed her maiden name after—I presumed—a divorce.

I got up to fetch a beer and leaned down to pat Fubar as he pushed in through his cat door. He smelled of cold air. Fubar skittered away from my hand, his truncated tail

twitching, and I let him go. Clearly, he was in his "I'm a
fierce predator who doesn't like mollycoddling" mode.
Leaning back against the kitchen counter to take the first
swallow of my Raging Bitch Belgian Pale Ale, I pondered
what I'd learned. Not much. The info about Velma's dad was
interesting, but I didn't see any connection between the Mal-
donados and Jackson Porter beyond his relationship with
Velma. Unless . . . maybe Victor Maldonado had unsuccess-
fully treated someone in Porter's family and a relative was
out for revenge? Even if that were true, I didn't see how it
would result in someone wanting to kill Porter. Maldonado,
maybe, but not Porter.

I returned to the table with my beer, ready for another
round of "Digging Up Dirt on the Web." Working on the
theory that one's nearest and dearest are most likely to want
to kill one, I searched for Elena Porter. I knew she had an
alibi that satisfied the police, but I wanted to learn more about
the woman. Elena was all over the Web, mostly at society
parties and fund-raisers with Jackson Porter. I studied a
photo of Elena and Jackson with Catherine Lang and a tall,
older man identified as her husband, Wilfred Lang, as they
raised their glasses in a toast at a diabetes fund-raiser. The
sight brought to mind Kitty's comments about Lang's death,
and I decided to search for articles about it. If it had been in
"all the papers" as Kitty had said, it shouldn't be hard to find.

I had just typed "Wilfred Lang+Vernonville" into the
search bar when the doorbell rang. Startled, I strode to
the door and opened it, Fubar on my heels. A sixty-ish man
with gray hair stood there wearing a dark suit and peaked
cap; a stretch limo idled in the street. I stared at him, uncom-
prehending.

"Miss Ferris?" he asked in a soft voice. "Are you ready?"
He studied my jeans and sweatshirt doubtfully.

"Ready?" Enlightenment dawned. Dinner. My parents. Ack! How had I forgotten? "Almost," I lied.

"I'll wait in the car, ma'am."

I got home from dinner with my parents well after midnight, stuffed with lobster thermidor, wild rice and shiitake mushrooms, and an elegant passion fruit tart. My dad had filled me in on the details of his latest projects, and Mom and I had enjoyed a good talk about various family members, what she might like to do while living in Alexandria, and my love life. That latter topic had yielded enough material for about eight seconds of conversation where Mom asked, "Is there anyone new in your life?" and I shook my head no. Mom sighed the "I want to be a grandmother before I die" sigh and patted my arm gently, thanking me for the crystal earrings I'd bought her at Diamanté before changing the topic to Clint and his latest travels. I fell into bed, exhausted, and didn't notice that my laptop was still on.

Tuesday morning, as I was eating my oatmeal with blueberries, regretting the third glass of the extraordinary Stag's Leap cabernet my dad had decanted—thank goodness for Lyle, the chauffeur—Fubar leaped onto the table and jarred the computer to life. Wilfred Lang smiled at me over a headline that announced "Vernonville Financier Missing." Letting my oatmeal get cold, I scrolled down to read the article from the *Washington Post*. The gist of it seemed to be that Wilfred Lang, who did something important on Wall Street but lived in Vernonville, had not returned from a hike when expected. His Mercedes was found at a trailhead in Shenandoah National Park and searchers were concentrating their efforts in that area.

I clicked on a link to a follow-up article and learned that

Wilfred Lang's body had been discovered by a young couple hiking in the Shenandoah Mountains for their honeymoon. He was several miles off the trail, in a back-country area not frequented by campers. Autopsy results showed he died of severe hypoglycemia. No backpack was found near his body, and the pathologist posited that he'd taken his usual insulin dose and then been unable to eat because his food supply had been lost or stolen. "We've got a lot of black bears in this area," the sheriff said, giving one possible explanation for how Lang lost his provisions.

The article went on to say that Lang's wife, Catherine, said her husband was adept at managing his diabetes but that she'd tried to get him to give up his solitary hikes when the disease was diagnosed. She and a friend had spent the weekend at a spa in Pennsylvania, and she hadn't missed him until he failed to return or call on Monday. The victim's daughter from an earlier marriage, Aileen Lang-Quincy, called for an in-depth investigation, asserting that her father was the victim of foul play.

Clicking to the next page, I found a lengthy obit of Wilfred Lang. Halfway through a list of his financial accomplishments and awards, I pushed the computer aside and took another bite of congealing oatmeal. "What do you think about that, Fubar?" I asked the cat, who was staring at my cereal bowl in a way that let me know he wouldn't be averse to finishing off any leftover milk. I put it on the floor for him and stroked his head as he lapped. "I'll bet you a year's supply of kitty kibble that the friend who was spa-ing with Catherine Lang when her husband disappeared was Elena Porter."

Fubar didn't take me up on the bet.

Twenty-one

. . .

Minutes before the mall opened on Tuesday morning, I burst through the door of Merlin's Cave determined to make up with Kyra and fill her in on what I'd discovered. She emerged from the stockroom at the back, her lips compressing a tad when she saw me.

"Don't look like that," I said. "I'm here to apologize. I shouldn't have said what I did about Dyson."

"It's okay," she said, breaking into a smile. "He's a jerk." She gave me a hug, the silk of her red tunic slippery under my hands. "I'm sorry, too. I shouldn't have said . . . you know. It's not true."

I hugged her hard in acceptance of her apology before letting her go. "Look what I found." I pulled out the articles I'd printed from the Internet about Wilfred Lang's death and asked her the same question I'd asked Fubar.

"Could be," she responded, sifting through the pages. "Are you saying you think they're in on some sort of conspiracy?"

"Like a twist on *Throw Momma from the Train*," I said. My dad had made me think about the possibility of more than one person being in on the murder with his joking about "the mistress and her new lover" killing Porter. The rest of the idea had come to me full-blown after reading about Wilfred's death. "Catherine kills her husband—"

"Why?"

"How should I know? Maybe he cheated on her or beat her or wanted kinky sex. Maybe she was tired of him. Point is, she kills him and Elena gives her an alibi. Then, Elena kills her husband and Catherine alibis her. See the symmetry?"

"I don't see how Catherine could've killed her husband. It says here that he died of hypoglycemia on a hike. It's not like she was with him to feed him a poisonous mushroom or tip him off a convenient cliff or something. I just don't see how this can be murder." Kyra looked apologetic for raining on my parade.

I chewed on my lower lip. She had a point. But the idea had seemed so *right* when it hit me. It couldn't be coincidence that Elena and Catherine had been together when each of their husbands died nonnatural deaths.

"It could be coincidence," Kyra argued, as if reading my thoughts. "They're best friends. They spend a lot of time together. They're probably more likely to be with each other than with anyone else other than their hubbies or kids."

"But doesn't it strike you as unlikely that two women in their fifties would both lose their husbands under unusual circumstances—to say the least—while in each other's company?"

Kyra smoothed a ruffle on her black and red tiered skirt. "It's unlikely that two sisters-in-law would have their husbands assassinated, but it happened to Jackie and Ethel Kennedy."

"That's different! The Kennedys are jinxed. The surprise is that only two of them were assassinated."

"Your chances of being hit by lightning are only one in three thousand or so over the course of your entire life, but there's one guy, a park ranger, who was hit seven times. I read it in a bathroom reader."

"We're not talking about lightning."

"I'm just saying that statistics don't prove jack. Besides, you don't *know* that the Lang woman was with Elena Porter, do you?"

"No," I admitted, my brain working furiously to come up with a way of finding out. Asking Catherine Lang or Elena Porter didn't sound like a good bet. Nor did asking Detective Helland to fish around in a closed case file from another jurisdiction. An idea came to me. "But I think I have a way to find out."

Aileen Lang-Quincy agreed to meet me in the lobby of the Four Seasons Hotel in Washington, D.C., that night when I called the number I found for Lang Enterprises. Her secretary had been reluctant to put me through, but when I said it concerned Wilfred Lang's death, Aileen Lang-Quincy came on the line and allotted me a few minutes before a company banquet. Driving toward D.C., I was glad to be headed into the city at rush hour and not toward the burbs like the poor commuters caught in a six-mile back-up near the Dale City exit. Traffic was moving so smoothly I abandoned my plan of taking the Metro in from the Springfield station and drove straight into Georgetown, lucking into a metered spot only four blocks from the hotel.

I'd taken the time to change into a cream-colored silk blouse and a pair of black wool slacks and topped them with a Burberry coat left over from my premilitary life, so the doorman at the Four Seasons didn't spare me a glance when

I walked in. I settled on one of the fawn-colored settees in front of a marble fireplace where Aileen Lang-Quincy and I had agreed to meet. On the mantle, elegant calla lilies graced white vases. Guests in formal wear—here for the banquet?—made bright splotches against the lobby's mono-chromatic palette.

A tall woman in a dull red Armani gown strode toward me, eyebrows raised enquiringly. "Emma-Joy Ferris? I'm Aileen Lang-Quincy." She offered a hand with short nails sporting a French manicure. Her hair was dark, cut in a short, asymmetric style, and her face was discreetly made up except for bright red lips. A triple strand of pearls draped the gentle swell of bosom revealed by the strapless satin dress. I'd read up on her and knew she was now the president of Lang Enterprises—not bad for a woman in her early for-ties.

"Call me EJ," I said, shaking her hand. Her firm grip let me know she was a no-nonsense executive, used to operat-ing in a man's world.

"And I'm Aileen." Seating herself gracefully on the set-tee, she arranged the folds of her gown around her ankles and leaned forward slightly. "You intrigued me with your phone call," she said. "My father died more than three years ago—how could you have new information about his death?"

"Potential information," I said, sitting across from her. "Before I say anything more, do you mind telling me why you thought your father was murdered, why you agitated for a more in-depth investigation?"

Aileen knit her dark brows, considering my request. "I guess there's no harm in it," she said finally. "I didn't have any proof of foul play, but I found it difficult—no, impossible—to believe that my father died the way they said he did. He'd been an insulin-dependent diabetic—type one—for almost ten years by then. It was a kind of diabetes that they call late onset, some sort of autoimmune disorder, I believe. Anyway, he was a highly intelligent man and a disciplined one. He was managing his disease well; the idea that he'd inject himself with insulin and then not eat didn't sound plausible to me." She massaged the palm of her left hand with her right thumb as she talked, and I knew the topic was still painful for her.

"You didn't buy the idea that he lost his food somehow? Maybe a bear swiped it, or he wandered away from his campsite and got disoriented?"

She shrugged one bony shoulder. "I can't sit here and declare those things categorically impossible. However, they seemed improbable enough to me that I badgered the authorities to look deeper. They searched for his backpack but never found it. My father was a very wealthy and powerful man, EJ." She gave me a significant look. "Many people benefited financially from his death, including me."

"Since you mention it," I said, glad that she'd broached the subject, "who were the beneficiaries in his will?"

She stiffened. "I don't see how that's any of your business." A luggage cart trundled by, pushed by a bellhop, and a small dog yapped at us from within a carrier stacked precariously atop a heap of designer suitcases.

"Probated wills are a matter of public record," I reminded her.

Taking a deep breath through her nose, she exhaled loudly. "I inherited controlling interest in Lang Enterprises, the Manhattan apartment, and the presidency of the company. I was in line for that job the next year anyway when my dad planned to retire. I've worked for the company since graduating from Stanford. Both my brothers inherited substantial property and other assets, and my stepmother got the house in Vernonville and a trust fund that ensures she never has to work again."

But she had worked again, I thought. She worked for Jackson Porter. "Were—are—you and your stepmother close?"

"What a funny question," Aileen said, giving me a quizzical look. "I was an adult when my dad married Catherine, and we've always been friendly but not intimate. Now, tell me why you called," she commanded, glancing at a gold Omega watch on her wrist. "I've got to go into the dinner. I'm giving opening remarks."

"And I've got to get to work, so I'll keep it brief." I explained about Porter's death and how Catherine Lang had supplied Elena Porter with an alibi for the time of Jackson's murder.

"I don't see how that relates to my dad's death," Aileen said, disappointed. She stood in one fluid motion, the gown swishing.

I stood, too. "I think your stepmother was returning the favor."

Aileen was quick. It took her only a split second to realize what I was saying. "You think Catherine arranged my father's death somehow and that Elena backed up a fake alibi? And now she's doing the same for Elena?"

I nodded. "I think it's possible. The newspaper account said Catherine was at a spa with a friend the weekend your father died. If that friend was Elena—"

Aileen made a disgusted sound. "You should leave security work for novel writing. *I* was with Catherine at the spa that weekend, not Elena. I'm the 'friend' the article referred to. This has been an utter waste of my time."

Before I could recover from my astonishment enough to

answer her, she had spun away in a swirl of garnet satin and was halfway across the lobby. I didn't try to call her back. Her announcement left me flummoxed, flabbergasted . . . I tried to think of other words that would encapsulate my surprise. None came to me, and I retraced my steps across the lobby and out the revolving door to my car, finding a ticket on my windshield even though the meter could only have expired a minute or two earlier. I jerked the ticket from under the wiper and glared at the back of the traffic enforcement officer giving the same treatment to an H3 half a block away. This whole expedition had been a disaster.

On the long drive back to Vernonville, I beat myself up for having leaped to conclusions without getting all the facts. I had made a complete and total idiot of myself. Even in the car, my cheeks warmed with the memory of Aileen Lang-Quincy's scornful look. I could only be grateful that I was unlikely to run into her again. Even worse than the humiliation was the realization that I was back to square one. Now that I had to consider Elena's alibi a legitimate one, I was left with a handful of suspects who appeared equally likely—or unlikely—to have murdered Jackson Porter.

I hadn't eaten before driving into the city and I needed food before I could think about the murder anymore. Kyra's cell went straight to voice mail, so I called Grandpa Atherton. He sounded happy to hear from me and invited me over for dinner. "You can try out my new night-vision goggles while you're here," he said.

Knowing that dinner at Grandpa's meant either cafeteria fare if we wandered over to the community dining facility, or canned soup and toast if we ate in his home, I stopped by a supermarket and picked up a deli-roasted chicken and a quart of pasta salad. Minutes later, the familiar scent of chicken noodle soup boiling on the stove greeted me as

Grandpa opened the door. "You can save the soup for tomorrow's lunch," I said, hefting my grocery bag.

"Thank you, Emma-Joy," he said, stooping to kiss my cheek. "I'll just put this on plates and we can eat."

I followed him into the kitchen and pulled a couple of Heinekens from the refrigerator while he divvied up the chicken and pasta salad onto paper plates. The tiny dining area off Grandpa's kitchen was stacked halfway to the ceiling with boxes of gadgets he'd bought online, and two computers, ham radio equipment, and other electronics took up the entire table, so we carried our plates into the living room and ate off metal TV tables. Grandpa didn't have a TV—he agreed with whoever said it was bubblegum for the mind—and his living room vibrated with books and mementoes of his CIA career: a hammered silver wall hanging from Nicaragua, a Hmong quilt, a cricket bat, a display of Soviet military insignia, a piece of a jacket that supposedly belonged to a young Fidel Castro, and more.

"So, what's on your mind?" Grandpa asked, wiping chicken grease off his fingers as we finished the meal. "Are you still fretting over that murder?"

"I wouldn't call it 'fretting,' " I said, leaning back against the green plaid sofa. "But it's eating at me."

"Fretting," he said with a decisive nod. "Your mom was always a fretter, too. I don't know where she got it because I've never worried a day in my life and my Dolores was the most serene person I ever knew. She had to be, what with all my activities in the sixties and seventies."

My grandmother had died almost two decades ago, and I knew Grandpa still missed her. He gestured for me to continue, and I told him about the theory that Aileen Lang-Quincy had blown out of the water and about the other suspects.

"It was a woman," he said decisively when I finished.

"Why do you say that?" I asked, swallowing a sip of warm beer.

"Because no man would strip a man and display him in a window," Grandpa asserted. "A man might cut off another fellow's privates to leave a message—don't mess with my wife, for instance—and I saw a chap once who'd been tortured and the naked body left in the street as a warning for potential informers, but this . . . this is a woman. If Porter was a womanizer like you say, it's some woman who thinks he did her wrong."

What he said made sense to me, but the physical difficulties involved made me less sure than Grandpa seemed to be. I flipped through my mental photos of Finola, Monica, Velma, Elena, and Catherine. "None of the women involved are exactly bodybuilders," I said. "I don't think they could have gotten him into the store by themselves."

"You'd be surprised what people can accomplish with a little adrenaline flowing through them," he said, then immediately contradicted himself. "Or maybe you wouldn't be."

He was remembering my time in Afghanistan, the firefight that had won me a medal and cost me my knee when Taliban forces set off an IED. "People can do extraordinary things when the situation demands it," I agreed, setting my empty bottle on the tray with a snap.

"I'll see what I can learn about the suspects for you," Grandpa said, his face lighting up. "Which one should I follow first? Maybe that Monica woman. Mothers can be ferocious when they think their cubs are in danger . . . even if the danger is emotional rather than physical."

"None of them," I said. "And no breaking and entering to check out their computers, either." I shuddered at the memory of how close he'd come to being caught at Gatchel's house. "I think it's time I bowed out of this and let the police do their thing. I really thought that my familiarity with the mall would help me identify the murderer, but so far I'm batting zero." My fantasy of confounding Detective Helland by apprehending the murderer and marching him or her through the front door of the police station was looking about as likely as my knee suddenly regenerating.

Grandpa unfolded himself from the wing chair he sat in and pulled me up for a hug. The waffle weave of his tan vest felt comforting under my cheek. "You're not a quitter, Emma-Joy. I'll tell you what will make you feel better. We'll go for a walk and I'll let you use my new night-vision binoculars. The higher signal-to-noise ratio in these fourth-generation devices is amazing. They've managed to negate some of the halo effect as well, so the binocs work better in an urban area with more ambient light."

Grandpa's enthusiasm made me laugh. "Let's do it."

I left Grandpa's place an hour and a half later, feeling more relaxed than I had in days. Something about the simple pleasure he took in spying on unsuspecting strangers transmitted itself to me. I stopped home to change into my uniform and feed Fubar and then headed to the mall. The turnover briefing from Edgar Ambrose and Dallabetta consisted of a quick "Quiet as a grave," and quicker good nights as they headed for their cars and, presumably, their comfortable beds.

I settled in at the desk and studied the camera screens, which remained boringly devoid of activity. After half an hour and several complete cycles through the mall's fifty-plus operational cameras, my eyes burned and I was having trouble staying awake. Not a good sign with seven and a half hours more to go before my shift was up. I scrunched my eyes closed to moisturize them and when I opened them, thought I glimpsed a dark, hooded figure skulking along the outside of the mall about where Kyra and Joel and I had staged our reenactment the other night. The screen switched to another view before I could verify what I'd seen, and I hastily clicked through the cameras to bring up images from the one in question. Nothing. Whoever had been there—if anyone—was gone. I drummed my fingers on the desk for a moment, then decided a quick patrol was in order. If nothing else, it might help me stay awake.

I mounted the Segway and purred through the empty halls toward the Dillard's wing and Diamanté. Whoever I'd seen might still be outside, but my instincts told me he or she was trying to get in. I slowed as I approached the turn, grateful for the Segway's almost silent operation. The corridor's inadequate after-hours lighting cast more shadows than illumination, and I hesitated before steering toward Diamanté. I saw no movement, no sign of breaking and entering at any of the stores I passed. When I drew level with the narrow hall that led to the restrooms, though, a change in temperature goose-pimpled my skin. Was it my imagination, or had I felt a draft? I stopped. Without the slight rush of air caused by the Segway's movement, I definitely felt a draft. The outside door was open.

Now would be a good time to call the Vernonville Police Department. However, after this evening's "cry wolf" fiasco with Aileen Lang-Quincy, I was reluctant to make the call and look like an idiot again if no one was there. I'd check it out first. I hugged the wall with the Segway, passing the men's room and then the ladies' room without incident. The large trash can was right where it always was. I peered into it. Empty. No trash or bodies. The exterior door when I reached it was ajar, open a scant half inch. Using my elbow, I nudged it wider and peered into the darkness. The cold bit at me, making me blink, but I saw nothing unusual or suspicious—no vehicles or hooded skulkers. I pulled it closed behind me, but it didn't latch properly and sighed open the same half inch. Hm. Had someone damaged the mechanism forcing the door just now, or had it happened earlier, perhaps in the course of a delivery? I cursed the mall's penny-pinching ways and the lack of a proper alarm system.

A faint sound behind me, not a footstep or anything identifiable, but out of place in the deserted hallway, made me spin around. Two figures loomed in front of me. Hillary Clinton stood ten feet away on my left, and Sarah Palin hovered close beside her on my right. Hillary had a gun pointed at my midsection. Damn politicians.

Twenty-two

· · ·

The vinyl Halloween masks made their heads look out of proportion to their bodies, which were clad in gender-obscuring navy sweatpants and black hoodies. Despite the disguises, I had a pretty good idea who I was dealing with. The sight of the gun had sent my brain into warp drive, and I knew the twosome could only be Velma Maldonado and her mother, or Elena Porter and her best friend, Catherine Lang. Velma and Monica, however, had no way of knowing I was working the midshift tonight.

"You know, I thought you two killed Jackson Porter together," I said, "because Wilfred Lang also died under odd circumstances and that made me wonder. But then I talked with Aileen and she told me you"—I looked at the gun-wielding Catherine—"were with her at the spa when your husband died. She was your alibi."

"More like I was hers," Catherine said in her low voice, apparently unperturbed that I had recognized them. Not good.

"You mean Aileen killed her father?" I was momentarily distracted from the present danger.

"My guess is she paid to have it done," Catherine said. "She'd never been interested in spending time with me before, and then she calls to suggest we 'get to know each other better' with a spa weekend and Wilfred ends up dead? You do the math. I wasn't about to rock the boat, though, because I was just as glad to be rid of him as she was. That man was . . . He deserved to die." She shuddered and the gun trembled in her hand. "Anyway, it gave me the idea when Elena told me about Jackson's latest affair, the way he was humiliating her with that Velma girl."

"You can't believe how much he was spending on her," Elena said from behind her Sarah Palin mask. "He was backing an off-Broadway show to give her her shot at fame. We don't have that kind of money—he was ruining us, mortgaging our future for that bimbo. I could have been famous if I hadn't given up performing when we had Robbie. Did he ever offer to back my career? Did he ever even want to listen to me play? No." She sounded sad and weary, but then her voice strengthened. "I had tolerated his infidelities before, but this was the last straw."

"So who shot him?" I looked from Catherine to Elena and back again.

"We're done talking," Catherine said. "As long as we stick to our story, no one can prove anything." She turned to face Elena as she spoke, and I imagined her glaring her partner to silence, although I couldn't see her eyes properly with the Hillary mask in the way.

"You could probably get rid of the masks," I suggested, hoping that pulling it off might cause Catherine's aim to slip so I could try something.

"Oh, no," Catherine said. "We're burglars. We've broken

in to rob the jewelry store, and we're wearing masks so we can't be identified on camera. You're about to play hero and try to stop us. Unfortunately, you get shot and die. Elena and I will make a big fuss about the inadequate security at the mall and donate a huge wreath to your funeral. I learned that from Aileen, too: put on an outraged face and call for an investigation and no one will suspect you. She called me, you know, after your talk at the Four Seasons, and mentioned you were working tonight." Her eyes, shadowed by the mask, mocked me.

I evaluated my options. I didn't like any of them. The door behind me was still cracked open, but I'd have to lean my weight against it to open it and that would give Catherine ample time to put a bullet in my back.

As if she were reading my thoughts, Catherine motioned me forward with her left hand, the one not holding the gun. "Get away from the door."

I inched forward on the Segway, glad for its bulk between me and the gun, even though I knew it probably wouldn't stop a bullet. Every minute I could extend the conversation was another minute to come up with a plan, so I said, "And Weasel? How did he find out?"

"The other guard? Was that his name?" Catherine asked. "How appropriate." It was weird not being able to read her expression; Hillary's fixed smile was disconcerting. "He saw the car that night and called Elena the next day, hinting at what he knew. He wanted ten thousand dollars for his silence. He got silence, all right. Permanent silence."

"What we in the military would call collateral damage," I said, looking for a way to drive a wedge between the two women. Divide and conquer. "And is that what Robbie was? Collateral damage? Pretty cold."

Elena gasped. "He died of an accidental overdose!"

I sensed an opening. "Oh, I don't think so. Your buddy Catherine here killed him because he was going to tell me what he knew. Did he overhear you plotting? Find blood in the back of the SUV? Discover—"

"Ignore her, Elena," Catherine said, her voice tenser than before. "Move around behind her so if she tries something—"

I leaned forward on the Segway, sending it straight toward Elena as she started to move. She reflexively jumped out of the way, bumping Catherine, and I shot past the pair of them, hunching my shoulders to make myself the smallest possible target. Leaning right, I turned into the Dillard's corridor as a bullet whizzed by, the sound of the shot deafening in the confined hallway. My ears ringing, I shifted my weight from side to side, directing the Segway on a serpentine path through the corridor. Footsteps sounded behind me, and I risked a look back to see both women emerging from the service hallway, masks still in place, Catherine leveling the gun. I leaned left hard and another bullet missed me.

My heart was pounding fast enough to rip its way out of my chest, and my breath came in shallow gasps. I forced myself to take a deep breath and think. Top speed on the Segway was only twelve and a half miles an hour, and I knew Catherine, at least, could catch me if she sprinted. My only hope was to hide long enough to call for help. Making it to another mall exit wouldn't do the trick; I'd be even more exposed and easier to run down in the empty parking lots.

I had emerged into the main atrium where the corridors crossed and the fountain lay straight ahead of me, with the food court on its far side. Deciding the Segway was a liability now—it hampered my mobility and made me too visible—I zoomed around the fountain and leaped off, taking care to land on my left leg. The Segway continued a few feet toward the food court as I dove into the greenery in the nearest planter, hoping the ferns and spaths and hostas would hide me.

"She's got to be right here somewhere," Catherine's voice said from only a few feet away. For once, I was grateful for the mall's cheapskate habit of only lighting the place dimly at night. Breathing as quietly as possible, I detected the scent of damp earth and what might have been lemonade—shoppers all too frequently emptied their drinks into the planters—and I quickly began to feel light-headed from lack of oxygen.

"Maybe she's in the food court," Elena whispered. "Behind one of the counters or under a table."

The squeak of rubber-soled boots on tile told me they were headed toward the food court. I took a peek and saw their shadowy backs passing the Segway, which had drifted to a stop near Legendary Lola Cookies. Reaching into my pocket, I withdrew my cell phone and hit redial because it was faster than punching in 911.

Grandpa answered, sounding completely alert, even though it was near midnight.

"Grandpa, send the police to the mall. I'm—"

Something heavy smacked down on my wrist, sending the cell phone clinking to the floor and skidding across the tiles until a booted foot crunched down on it. Wrist aching, I raised my eyes to see the Hillary Clinton mask looming over me, gun raised. Apparently, Catherine had smashed the gun into my wrist. "Get out of there," she commanded. Elena stood several feet to her right, Sarah Palin mask shifted upward slightly so her mouth was exposed. Easier to breathe that way, I guessed.

I swung my legs over the side of the planter, momentarily disgusted by the sight of chewing gum stuck to my uniform slacks. Without thinking much about the move, I brought my legs into my abdomen and exploded them outward, pushing off the planter with my arms at the same time so I launched myself at Catherine. My feet thudded into her chest, and she staggered backwards, overbalancing and collapsing into the fountain with a spray of cold water. I landed jarringly on my back, knocking the breath out of myself. A glint of light on metal sailing through the air told me Catherine's fall had loosened her grip on the gun. I heard it land and twisted to reach for it as Catherine yelled, "Elena, get the gun!"

I struggled to my feet as Catherine surged out of the fountain, Hillary face smashed on one side and hanging askew past her chin. She ripped it off with a snarl and tossed it behind her. It gave me some small comfort to know police would be able to identify her now from her image on the cameras, if we were within range of one that was actually working. I readied myself for her charge as Elena said, "I've got the gun."

Catherine and I looked at her, and a satisfied smile leaked across Catherine's face. It vanished as Elena turned the gun on her and fired. The bullet went wide. Catherine's eyes widened with fear and she held both her hands out. "Elena, what—?"

"You killed my son," Elena said, her voice level and cold with none of her earlier hesitation. She stood braced with the backs of her thighs against the planter, arms extended at shoulder height, gun pointed at Catherine Lang. I stepped backwards surreptitiously, removing myself from the line of fire.

"I didn't!" Catherine said. "It was an overdose. I wouldn't—"

"I could forgive you sleeping with Jackson, but—"

"Wha—?" Catherine tried to look astonished, but even I could see she was lying. Her dark hair lay plastered to her cheeks, and her eyes darted from side to side. "I don't know what—"

Another bullet splintered into the fountain three feet to Catherine's left, sending up a geyser of tile shards. I instinctively covered my head with my hands, and the ceramic bits plinked harmlessly to the ground.

"Of course you did," Elena said. "Why else would you go to work for him after Wilfred died? It's not like you needed the money. I've known for months that you two were going at it like bunnies in his office when the rest of the staff went home. I put up with it because I couldn't stand the thought of losing both of you. How pathetic is that? The only good thing about his taking up with that dancer was that she put your nose out of joint. How's it feel to be cheated on, huh? If I'd had doubts about whether or not you were screwing him, you erased them with how eager you were to humiliate him by stripping him naked and sticking him in the window. And then you took those photos and posted them online, making sure even more people would see him like that."

"He was a louse," Catherine said, trying to keep her tone reasonable, but I heard the edge of panic in it. "You deserve better than him, Elena."

"I deserve better than both of you." She aimed again, squinting one eye closed. "This is for Robbie." She fired. The recoil knocked her back, rustling the plants behind her.

Catherine let out a howl of pain, clutched at her abdomen, and toppled into the fountain again. This time she lay still, floating faceup.

Elena swung the gun toward me, resolve hardening the lines of her pudgy face.

"Uh, don't look now," I said, "but there's a snake behind you."

"Right." Elena laughed, just as Agatha's cold, reptilian snout nosed her arm. Elena whirled and sighted the python. Only three or four feet of the snake's length protruded from the bushes, but it was enough to give a sense of her size and power. Her tongue flickered out. "Oh God, oh God." Elena scrambled away from the planter and fired at the snake, shots spraying everywhere. I lost count of the bullets, but within twenty seconds the gun clicked empty. Elena flung it at Agatha, who eyed her without blinking, unmoved by the hail of bullets.

Seizing the opportunity, I lunged at Elena and got my arms around her, hooking my foot across her ankle and pulling it back, sending her to the floor. Unfortunately, my knee gave out, and I sprawled atop her cushy body just as someone shouted, "Freeze! Police!"

I looked up to see Jay Callahan approaching, business-like, a Sig Sauer held in front of him. "I knew you were a police officer," I said with satisfaction.

"I just said that to get her attention," he said with a small smile, slipping the gun into a holster at the small of his back.

"Right," I said skeptically. He offered me a hand and pulled me up. His hand was strong and warm, and he maintained his clasp even after I was on my feet. "Got any handcuffs on you?"

"Sorry." He shrugged. I tugged at my hand and he let go slowly.

Trusting that Elena wasn't going anywhere—she had curled up in a ball and was making little whimpery noises—I took two steps to the fountain to check on Catherine. A faint pulse thrummed in her wrist when I grasped it. "Call an ambulance," I told Jay, pulling her toward the edge of the fountain. Water sloshed over the edge. In the dim light, I couldn't see how much blood she'd lost, but she was chilled and unconscious.

Jay made the call quickly and helped me lift Catherine's wet, limp body out of the fountain and settle it gently on the tiled floor. He took off his jacket and laid it over her as I put pressure on the sluggishly bleeding wound in her abdomen.

"Holy crap!"

Jay was staring past me, over my shoulder, and I turned my head quickly. Agatha had slithered out of the planter and was making her way toward the fountain with smooth undulations of her heavy body, completely uninterested in us or the night's excitement.

"That is one big snake," Jay said, awe in his voice.

"Her name is Agatha," I said. "Kiefer will be glad she's turned up. Speaking of turning up"—I gave him a sharp look—"what brought you here in such a timely fashion?"

"I happened to be in the garage and I heard shots," he said. "So—"

"You spend more time in garages than most cars."

Jay ignored my interruption. "—so, of course I came to see what was going on."

"Of course," I mocked. "You know that most people—civilians—run *away* from bullets, not toward them?"

Before he could answer, what seemed like a horde of people descended on us: EMTs, uniformed police, Detective Helland, and Grandpa Atherton. The EMTs pushed Jay and me out of the way as they gathered around Catherine, the cops swooped down on Elena, another officer led Jay away, and Detective Helland approached me, immaculately suited even at this hour, with the look of a man about to wreak bodily harm on a completely undeserving mall security officer. Before Helland could reach me, Grandpa Atherton hurried forward and put a fleece jacket around my shoulders. I hadn't even realized until that moment that I was chilled by the fountain water that had soaked me when we moved Catherine. "You okay, Emma-Joy?" he asked.

I nodded, putting my hand over his bony fingers where they rested on my shoulder. "You were right about it being a woman," I told him. "Two of them."

His blue eyes twinkled. "That Shakespeare fellow got it right when he said, 'Hell hath no fury like a woman scorned.'"

"It was William Congreve, actually," Detective Helland said in a steely voice, his blue eyes boring into mine. I felt a tingle that wasn't completely fear or cold zip down my spine. "And a woman scorned has nothing on a detective left out of the loop by a meddling, justice-obstructing, go-it-alone mall cop."

Twenty-three

. . .

Kyra's voice followed me out to the kitchen almost a week later as we waited for *Dancing with the Stars* to start. "I can't believe the DA is going to let Elena Porter off with such a light sentence."

I opened the fridge to get two more beers. "She's testifying against Catherine Lang. She says it was all Lang's plan and that Lang's the one who shot Jackson Porter and Weasel. The police found the Christian graffiti under a layer of new paint on Lang's MDX. The gun she used at the mall—the same one that shot Porter and Weasel—was registered to Wilfred Lang."

"Is she admitting to it?"

"Heck, no. As soon as she recovered enough to start talking, she started blaming Elena. She says Elena came to her with the plan and asked for her help. She says she loaned Elena the gun and helped her with Porter's body after the fact. A jury will have to sort it out."

"What about Robbie?"

I returned to the living room in time to see Fubar swipe a paw at the last piece of sushi takeout we'd brought home for dinner. "I saw that," I told him.

He licked his paw and pretended he didn't know what I was talking about and wouldn't eat sushi if we begged him to.

I handed Kyra a beer. "I guess we'll never know for sure. Lang's maintaining she had nothing to do with it, although Elena thinks she made Robbie shoot up at gunpoint."

"How did Lang or Porter's wife or whoever get a key to Diamanté?"

"Lang actually worked there when the store was a formal-wear rental place. I remember she told me once she'd met her husband at the mall when he was getting decked out for a wedding. She even said she met him 'here' when we were standing in Diamanté. I knew the store used to be a formal-wear rental place; I just didn't put two and two together. Mea culpa." The thought rankled. I'd had most of the pieces to the puzzle and just hadn't fitted them together right until Catherine and Elena ambushed me. Thinking about that night brought Agatha to mind. "Did you see the crowds around the Herpes Hut today?" I asked.

Kyra nodded, grinning. "Kiefer's really capitalizing on the whole 'hero snake' thing. Pretty clever the way he's using the publicity to nudge the police into tracking down Dawson and his LOAF buddies. Think Agatha will have to testify if it comes to trial?" She chuckled.

"Unlikely." I imagined the big snake in the witness box, flicking her tongue to point out Dawson as the culprit.

"Are the police going to go after that Lang-Quincy woman?"

"Aileen? Nope." I plopped down onto the sofa, and Fubar

leaped up beside me. "There's no percentage in it. The death was ruled accidental, the body was cremated, and Catherine Lang stands by her alibi. If Aileen hired it done, the killer has been discreet for years and isn't about to start blabbing now."

"I'm sure the police don't want to have to admit that they might have blown the investigation into Lang's death, either," Kyra said cynically. "Although I will say it was gracious of Detective Helland to mention you at the press conference: 'Fernglen Galleria's Officer Emma-Joy Ferris provided significant assistance to the police.' See, I memorized it. I also clipped the article from the *Vernonville Times* if you want to add it to your scrapbook." She grinned.

"Pass." I wouldn't admit it to Kyra, but I'd felt a tiny tingle of satisfaction at Helland's praise. It somewhat made up for the way he'd chewed me out the night Catherine and Elena tried to kill me.

The familiar theme music came on and Kyra muted it. "I think you're wrong about Jay, by the way," she said as we watched the stars parade in with their professional partners. "He makes one dee-lish-us cookie, and he's too laid back to be a cop or agent or whatever."

"Really?" I eyed her, wondering under what circumstances she'd gotten to know Jay Callahan so much better. I hadn't talked to the man since the night we captured Catherine and Elena. We'd crossed paths once or twice at the police station where we'd each been summoned for numerous interviews with detectives, DAs, and investigators, but we hadn't had a chance to sit and chat. He might think that by helping me with Catherine and Elena he'd allayed my suspicions about his activities. He'd be so wrong. He might have Kyra snowed with his sweet talk and luscious cookies, but I was keeping an eye on Mr. Jay "Cookie Man With a

Gun" Callahan. I was going to find out exactly what he was up to at Fernglen, and I knew darn well it wasn't selling cookies.

"Not that I'm saying you were ever uptight, or anything," Kyra added hastily, a mischievous glint in her eyes, "but you've relaxed a bit this past year. I think working at the mall is good for you."

"Really?" I said again. I tapped a business-sized envelope against my thigh. The letter had come today, offering me an in-person interview with the police department in the bustling metropolis of Galax, Virginia, about four hours southwest of here, not far from the North Carolina border. With any luck, it'd be buh-bye Fernglen Galleria and hel-lo Galax before the summer.

But I knew Kyra would be sad at the thought of me moving, so I didn't hand her the letter as I'd planned. Truth to tell, the idea made me a bit sad, too. Grandpa Atherton popped into my head, as did Kyra, Joel, and, surprisingly, Detective Anders Helland. I didn't want to jinx the job by talking about it before it was a done deal, I told myself. Sliding the envelope unobtrusively under a stack of guitar sheet music, I slipped Fubar the last piece of sushi, cranked up the volume on the TV, and made a bet with Kyra about which of the male pros would find an excuse to take his shirt off on tonight's show.

NEW FROM ANTHONY AND BARRY AWARDS WINNER

JULIE HYZY

GRACE UNDER
PRESSURE

Everyone wants a piece of millionaire Bennett
Marshfield, owner of Marshfield Manor, but now
it's up to the new curator, Grace Wheaton, and
handsome groundskeeper Jack Embers to protect
their dear old Marshfield. But to do this, they'll
have to investigate a botched Ponzi scheme, some
torrid Wheaton family secrets—and sour grapes out
for revenge.

penguin.com

Jessica would be and she said, "Yes."

"Great. So it's all set. Right?"

"Yes." What would she wear? How would she look in a dress-up dress? Would she be able to wear flats or would Aunt Jessica insist on those pumps with heels?

"So do you want to double-date or go alone? And do you want to rent a limousine and go out to dinner first? If we do that, we'll have to double up with some others. Budget problems."

"Could we talk about this when I get back?" Anna asked. "My mom doesn't like it if I talk a long time on long distance."

"Oh, sure. When will you be back in Madison?"

"I'll come back two days after Christmas," Anna decided she would have to return early to shop for a dress. They didn't sell ball gowns in Saint Olaf's, that's for sure.

"That your boyfriend?" her brother Olaf asked when she hung up the telephone.

Anna was still in shock from the telephone call. She shook her head and said, "That's a friend named Lars. I run with him."

"What did he want?" her mother asked.

Anna turned and looked at her mother with a puzzled expression in her eyes, "He wanted me to go to a dance with him."

"Then he *is* your boyfriend," Olaf shouted.

"Go outside," her mother said to her oldest son. Then she looked directly at her daughter and said, "I don't know why you look so surprised. You're a pretty girl. I knew some boy was going to figure it out one of these days. Do you need a dress?"

"Yes." She was surprised that her mother seemed so interested. Most of the time she worked so hard and said so little that this sudden question about dresses was startling.

"Your father and I didn't know what to buy you for Christmas," her mother said. "A dress will be just fine. Shoes, too."

Anna's heart sank. She was going to feel silly enough at her first dance. If she had to wear some country dress that her mother picked out from the local mall, it would be horrible.

"Cash is all you'll get for Christmas this year," her mother decided. "Your aunt can help you spend it. May be some good sales in the city right after Christmas."

Anna rushed over and kissed her on both cheeks, hugging her tight. Her mother pushed her away and laughed, "You're getting so tall you almost knocked me over. Mind if you kiss that boy, don't knock *him* down." Then she laughed and laughed as Anna blushed bright red.

Chapter 41

Willow was sorry they were wasting any of their time in Mexico visiting people, but Carlos and his mother seemed determined to take the Winstons to visit their friends the Beltrans. Mostly, they seemed to want to show off their house.

This whole trip had been frustrating, Willow decided. She'd never really managed a minute alone with Carlos and she still didn't have a date for the New Year's Eve ball. When she'd started out, she was sure that Carlos was crazy about her but now she was no longer so sure. Seeing him in his own country, with his own surroundings and family around him, made him seem different to her.

For one thing, Carlos seemed younger at home and that should have been encouraging but it wasn't. A younger Carlos also meant a less serious Carlos. Since Carlos had always been kind of a joker in his conversation, Willow wasn't sure when she could really believe what he was saying. Willow was beginning to have more than a few doubts about how serious he really was when he called her his love or his beautiful one.

The Beltrans' house turned out to be on the side of a very tall hill on the way to Mexico City. They were invited to spend the day and evening there and then go into Mexico City for some sight-seeing before their 6 P.M. plane the next night. Willow knew that Carlos and his family had been very nice to them but she wished their visit included more outings with just young people. It seemed to her that everywhere they went, there were a lot of older people she was supposed to be polite to.

When they left the highway and began the long, steep climb up the hill to the Beltrans' house, Willow held her breath. It was a one lane street and there were places where even that lane didn't look wide enough for the limousine they were riding in.

Willow moved closer to Carlos and whispered, "What happens if we meet a car coming down?"

"We back down," Carlos explained casually. "Don't worry, Willow, my love, there are no cars coming to meet us. Señor and Señora Beltran are expecting us."

Mrs. Montoya turned and smiled at her son. "They will be so happy to see you, my son. They want to hear all about Luisa. After all, she hasn't been home since her birthday in April." Then his mother sighed and said, "I know they hoped she would find a way to be here with us for Christmas. Not a very dutiful daughter, I fear. Brilliant but not dutiful."

"Luisa is studying," Carlos said, and Willow was startled at the irritation in his voice. Always before, when he spoke to his mother, he was even more courteous than usual.

"She found time to visit you in the States," Mrs. Montoya said.

"Who is Luisa?" Willow asked.

"Luisa Beltran," Carlos answered. "My dearest friend. She's the girl I went to see in New York at Thanksgiving."

Willow felt a stab of fear go through her body. She was grateful that Brittany began to talk very loudly and very enthusiastically about the view, pointing out the window and drawing everyone's attention away from Willow.

They arrived at the top of the hill then and two servants dressed in white pants and shirt ran to open the limousine for them. As they stepped out, Jessica looked up at the huge white house and said, "I can see why you wanted us to see this house. It's like a castle."

"It was a castle," Carlos explained. "One of the summer homes of the Empress Carlotta and then it passed to the Beltran family. They built the two wings on it and Luisa's grandfather added the turrets and viewing bridge. I hope you brought your climbing shoes, Jessica, my dear. There are four floors and twenty-two bedrooms."

"First we will have coffee," Mrs. Montoya said.

Brittany took Willow's hand and said, "I need to walk just a little bit. Come with me." The two girls practically ran down the path and to the other side of the street where they were out of view. Once there, Willow began to cry silently, painfully.

Brittany put her arms around her sister's shoulders and let her cry it out. As the sobs came out in great gulps of disappointment, Brittany hoped with all her might that no one would come looking for them until the worst was over. Finally, Willow raised her tear-streaked face and asked her sister, "Did you know he had a girlfriend?"

"His mother tried to tell me the other day. I told you about that," Brittany answered. "And this morning she told me he was engaged."

"He's too young to be engaged," Willow

sobbed. "He's only twenty. I'm only four years younger than he is. It's not fair."

"Maybe it's all his mother's idea," Brittany said. "Maybe he likes you best."

"No, he doesn't," Willow said. "I can see now that I've given him a lot of opportunities to say he liked me — and he's always avoided me. He's just a big flirt and I really don't like him anymore. I feel so foolish." Willow wiped her eyes with her hands and smiled at herself. "I sound silly, don't I?"

"You sound hurt," Brittany said. "He *is* a flirt," she added. At that moment, she genuinely hated Carlos.

"You'll have to get over it," Brittany pointed out. "He lives at our house and we're his guests here. He's never really promised you anything or told you he loved you or anything like that, has he? You *do* keep changing who you think you're in love with. You know that."

Willow sighed and shook her head. "Everytime I would get close to him, he'd sort of duck away. I think — I think he's just self-centered and . . ." Words failed her and she burst into tears again.

Brittany watched her sister cry and eventually suggested, "We could say you were sick and needed to rest for a while. You could always be carsick."

"Would you help me?" Willow asked.

So Brittany went into the house first and arranged to have Willow taken straight to her room, bypassing meeting the Beltrans or seeing Carlos.

Willow waited until the maid put her bag on the luggage case and opened the windows to the beautiful morning sun. When the maid left, Willow threw herself on the bed and covered her eyes with her hand, saying, "I'll just stay here until we leave. By then maybe I'll be able to look at him without feeling foolish."

"What do you want me to tell Mom?"

"Tell her I'm carsick," Willow answered.

Brittany closed the blinds and left the room. Three hours later she returned with a glass of milk and a sandwich on a tray. Willow was lying in the same position, looking up at the same canopy roof on her bed.

"You'll have to sit up to eat," Brittany said.

"I can't eat," Willow wailed. She rolled over on one elbow and looked at her sister. "What's he doing?"

Brittany made a face and said, "He's having a great time. No one seems to think it's weird you're carsick. Seems it happens a lot to people who go up that hill."

"He didn't ask about me?"

"Not really," Brittany said. "We toured the house and had lunch and we're getting ready to see some ruins. I'm supposed to find out if you feel good enough to go."

"He's very self-centered," Willow said thoughtfully. She took the sandwich and bit into it. "Crunchy," she observed.

"It's a *torta*," Brittany said. "That means it's made on a hard roll and has beans on it as well as turkey and cheese. Good, huh?"

"Very," Willow said. She washed the last bite down with the milk. "I've decided what to do about the New Year's Eve ball."

Somehow, Brittany knew exactly what was coming but she asked anyway, "What?"

"I'm going to call Lars from Madison and tell him I've changed my mind. That I want to go with him."

"Good idea," Brittany said. What else could she say? If Willow wanted to go to the dance with Lars, he would say yes. And after all, Willow was her sister and she really was hurting. Brittany stood up and said, "So you're not coming to the ruins, I take it?"

"No." Willow stretched and yawned. "I'm going to play sick till tomorrow. But I'll tell you one thing, I'm not going to let this ruin my life."

"Just your trip," Brittany said.

Chapter 42

The next morning, Willow was down for breakfast at the same time as the others. Her host and hostess apologized profusely for the steep climb and Mrs. Beltran said, "I have some Dramamine you can take for the trip down."

"It was silly of me to get carsick," Willow said. "I missed all the fun." As far as she could tell, everyone believed her story including Carlos, who hovered around her chair and insisted on bringing her choice tidbits from the breakfast sideboard. "You must try this cheese," he said. "It's a famous goat cheese from Oaxaca. I tried to find some in the market the other day but it was all gone."

She ate the goat cheese spread on a tortilla and washed it down with orange juice. She went through all the motions of being the same old Willow as before except she did nothing at all to be alone with Carlos. Nor did she flirt